Indian Air Force

The Case for Indigenisation

INDIAN AIR FORCE

THE CASE FOR INDIGENISATION

Edited by

Air Commodore
Jasjit Singh
AVSM, VrC, VM (Retd)

KW
KNOWLEDGE WORLD

KW Publishers Pvt Ltd
New Delhi

in association with

Centre for Air Power Studies
New Delhi

2011 | **F P B A** | BEST PUBLISHERS AWARD (ENGLISH)

The Centre for Air Power Studies is an independent, non-profit, academic research institution established in 2002 under a registered Trust to undertake and promote policy-related research, study and discussion on the trends and developments in defence and military issues, especially air power and the aerospace arena, for civil and military purposes. Its publications seek to expand and deepen the understanding of defence, military power, air power and aerospace issues without necessarily reflecting the views of any institution or individuals except those of the authors.

Jasjit Singh
Director General
Centre for Air Power Studies
P-284, Arjan Path
Subroto Park
New Delhi 110010

Tele: (91-11) 25699131
E-mail: diroffice@aerospaceindia.org

ISBN 978-93-81904-49-7

Contents

Contributors

Air Commodore **Jasjit Singh** AVSM VM VrC (retd), Director General, Centre for Air Power Studies.

Air Marshal **P.K. Mehra** PVSM AVSM VM (retd), Former Air Officer Commanding-in-Chief, SWAC, IAF.

Air Marshal **N.V. Tyagi** PVSM AVSM VM VSM (retd), Former Deputy Chief of the Air Staff.

Air Marshal **A.K. Nagalia** PVSM AVSM VM VSM (retd), Former Deputy Chief of the Air Staff.

Group Captain **S.S. Sharma**, Senior Fellow, Centre for Air Power Studies.

Group Captain **S. Bhanoji Rao** VSM, Commanding Officer, AQAW(A), Jabalpur.

Air Marshal **T.M. Asthana** PVSM AVSM VM (retd), Former Commander-in-Chief, Strategic Forces Command & currently Distinguish Fellow, Centre for Air Power Studies.

Group Captain **Manoj Kumar** VSM, Senior Fellow, Centre for Air Power Studies.

Shri Shiv **Ram Krishna Pande**, Associate Fellow, Centre for Air Power Studies.

Ms **Debalina Chatterjee**, Associate Fellow, Centre for Air Power Studies.

Air Vice Marshal **A. Agrawal** VSM (retd) Former Senior Maintenance Staff Officer, SWAC, IAF.

The Challenge of Indigenisation: The Case of the Aircraft Industry

✧ JASJIT SINGH

No country is really independent unless it is independent in matters of its armament.

— Jawaharlal Nehru

It appears curious and inexplicable to most students of national security and defence that in spite of an aircraft industry that has expanded enormously since 1939 when it was set up, India has been forced to import almost all types of complete aircraft from foreign sources. A small degree of self-reliance was achieved by licensed manufacture of some of the aircraft. But the high-technology systems and components for these also were imported. At one level, this can be explained by the reality that the country was deindustrialised during the two centuries before independence. The Industrial Revolution had started in England three centuries before India's independence. As industrialisation grew and expanded geographically to Europe and North America, muscle power gave way to machine power for economic productivity.

Growth and advances of technology, especially in its military application, as the natural consequence of the industrialisation of England and Europe, also provided significant military advantage over the local and regional regimes and became the source of capability to establish empires in the rest of the world. The colonial powers of Europe did not set up any industry in the countries they ruled, and focussed on military technological superiority and further advancement of their own industries with resources and raw materials from the colonised countries. Japan, however, did create numerous industries in Manchuria when it invaded China. China had also grown with massive transfer of military and civil industries, lock, stock and barrel by Stalin's Soviet Union in early 1950.

While some "sunset industries" like textiles had been transferred to India by the British (after British labour costs began to rise), India's industrialisation really began after independence. In fact, there was serious difference of opinions among the leaders of the Indian National Congress which had spearheaded the struggle for independence, on whether India should adopt a village-based cottage industry or try and invest in heavy industries like steel, cement and power generation, etc. Perhaps both strategies could have been followed if financial resources and techno-economic aid had been forthcoming. Nehru's vision of a modern industrialised India with village-based development appears to have provided the mixed economy which over the years has succeeded in moving the country toward substantive socio-economic development. From our perspective of indigenisation of military weapons, especially aircraft and their peripherals, we have lagged behind perhaps due to the Indian mind emphasising on "cutting edge" technology. But the Indian mind also tends to focus much more on the theoretical rather than the practical application of that theoretical knowledge: for example, there is great emphasis on political science and very little on international relations, etc.

We need to constantly keep in mind the reality of the centuries of deindustrialisation which had the country way behind the developed countries and even behind China, which got significant infusion of industrialisation. Hence, India has had to condense into decades, its industrial technological revolution, which the developed world achieved in centuries with the added benefit of resources from the colonised countries. Contrary to conventional wisdom, India did/does not possess any significant natural resources. Its only asset for two centuries has been its human resource which was fully exploited by the British in areas ranging from transportation of labour to work in plantations as far as the Caribbean, Fiji, South Africa, Kenya, Myanmar (then Burma), Malaya, etc., though the greatest exploitation was of Indian soldiers in the Imperial

Wars. The raw materials produced by the country like cotton, iron ore, etc., were exported to run textile mills in England. Hence, we need to judge our ability/inability to achieve self-reliance in armaments keeping in view the handicaps that our history placed on us in the past when the developed industrial countries enjoyed the benefit of unlimited access to resources.

It is also true that HAL (now Hindustan Aeronautics Limited) has manufactured many hundreds of combat aircraft, and overhauled thousands of aero-engines for combat and transport aircraft. But, more important, after independence, it started on the ideal vector which would rely on three parallel processes: (i) indigenous design and development even if it required collaboration with foreign expertise; (ii) licensed production of weapons and equipment in the country, presumably including every sub-system and component down to the nuts and bolts; (iii) direct import of urgent and high-technology aircraft and systems to meet operational requirements, with licensed manufacture to complete the full complement of aircraft required. When looked at closely, the last process mostly has become another aspect of the second process, that is licensed assembly and production for an aircraft/system designed abroad in which HAL was not, and could not have been, a party. When the government proudly announced, every time a contract was signed, that this would be accompanied with TOT (Transfer of Technology), what it really meant was that production technology would be available.

The official terminology in the Ministry of Defence was a choice between "buy" and "make," the former without any licensed manufacture and the latter, including manufacture under licence. A typical example is that HAL manufactured around 600 MiG-21 variants. But when HAL designed the "combat flaps" to enhance the air combat capability of the aircraft, it could not introduce that in the fleet. Similarly, when it was finally decided to upgrade the MiG-21, the Russians had to be involved in the process and paid for their labour though they were not really needed.

The Chinese, of course, do things differently. For example, they purchased the Sukhoi Su-27 air superiority fighter from Russia in early 1990 under a contract that specified 24 aircraft outright imported and the balance to be assembled and manufactured in China. It acquired the Su-30MK after that on similar terms and realised that the platform was the same as that of the two-seat Su-27 trainer. It copied most of the systems of the Su-30 and cancelled the Su-27 contract and began to manufacture it modified to the Su-30 standard, and called it the J-11. The Russians were livid; but they needed the hard currency and exports to China, especially of the high-powered jet engines which China (like India) is unable to produce indigenously.

Looking back at the triple process of building indigenous capacity while meeting the operational demands of the Indian Air Force (IAF), the third process, viz., outright buy, especially high-technology aircraft and systems, has continued. The second process of relying on licensed production actually received a boost after the Sino-Indian War of 1962 when the IAF was authorised to expand from 25 squadrons to 64 squadrons. The Soviet Union did not demand hard currency payments which it would have been unable to spend given the complete ban by the West on economic and trade relations with it. For an India perennially short of hard currency, trade with the Soviet Union on rupee payment appeared as a boon in spite of the rupee-rouble exchange being pegged on a basket of Western currencies, thus, significantly costlier to India than its face value. But Soviet aircraft and systems rapidly increased in technological quality and served the IAF's (and the other two armed forces') operational purposes.

Moscow soon began to offer even long-term credit at very low interest rates to ensure that the rupees it earned in this trade would sustain for a long time to enable it to use them to purchase consumer items like medicines, rice, tea, hosiery, textiles, etc. from India. HAL set up additional plants for the licensed manufacture of Soviet designed aircraft (at Nasik in Maharashtra) and engines (at Koraput in Orissa) at two opposite ends of the country. Incidentally, Koraput is not even connected by rail (or an airfield anywhere close by) and all engines manufactured and overhauled at this factory had to be moved on hired trucks thousands of kilometres away from Nasik IAF air bases across the country. This inevitably led to increased costs and inefficiency, with an impact also on aircraft serviceability in the operational squadrons. The direct negative result of this process was that licensed manufacture of Soviet aircraft and arms became the dominant part of the three parallel processes we identified above. Above all, successive governments became complacent.

There is no doubt that the efforts to diversify the sources of supply had become a way to achieving a lower level of self-reliance since it reduced the dependence on any one country. But in the ultimate analysis, this had long ago settled down to two-odd countries: the Soviet Union and two European manufacturers (the UK and France) of aircraft and associated weapons and equipment. On the other hand, piecemeal acquisitions (like that of the Jaguar) only led to cost escalations and we denied ourselves economies of scale. But none of them was converted into joint ventures and nor was design data transfer part of the licensed manufacture contracts. So we could not even modify the aircraft we were manufacturing in the country.

The major casualty of this complacency was the first of the three processes identified above: indigenous design and development. It is pretty obvious that indigenous design and development is the foundation on which overall indigenisation for self-reliance can be built. The other two processes could at best serve as an interim step till a country reached self-reliance in design and development capability. Hence, India's march toward indigenisation is at best a one-legged effort and it will be a very long time before Indian pilots would be able to fly a modern Indian designed combat aircraft. I recognise that many people would angrily question the above conclusions at the very start of this study. I can hear loud noises about the Light Combat Aircraft (LCA). But this actually proves the central point being made.

The LCA was conceived in 1979-80 as an incremental approach to design and development of a low cost fighter for battlefield support to the land forces to replace the MiG-21 beginning 1985-86 and building 450 aircraft as the "workhorse of the IAF" as Mr Arun Singh, the Minister of State (MoS), Defence, used to say. Three key deficits of the otherwise excellent MiG-21 (which shot down two F-104 Starfighters of the Pakistan Air Force in the 1971 War in low-level air combat) were sought to be removed in the process of designing the new aircraft. The first, repositioning of the air intake (no longer required to be so critically managed as that in the MiG-21 which was to operate at Mach-2 at 22-km altitude) to the side intakes to hopefully make the aircraft less susceptible to bird strikes which accounted for total loss of the aircraft in nearly a quarter of our flying accidents. The second was to install a better modern air interception radar with a head-up display in the nose now freed from the imperatives of the nose intake. Third, there would be space for a cockpit air-conditioning system as compared to the existing MiG-21 which instead has a cockpit heating system needed above 14/20-km altitude. The bulk of our flying was being done at low level and the Air Force was expected to engage the enemy in air combat at very low altitudes and penetrate hostile air space at tree-top level. The MiG-21 cockpit temperatures in the north Indian summer would normally reach over 70 degrees Celsius within two minutes after take-off. Pilots would, on an average, lose as much as 3.5 kg weight in a 40-minutes low-level sortie (I proved it once in 1975)!

Third, the MiG-21 then was flying with 475 kg of ballast weight split into small pieces in most of the front fuselage to maintain the critical centre of gravity of a partially unstable aircraft design. The aircraft had a limited range and payload (like most Soviet aircraft of the 3rd generation in keeping with their defensive orientation) and their low cost allowed large numbers to be deployed defensively. Hence, the penetration range of the aircraft in a ground attack role, or its time for air combat was limited. Utilising 475 kg for internal fuel would have dramatically enhanced its range as compared to the MiG-21.

Unfortunately, the decade of the 1980s was spent on one side in hyping the standard of preparation and Air Staff Requirements (ASR) to make it the dream of a fighter pilot! But someone forgot to increase the weight to accommodate everything that would make it a 21st century combat aircraft at par with the best in the world. On the other side, a vicious tussle raged as to who would head the new national project in or outside HAL? Ultimately, the proverbial Indian compromise was adopted and an ad-hoc organisation (more of it later) called the Aeronautics Development Agency (ADA) was set up as a registered society (to make financial management easier) but under the Defence Research and Development Organisation (DRDO) by milking HAL of designers and engineers. The critical point is that three decades after the design of the first and so far the only HAL designed multi-role combat aircraft, the HF-24 Marut, was commenced, the LCA finally started to move ahead with design feasibility that the IAF had major difficulties with. During those three decades, aviation technology had advanced exponentially and our early designers who formed part of the HF-24 design team, led by a German group under Dr. Kurt Tank, had retired. In the absence of institutional memory, the mistakes committed during the HF-24 were repeated in the LCA. In short, in 2013, the LCA has yet to reach its Initial Operational Capability (IOC) although the IAF has placed orders for 40 aircraft to demonstrate its commitment to the programme. And with a new engine, the GE 414, the aircraft would have to undergo significantly extensive development processes.

What lessons can be drawn from the above sketch? Some of the ones relevant to our present study can be briefly outlined as follows:

- Design and development form the critical foundation of indigenisation and self-reliance.
- The Design Division of HAL set up after independence has been emasculated over the decades. So much so, that the country is importing a basic trainer for *ab-initio* training from abroad after a lapse of four years.
- The final marginalisation of HAL's design and development capability was achieved by establishing the ADA under DRDO management, increasing the stakeholders and decision-authorities in the government and sidelining the IAF.
- The combat force level of the IAF is facing an unplanned 24 percent drop. It has happened when both our potential adversaries have pursued a massive modernisation of their air forces.
- What was true at the time of independence is true today. **The Indian Air Force is the primary stakeholder in the aircraft and systems**

that it acquires and employs in defence of the country and its air warriors keep ready for the worst in peace and war.

- The Indian Air Force is expected to increase its force level to 42 combat squadrons by 2022 and possibly 49 squadrons by 2030 or so.

If this is so, should not the IAF play a greater role in the critical area in the processes of design, development and acquisition of the tools with which it has to function even at short notice perhaps against immense odds and yet win the wars of the nations? If the answer is yes, then the question is, how can that be achieved within the norms and parameters of Indian democracy?

Indian Navy Model

The most simple and efficiently workable approach to indigenise design and development up to, and partly including, the manufacture of aircraft and weapons systems besides their integration with the platforms is to adopt the model that the Indian Navy has followed since independence. It needs understanding that this policy was inherited from the British since the Admiralty had directly controlled warship design and construction to meet their operational requirements over the centuries. Hence, the Naval HQ now has a Directorate of Naval Design under the Chief of Naval Staff (CNS) and also the Controller of Warship Construction which allows it to direct the construction also. Most of the dockyards constructing and refitting warships are headed by naval officers. The third element is the WESEE (Weapons and Electronic System Engineering Establishment) notionally under the Ministry of Defence though managed under the Chief of Material in Naval HQ in close cooperation with the Scientific Adviser to the Defence Minister. It has highly qualified technical experts from the Navy and the scientific community on its strength. The Indian Navy's advanced capabilities in information warfare, cyber capabilities and warfare, etc. are all due to the enormous design and development work being carried out in WESEE. One possible reason for its success is that the electrical and electronic branch officers have very few vacancies at the top ranks; and WESEE provides professional challenges and satisfaction, besides the potential for employment in the corporate sector in later years. The IAF used to rely on a similar institution called the Directorate of Technical Development and Production (DTD&P). Two dedicated DRDO laboratories work in close cooperation with the Indian Navy beside a large number of qualified naval officers being assigned to a number of DRDO laboratories.

The key factor that emerges from a closer study of Indian naval warship design and construction strategy is that its four components outlined above function in deep harmony. The Ministry of Defence has been providing it full support for the past six decades. The success of the Indian Navy in indigenous design and development has been well recognised. The INS *Delhi*, a 7,000-odd ton destroyer which many in the international community interpreted to be a cruiser, was an instant success, when it was launched in 1997, and other Delhi class ships have, if anything, surpassed its performance and capability. Many of the critical systems like guided missiles are still imported and integrated into Indian naval warships. It may be recalled that the Defence Minister, Shri A.K. Anthony had stated a couple of years ago that the Indian Navy from now on will not be importing any warships. The Chief of Naval Staff had recently stated that out of 44 warships under construction, 22 are being constructed in India. This indeed is a remarkable achievement, unparalleled by any other component of armed forces in India.

It is an example worth emulating by the IAF if it has to push for indigenisation of its aircraft and their support services without having to pay the price of depleted combat force levels and/or poor serviceability and sustainability of its aircraft due to poor product and spares support of even imported aircraft and those manufactured under licence. And the Ministry of Defence should support such a redirection. It needs to be clarified that the British relied totally on their private industry to design and develop aircraft of all varieties. At the government level, it was the Ministry of Supplies that dealt with the industry and placed orders on the industry on behalf of the Royal Air Force, with the UK Defence Ministry acting as the key organisation which also included the top hierarchy of the Air Force, what with a Minister of State heading the branch. When

India became independent, the Ministry of Supplies was the agency to approve demands and approve acquisition.

But the Industrial Resolution of 1957 brought all defence activities and aircraft acquisitions under the Ministry of Defence which also separated itself from the Air Force leadership once the IAF and other armed forces became subordinate Services. But this also created a lacuna in that transport aircraft, airliners and general aviation remained in a limbo. In due course, the airliners were brought under the Civil Aviation Ministry, and military transport aircraft under the responsibility of Ministry of Defence in keeping with the Industrial Policy resolution. General aviation has remained in a limbo even now. The extensive review of the higher defence organisation triggered by the Kargil War provided only a weak, partial solution by changing the nomenclature without any reforms or reorganisation as such in terms of creating an integrated Ministry of Defence. But that is a vast and different issue that need not be dealt with here although the organisation of the defence establishment and the place of the IAF in it are crucial issues that affect indigenisation.

Design and Development Integral to IAF
The second option would be a variation of the Indian Navy's example to suit existing realities and the IAF's specific needs. Air Chief Mshl P.C. Lal had reorganised the Air Headquarters (HQ) in January after he took over as Chief of the Air Staff. If pursued as the directorate responsible for new projects, it had the organisational potential to become equal to the Naval HQ's Directorate of Naval Design. In essence, it separated many distinctly different issues under separate directorates. For example, instead of the all-embracing Policy and Plans Directorate, he separated administrative plans from aircraft and weapons acquisition plans. What is of interest to our present study is that a Directorate of Projects was created under the Deputy Chief of the Air Staff. As the name suggests, this was to become the embryo for managing projects for the Air Force. Alongwith it, the Directorates of Systems Analyses to improve decision-making, and of Air Staff Publications to produce the requisite literature were also established. The close coordination of the Directorate of

Projects with the Directorate of Technical Development and Production (DTD&P), and the Scientific Adviser to the Chief of the Air Staff would have been the natural way forward. Unfortunately, this did not happen. So much so, that when the Air Force decided to integrate and create a new weapons aiming and navigation system of the newly acquired Jaguar in 1979, the task was undertaken by an ad-hoc group of IAF personnel (with a test pilot as the key person) who created the Darin system that made the IAF Jaguars far superior to the British and French aircraft. The process is now producing the Darin III, the third development in the series.

Similarly, Air HQ has taken the initiative to indigenise as many line items as possible for the MiG-29 and the process is proving to be enormously successful. Our purpose in identifying these efforts and earlier organisations is to highlight the need and potential of establishing design and development of aircraft as an IAF responsibility with adequate interface with HAL management. Incidentally the old system of appointing Air Force officers as Chairman and General Managers is hardly conducive to the larger issue of indigenisation as the history of the past six decades shows.

As noted earlier, the ADA was established in the mid-1980s as an ad-hoc ad interim organisation with a specific task to design and develop the LCA with manpower seconded from HAL but with the organisation delinked from HAL as an independent registered society. Rationally, its original task has been long finished though the weakness in design (like the airframe being much heavier than the design stipulation) has not led to its performance meeting the ASR against which the LCA was finally approved for design and development. Since it was done under the initiative of the DRDO, the head of DRDO continues to be the Chairman of the society and, thus, the head of the ADA. DRDO designed the aircraft, but had to go to HAL for producing the product. In spite of excellent cooperation between the ADA (read DRDO) and HAL, there have been serious problems in productionising the design. Historically (and I can cite many examples), this was to be expected and logically ADA should have been merged with the HAL design bureau once the technology demonstrator was ready.

In fact, ADA failed to even start a follow-on design project in the early 1990s which could have begun to mature by now. I had argued in favour of doing so at the LCA progress review attended by the then Defence Minister, Shri Sharad Pawar, in late 1991. This may be fairly accurately ascribed to its one-shot task and goal of designing the LCA and it had no stake in becoming the design and development hub for all or at least some of the IAF aircraft needs. Nor did DRDO, the controlling authority of the ADA, appear to have looked at it from that perspective. It had made progress in many areas of design and development of aircraft; and a great deal of the research work had been outsourced to nearly 300 academic institutions. There is no reason why it could not have undertaken at least the design and development of a primary trainer which, it was clear at that time, the IAF would require badly after the HPT-32 had been in service for around 15 years.

The best course in the interest of the country even at this stage is to bring the ADA under the Air HQ as its design and development capability. DRDO can then concentrate on strategic systems like long-range highly accurate ballistic missiles (hence, usable with conventional warheads), manoeuvrable reentry warhead/vehicle (which has been operationalised by the US, Russia and China already), and Ballistic Missile Defence (BMD) (especially with boost-phase interception), which may have a long gestation period, and withdraw from areas like design of an odd aircraft. In order to optimise the output of the ADA, probably on Air Marshal at the top (possibly a second Deputy Chief of the Air Staff) may have to be nominated for this role; and this, in the era of the A.V. Singh Committee implementation when the Air Force is looking for suitable jobs for the authorised strength of Air Marshals would serve the dual purpose of taking on key tasks within the existing force level. There are many highly capable technical officers and test pilots in service who could usefully take on the responsibilities of managing the ADA. The other alternatives would be substantive expansion of the ADA to undertake all design and development tasks in the aviation sector or at least take on the responsibility for future IAF needs rather than continuing the ad-hoc programmes. In addition, some coordinating mechanism has to be evolved between the ADA and HAL so that design-to-production synergy can be built up. In conclusion, one can assert that the best course of action is to follow the known experience of the Indian Navy and bring the ADA under the IAF to form the critical design and development agency for future aircraft and systems. If, for some reasons, the ADA cannot be brought under the IAF which is the primary stakeholder for military aircraft, then logically, the ADA could be merged with HAL. Leaving the ADA as an interim ad-hoc institution for decades in such a critical area would be a gross mistake.

Research and Development
Two issues demand serious attention. The first is that a Research and Development (R&D) laboratory is required to be established in the Air Force to undertake a variety of tasks like new weapons and system integration, etc. It is worth noting that the US Air Force (USAF) has a number of its own laboratories for R&D for new capabilities in the aerospace domain. And they compete with each other to ensure that the USAF remains the world leader in aerospace technology. One has only to look at their programmes to understand how and why the US is far ahead of even highly industrialised Western countries, and the USAF remains the preeminent air force in the world.

Aircraft design and development is deeply linked to the R&D expenditure in the aerospace sector specifically and national R&D investment in general. Hence, looking beyond the aircraft industry and design and development issues in enhancing indigenisation, the second major issue that deserves attention is that Indian expenditure on R&D is pathetically low for a country that is already at the cusp of being a major power. Over the past three decades, the total R&D as a percentage of national Gross Domestic Product (GDP) has not exceeded 0.8 percent; and out of this, nearly 0.7 percent is spent in the government agencies like DRDO and Department of Science of Technology in its laboratories. There is a serious risk if we do not take remedial measures; industrial production, already on the decline, may further go down in the coming years and the great Indian dream may come to nought. In that case, there could be serious domestic violence adding to the problems of economic growth.

According to *Battelle R&D Magazine*, global R&D spending was expected to grow by about 5.2 percent to more than $1.4 trillion in 2012. Most of the global funding growth is being driven by the Asian countries, which were expected to increase nearly 9 percent in 2012. The share of global spending on R&D explains clearly how some countries like Japan and China have advanced so much (see Table 1 for details). While the US, spending almost a third of the global R&D expenditure, is obvious as the largest spender, this also has to be seen in the context of the United States' economy and, more important, the advances in technology that have been funded for over a century. At the same time, the major driving force for US R&D funding at such high levels is that the country clearly wants to stay ahead in technology compared to any other country though some day, another country may close the technological gap. But only a large country like China may be a real challenge some day as a peer.

Table 1: Share of Global R&D Spending

	2010	2011	2012
US	32.8%	32.0%	31.1%
Asia	34.3%	35.5%	36.7%
Japan	11.8%	11.4%	11.2%
China	12.0%	13.1%	14.2%
India	2.6%	2.8%	2.9%
Europe	24.8%	24.5%	24.1%
Rest of the World	3.0%	3.1%	3.2%

Source: "2012 Global R&D Funding Forecast", *Battelle R&D Magazine*, December 2011, p. 3.

As may be seen from Table 1, India is one of the very low spenders on R&D. China has been spending an average of 13 percent of the global expenditure on R&D and the results are clear in terms of the technological advances supporting economic growth in an inter-active process. China spends nearly 13 percent of the global R&D expenditure whereas India accounts for a mere 2.8 percent or so, during the three years under review in spite of the fact that its average annual GDP growth for the first decade of this century was in the order of 8.4 percent! This may well be the reason why the industrial growth (as a percentage of GDP) has been slowing down in recent years since it obviously depends heavily upon licensed production (as in the case of the aircraft industry) rather than innovation through research and development even if it is only a case of reverse engineering, like China does in many cases. At the rate China is investing in R&D (besides US offshore R&D operations in China), it is likely to surpass US R&D spending by 2023 (See Fig 1).

Fig 1: China's Annual R&D Spending

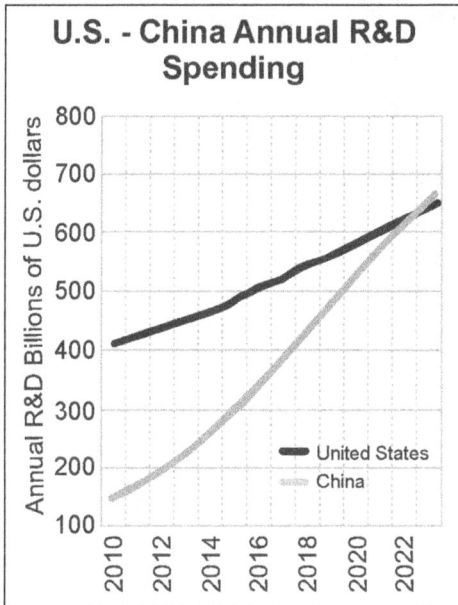

Source: "China's R&D Momentum," *Battelle, R&D Magazine*, p. 29

Note: China's double digit growth in R&D spending is expected to match and surpass that of the US by about 2023, if several forecasting criteria are maintained. This forecast is based on Chinese R&D continuing at an average 11.5 percent per year and US R&D growth averaging about 4.0 percent per year for the next 13 years. Present US R&D annual growth is only about 2.1 percent but has been more than 6 percent over the past six years. China's R&D growth over the past 15 years has consistently exceeded 10 percent.

What is perhaps more relevant is that China's rate of growth of R&D spending has far exceeded its national GDP growth rates over the past two decades or so. In 2011, China's Ministry of Finance had announced its allocation of $125 million to promote the application of China's R&D results into the commercial sector with the aim of accelerating the transfer of science and technology achievements into production and promoting corporate technology innovation—steps crucial to competitive industrial production growth. Secondly, unlike India, where nearly 0.6 percent of the GDP on R&D is from government funding, and the balance amounting to only 0.2 percent of the GDP is spent by the business/private sector, in China's case, the reverse is the norm, the general impression of state run institutions being the norm notwithstanding.

The post-1991 growth in India's economy has been remarkable and averages around 8.4 percent for the first decade of the new century. The service sector has shown the highest growth rate among the three segments of industrial production, agriculture and service sector. With the economic meltdown since 2008, it was inevitable that Indian economic growth would also slow down although it has remained one of the two major countries (China and India) with a fairly high economic growth. Even industrial growth has been fairly high. This is no doubt due to Foreign Direct Investment (FDI) which has brought with it the knowledge and means of industrial *production* and not necessarily any meaningful investments in R&D for future growth in India. A RAND study had looked at the composition of national gross expenditure on R&D in different countries over a period of ten years average from 1995 to 2005 (see Table 2). The expenditure has also been depicted in sector-wise distribution.

What strikes one is that India is the only country among those examined where the industry's contribution to R&D is significantly lower than that of the government. Obviously, the reforms have not touched the core activity for future industrialisation and stares at the reader as the weakness in the industrial revolution that India must pursue if it has to sustain its growth rate over the coming decades. It is regrettable that the industry's contribution and investment on R&D has remained poor.

Such low investment in national R&D by the industrial sector runs contrary to the expectation that the private sector should/would get involved in the aerospace industry. The government needs to look into this fundamental lopsided weakness.

As may be seen, in the United States, which stands as a model of technology driven economic development, the private industry's investment in national R&D is over six times that by the government. In India, a handful of industries like the pharmaceutical industry have invested substantially in R&D after 2000 and their growth has been remarkable as a consequence of this approach. It appears that the early successes of some of the government initiatives in nurturing new biotech companies are responsible for this change in the scenario. But, this has not happened in the other sectors. This stands as a powerful reason for the IAF to get involved in R&D in the aerospace sector like the US Air Force relying on a number of laboratories under it often in competitive programmes between the laboratories such as the hyper-velocity vehicles for the future as part of the USAF programme of Prompt Global Strike [as distinct from the Defence Advanced Research Projects Agency (DARPA) which undertakes R&D for the Department of Defence].

Table 2: National Gross Expenditure in R&D (GERD)
(Average from 1995 to 2005 as a percentage of GDP)

	USA	CHINA	INDIA	
GERD	2.6	1.0	0.8	Gross Expenditure in R&D
GOVERD	0.3	0.3	0.6	Government Expenditure in R&D
BERD	1.9	0.6	0.2	Business Expenditure in R&D
OTHERS	0.4	0.1	0.0	

Source: RAND Report, *China and India, 2025* (Santa Monica: RAND, 2011)

In conclusion, one has to reemphasise that design and development is the critical foundation of the aircraft industry and, hence, every step taken toward self-reliance through indigenisation must give it the greatest emphasis. This is where India has been remiss. The Indian Air Force has the greatest and most crucial stake in this process and possesses the capabilities to undertake the tasks with minimal reorientation. The ADA should be brought under Air HQ to begin moving toward the Indian Navy model of design, development and manufacture. This model has proved its value over six decades and now stands at the cusp of self reliance in meeting the future needs of the Indian Navy, even designing and building India's first aircraft carrier at the Cochin Shipyard. The nuclear submarine, no doubt, took quite some time as should have been expected; but the sea trials of the INS *Arihant* are scheduled in the near future. The earlier the government agrees to transfer the ADA to the IAF, the earlier we would put our aircraft industry on a sound footing for the future and move away from ad-hoc experimentation which had led us into the present cul de sac.

The second aspect of design and development is that designers are unique in their education but more so in their conceptual abilities. Hence, they deserve to be handled and utilised differently. The Soviet Union, in fact, went all out to do so: its aircraft were known by the names of their designers and the designers occupied the place of the head of the aircraft manufacturing facilities of that enterprise. We have tended to marginalise not only design and development but also our designers. Scientists from institutions like the National Aerospace Laboratories (NAL) in India would perhaps be the best heads of the Design Division of HAL or even as Chairman, HAL. Curiously, Dr. Valluri, who headed NAL and Raj Mahendra who for a long time had headed HAL's design bureau Dr. Valluri and who was keen to involve, were finally sidelined when the ADA was established; and so was (later) Air Mshl P. Ramachandran, an outstanding test pilot, operational fighter pilot and one of the finest officers that the IAF had, who was the key person in developing the Darin weapon aiming and navigation system for the Jaguar in the early 1980s. Personalities matter when national programmes are to be carried out. But we made another mistake: waiting for the LCA and not seeking an alternate operational aircraft for the IAF which simply led to unplanned decline of the combat force level, seriously jeopardising national security.

Looking ahead, the offsets clause offers a unique opportunity to find foreign investments as well as the relevant technology from the prime manufacturers, provided we handle it correctly. The first issue is that offsets must not be seen as a source of FDI only. They must be viewed as the route to enhance the technological capacity of the country and, hence, expedite the ongoing industrial revolution. Second, all the aircraft and systems that we have bought or are likely to buy (which are not joint ventures) have already been designed. Hence, little design technologies can be accessed as such. But all such aircraft have a life of 30-40 years during which they will require technological upgrades almost every decade.

The offsets should be geared to undertake such tasks and, hence, enable design and development in R&D establishments, preferably in the private sector, with collaboration with the prime manufacturer which should employ increasing numbers of Indian scientists and designers to work on the system engineering and upgrades. This process should create the requisite design and development capabilities in India in less than one generation besides supporting the larger national techno-economic base. It may look impossible but the steps like those of the Chinese Finance Ministry referred to above should become the norm. Above all, we need to enhance the investment in national R&D efforts, especially in the private sector, facilitated by the government but not directed by it.

Forecasting the Trends of Aerospace Power and the IAF: 2025

✿ P.K. MEHRA

Introduction

Wars in the last two decades have highlighted the need for aerospace dominance but the ensuing race among nations has made its achievement all the more difficult. The third dimension having grown in depth and importance, is the winning formula and, hence, the focus has shifted to beyond the atmosphere into space. Aerospace power delivers the range/ standoff, precision, lethality and, most importantly, quick response, through speed and information at the place of choosing since it overcomes all physical hurdles and its characteristics are war-winning. Practitioners of aerospace power are convinced that risk can be considerably reduced in all operations whether offensive or defensive through dominance in aerospace power. A number of countries among the developed world are far ahead in aerospace technology but there are only a few countries that have the numbers which can make a difference in a war. Efforts are being made by the stragglers to catch up and the gap appears to be narrowing primarily because the big aerospace powers have slowed down their development. It is very timely to study the trends in aerospace power development in major air forces since the Indian Air Force has to reverse the downsizing and obsolescence, and needs to arrest this downslide without delay.

There is a competition to develop aerospace fighting systems to get ahead but with shrinking budgets in most of the economies, the countries can remain in the race only through cooperation/collaboration, innovative development and superior technologies. Recent events have shown that greater connectivity has led to dependencies among various countries and this is one of the factors responsible for bringing about alliances in international relations. Our world has also seen the shift from bipolarity to single superpower and will see that to multipolarity in the future. These movements have resulted in changes in the alignment of various nations in order to ensure fulfilment of their own national interests. This era of key alliances can accelerate development in aerospace power through the removal of economic and technological constraints and will lead to interoperability with allies having similar capability.

Geopolitical Scenario and its Impact on India
It is an accepted fact that global aerospace dominance is the key to winning wars in the future and this can be achieved only through global alliances, both political and military. Hence, while studying the trends in aerospace power development, one cannot ignore the international geopolitics. Besides the need for alliances among different countries for unhindered functioning of air and space elements, the technology development needs a handshake to overcome both economic and knowhow limitations. Even with the global reach of land-based and carrier-borne aircraft, adequate aerospace power cannot be made to bear without a foothold in the area of conflict. This desire to maintain effective control over a conflict needs like-minded nations to develop the means together and take part in the conflict as allies. Globalisation and mutuality of interests have even brought about equations between countries on different sides of the globe. Similarly, there are many examples of neighbours building military and political alliances but equally there are regions where discord prevails amongst neighbours.

The way nation-states have come together in a formal or informal manner, building bilateral or multilateral relationships with one another in the last fifty years, is a pointer to the way the political and military alliances are expected to take shape in the next decade and a half. There have been a few political/economic/social international groupings of note in the last fifty years. Both the European Union (EU) and Association of Southeast Asian Nations (ASEAN) are not very old but have grown in strength and cohesion. The other associations like the Non-Aligned Movement (NAM), South Asian Association of Regional Cooperation (SAARC), Burma, India, Malaysia, Singapore, Technical Cooperation (BIMSTEC), Indian Ocean Region Association for Regional Cooperation (IORARC), Gulf Cooperation Council (GCC), and Organisation of Islamic Conference (OIC), East African Community, South African Development Community, Union of South American Nations (UNASUR), etc have either remained static or have gone through a metamorphosis lately. These unions and associations have socio-economic issues and nation-building as their agenda, without any military character, but the EU as well as ASEAN, also confer collective responsibility in enhancing peace and security on their member states. Defence Ministers from ASEAN + 8 met recently in Vietnam for the first time, to formally come together and establish a regional security dialogue at the ministerial level for peace, stability and development in the region. The EU is an economic and political union of 27 member states, and is growing. The EU was not meant to be a military alliance since the North Atlantic Treaty Organisation (NATO) was considered adequate but after the Kosovo War, there was an agreement to establish a credible military force without prejudice to NATO. A number of changes have taken place in the structure and constitution of the military force now called EUFOR and it has successfully taken over peace-keeping tasks in Africa, former Yugoslavia, etc. Recently, the UK and France have a signed defence agreement to create a joint expeditionary force, shared use of aircraft carriers and have even gone to the extent of working together to improve the safety and effectiveness of their nuclear weapons. Even though there are all round defence budget cuts among EU countries, the EU is still formidable considering that their combined defence budget was over Euros 200 billion in 2008, second only to the US defence budget.

In addition to the military groupings mentioned earlier, there are some military cooperation agreements and protection arrangements, namely the US-Japan, US-South Korea and the special US-Taiwan relationship Act, which are still in place. Some other cooperation arrangements, ostensibly for anti-terrorism, like the Shanghai Cooperation Organisation (SCO), and USA-Pakistan have also emerged. Defence diplomacy has played a major role in bilateral military cooperation between different countries. These bilateral initiatives have brought about strategic partnerships and even though unstated, have been built up to further their common agenda and aim in a specific region. All these bilateral and multilateral groupings will have an impact when seeking global aerospace dominance.

India is a member of a number of groups either as a full-fledged member or as an observer but what is of note is the number of bilateral strategic partnerships and defence cooperation agreements with a number of countries. The oldest membership is of NAM and there has been a bilateral strategic partnership with the erstwhile USSR. The bilateral defence agreements have elevated the relationship to a higher plane through regular exercises with other air forces instead of only a buyer-seller relationship with some countries. The joint development of the Su-30MKI was the first joint venture with Russia to co-develop an aircraft and now this level of cooperation has got a boost through the joint funding and technology sharing to develop the fifth generation aircraft and also Multi-Role Transport Aircraft (MRTA). India took nearly four decades to graduate to cooperation and joint development with the USSR/Russia; it is not known when the new relationship, if ever, with the USA will mature to this level. Although these bilateral and multilateral relationships are in a state of flux, a partnership in Design and Development (D&D) can be a reality thanks to the economic climate and the dependencies. How will this global scenario affect the geopolitics and will it lead to a race in building aerospace power among the budding superpowers and the aspiring regional powers?

Nature of Conflict Expected in the Future
The international relations have undergone a sea-change thanks to globalisation but it does not mean that wars will not take place. It is only the nature of wars which will change but as long as there is a state which is weaker than the other, the issue of dominance will come up and in case the nations are equal in stature, then the competition to

corner resources between them may lead to conflict. The chance of a World War III on the same scale as the earlier two World Wars is remote but the possibility of conflicts at different levels remains. Economic interdependence, competition for natural resources, globalisation, food, water, energy security and the role of non-state actors will determine the kind of future conflict. The proliferation of Weapons of Mass Destruction (WMD) and more and more countries acquiring strategic strike surface-to-surface missiles and weaker nations preparing for asymmetric warfare will require different *inter-se* priority, diplomatically and militarily. The Asia-Pacific region has recently been witness to muscle flexing between China and Japan but the lesson to be drawn is that economic power and control over scarce resources are ruling supreme during this period of recession. Use of North Korea as a proxy by China may not lead to war but the situation will remain tense. China has embarked on the path to become a great power and is building up its economic and military might to become a superpower in the years to come. The problem is that we are unable to link China's capabilities with the path to superpower status that it is likely to follow. The dragon is rising peacefully but will not hesitate to show its fangs when the time comes. Our boundary dispute does not have an immediate solution and China has now gone to the extent to terming Arunachal Pradesh and Jammu and Kashmir (J&K) as disputed territories, has recognised Pakistan Occupied Kashmir (POK) as part of Pakistan. These pinpricks are constant reminders that in spite of the fact that Confidence Building Measures (CBMs) are in place, India needs to develop both economically and militarily. China has been carrying out successful diplomacy in the South Asian region, West Asia, Africa, Central Asian States and even in Afghanistan. It has been able to maintain very good relations with both Saudi Arabia and Iran, which speaks volumes of its diplomatic skills and deep pockets. Both China and India are rapidly growing economies with a huge appetite for natural resources, energy, water, food, etc and, thus, may have to compete in the world market but the probability of war is low.

Wars in Iraq and Afghanistan have shown that even a superpower with the most sophisticated weaponry and equipment cannot defeat a determined, fanatical rag-tag group of mercenaries unless local support turns against them. The *jihadi* militants are the unseen face amongst the local populace who, having perceived the US weakness, are likely to continue their form of terrorism and expand it into other regions. The corollary is that aerospace power has to be specially equipped and trained along with other surface forces when it comes to fighting them.

The situation in South Asia varies between strong unrest and relatively reduced activity but the evidence and statements being made about the role of the state in promoting *jihadi* activity against India has added to the disquiet. Bangladesh appears to be calm with a democratically elected government maintaining control over the situation but it is a situation of wait and watch. Whereas Pakistan is continuing in a denial mode and is regularly being targeted by militants and is also facing the Shia-Sunni divide. Without an economic upturn, diplomacy and leadership by India, peace will continue to elude South Asia and the regional initiatives will remain just on paper. The spread of terrorist activity based on religious fundamentalism will keep the region on the boil. India will be faced with irregular warfare and the Indian Air Force should be prepared to fight this kind of war under a nuclear overhang. Both China and Pakistan are nuclear powers and are cooperating extensively in developing their strategic strike capability and as long as India does not possess the capability to thwart a ballistic missile attack, as well as a credible deterrent, this will be their principal weapon of choice. Considering the build-up taking place in our region, the Indian Air Force must build the capability, and organise, locate and develop infrastructure to be able to fight a war on both fronts.

Technology Scan

It is very difficult to visualise the kind of aerospace technology that will be available in the next 50 years. In fact, our experience of technological developments in aircraft and systems in the last 100 years could have been a subject of science fiction in 1911. A time horizon of 15 years, however, keeps this study within the realm of reality. Ever since it was realised that air power plays a decisive role in any conflict, there has been a constant and continuous effort to gain a lead over competitors and potential adversaries. The earlier generations of aircraft saw much research in airframes, engines and weapons for speed, manoeuvrability, increased thrust and different air-to-air and air-to-surface weapons but now the focus is on developing the systems. Once the designers saw that they were reaching a plateau, research was refocussed on defeating the systems/weapons already in the possession of the potential adversaries. The present focus areas are stealth, improved sensors like radars, precision weapons, engines offering super cruise capability and synthesising information.

There has always been a close linkage between doctrine and technology, with one spawning the other, but this linkage of late has become more and more one-sided with already proven technologies guiding the development of doctrines, especially in the field of stealth, precision weapons, sensor electronics, cyber, etc. It is evident that newer technologies do make the older ones obsolete and, thus, lead to revision of the doctrines but this happens only when revolutionary changes in technology take place.

Technology development could be evolutionary or revolutionary. Simply stated, F-35 technology is evolutionary but the technology of the F-22 and B-2 was revolutionary. Obviously, revolutionary technology takes time to develop and is expensive but since it is path-breaking, it places the user high beyond the reach of competitors till the competitors either develop a similar level of technology or are able to counter this threat through an antidote.

It is very difficult to define what the sixth generation aircraft will be like but the lead is likely to remain with the USA. There is a possibility that the USA may develop a sixth generation aircraft building upon the fifth generation technologies because of the shortfall in its existing fleet/resources and decision to induct matured technologies. The past experience of developing revolutionary technologies has shown that it has taken more than 15 years to field and integrate a new platform. In case, we consider evolution from the existing technologies, then the following can be surmised.

- There is considerable research going on to defeat stealth, hence, the believers in stealth will try to make the aircraft even stealthier.
- Development of metallurgy/composites to allow the aircraft to change its shape to make it more efficient at all speed ranges and during manoeuvres.
- Development of variable cycle engines to make them operate more efficiently in both supersonic and slow speeds.
- Use of micro-electronics to develop extremely sensitive and highly networked sensors to provide a comprehensive picture to the pilot and operators on the ground.
- Smart weapons, which can loiter, change the aim point and reconfigure to obtain the desired effect on the target. The directed energy weapons when integrated would obviate the need for very high manoeuvrability.
- There is much more research going on in the field of Unmanned Aerial Vehicles (UAVs) and, hence, depending upon the maturity, sixth generation aircraft could be optionally manned.
- Use of the multiplexed fibre optics bus instead of wires will reduce weight and harden against jamming, spoofing, electromagnetic interference and cyber attack.

Air Operations in Joint Warfare
In order to forecast the trends in aerospace capabilities, it is necessary to understand the way air power has manifested ever since the use of aircraft in operations. During the two World Wars, the task of the aircraft changed from reconnaissance to close support, air defence, interdiction and then to strategic bombardment. This change in a time span of less than three decades showed the versatility of air power and the subsequent developments in technology brought to the fore the inherent potential.

Each one of the fighting arms wishes to use this potential of aerospace power to its advantage and wants a larger share of the pie designated to support its operations. Air forces the world over are more keen on defending the air space and ensuring that surface operations are not affected by enemy interference. The Indian defence forces have largely understood this concept but it is yet to find universal acceptance. Interoperability, greater connectivity, regular exercises, confidence building, correct strength in terms of both technology and size and clearly delineated responsibilities of each of the air arms of the three Services will go a long way in optimum utilisation of resources. In India, we have examples of both good and inadequate jointmanship during the operations in the past. Although success may have been ultimately achieved, operations conducted after joint planning have seen more efficient use of resources and quicker success.

What Should be the Focus of Aerospace Power Development?
The foremost requirement is to achieve global aerospace dominance. The tools for achieving dominance are advanced technology, size of the force, doctrine and organisation. So far, the focus has been on manned aircraft but it is shifting gradually to unmanned aircraft virtually in all the major air forces. The question is whether this change is being driven by a long-term view or to beef up forces for the current war? Moreover, are the air forces being prepared for major organisational and doctrinal changes? Whenever there is a mention of power projection, it is the US forces which come to mind. What will be the status of US aerospace power in the next 15 years with dwindling size, delays in replacement of legacy aircraft by the F-35, development of very potent fifth generation aircraft by Russia, China and India, with near parity in space amongst these powers? It is intended to study the game changing trends in aerospace development through a discussion on various D&D programmes in the entire gamut of aircraft, systems, weapons, missiles, combat support systems, space-based systems with a direction for India to progress our own indigenous programmes.

Manned Aircraft
There is a considerable slowdown in developing new fighter aircraft because of the prohibitive cost of development, downsizing, reduced defence budgets, recession and also a shift in focus to unmanned aircraft accepted as most suitable for the current wars. The USA, Russia, China

and India are the only countries developing more advanced aircraft which fall into the fifth generation category and that too in collaboration. There is some mention of the sixth generation aircraft in the media and that too only in the USA but the US Air Force (USAF) has not firmed up the requirements so far and no development programme has been initiated. The USA has all along maintained its lead by taking up generational developments in time so that they are able to field the next generation aircraft before their competitors. Since a development programme takes about 12 to 14 years even in the USA, using already developed technologies, it is evident that there is unlikely to be a revolutionary concept in the next generation. The USA has decided to manufacture only 187 F-22 aircraft and is totally focussed on the F-35 variants. Technologically, the F-35 is a wholly US aircraft but there are eight countries that are tier 1 and tier 2 partners. The programme is about two years behind schedule and way over budget and the partners are wary that there will be no transfer of technology, and major maintenance will be under the central control of the manufacturer. Meanwhile, the manufacturers of the legacy aircraft are proposing to upgrade or replace the legacy fourth generation aircraft with 4+ and 4++ generation (F-15 silent eagle, F-18C/D, SAAB Gripen NG, Euro fighter tranche 3, Su-30 variants and MiG-35 aircraft), etc so that the air forces can retain the combat potential through numbers. The question begging an answer is: what are the potential adversaries likely to field in the next two decades?

China has the largest number of development programmes running to replace old aircraft. Some of these D&D programmes could be to select a winner in the competition and fully develop rivals to the F-22, F-35 and other 4++ generation aircraft. The well known designs being developed by Chengdu and Shenyang Aircraft Corporation are the J-10 (similar to the Lavi), J-13 (possibly a twin engine version of the J-10), and J-14 (similar to the Russian MiG 1.44) and J-15 naval fighter (similar to the Su-33). From the available information, it appears that the fifth generation J-14 will have considerably reduced radar signature and will be optimised for an air combat role but not as good as the F-22 or Fifth Generation Fighter Aircraft (FGFA) PAK-FA. Other developments of note are the indigenous

Light Combat Aircraft (LCA) and its future versions in India and the joint venture between Russia and India to develop a fifth generation aircraft. Japan and South Korea also have the capability to do so but haven't taken a final decision. India, by virtue of its size, aspirations, neighbourhood and the geopolitics of the region, needs to nurture and develop its indigenous D&D capability and the aviation industry. The LCA programme has been a successful technology demonstrator and much more can be expected from the team at the Aeronautical Development Agency (ADA). Now there is a need to develop other operational versions of the LCA and may be even the Medium Combat Aircraft (MCA) by using the proven technologies but with the user having a controlling stake in the programme. There is no aircraft design which has not undergone changes in shape and size after winning the technology demonstration/competition and, hence, the IAF should not shy away from proposing development of an aircraft, which will be operationally relevant for the next forty years. Even at the expense of repetition, a dispassionate hard look needs to be taken to ensure that the LCA or its other versions are developed to meet the future requirements considering the induction and development of aircraft in the neighbourhood. Both quantity and quality are required but the foremost criterion should be self-reliance and to get the numbers through indigenous development. The LCA development has shown that the technologies so far developed are mature and, thus, can be used to build an operational aircraft to meet the IAF's requirements.

Military transport aircraft normally do not attract as much attention as commercial airliners but there have been a few game changers of note, and others which have heralded the arrival of a new manufacturing country on the scene. In recent years, development of the C-17 has been a game changer for strategic airlift. Other ongoing developments are the A-400M by Airbus, An-70 by Ukraine, C-X medium airlift aircraft by Japan, a heavy lift heavier than A-400M aircraft by China, Indo-Russian joint development of the MRTA IL-214 and KC-390 by Embraer Brazil. All these developments are evolutionary and intended to meet the growing need of special purpose airlift, special operations and replacement of existing aircraft. The joint development programme being pursued by

India and Russia is a very good example for a successful venture in terms of cost, timeframe and export potential. Both Lockheed Martin and Boeing are experimenting with their own versions of futuristic aircraft to replace the C-130 with a Short Take-off and Landing (STOL) speed agile version with Take-off (T/O) speed being 70 knots, cruise speed 0.8M, max payload of nearly 30 tons, target Runway (R/W) length of 2,000 ft. This new development is in the wind tunnel testing phase and will require extensive technology development to achieve these requirements through use of upper surface blowing, blown flaps, use of nozzles and flaps to obtain the performance. The USAF has already issued a Capability Request for Information (CFRI) for the C-130 replacement to complement the C-17 with reduced performance and capability to operate from unimproved/ unprepared surfaces. It is possible that the futuristic aircraft design stated above may be proposed by Boeing and Lockheed Martin.

Unmanned Aerial System (UAS)
If the current development of new aircraft looks bleak, it is primarily due to the shift in focus to developing the Unmanned Combat Aerial Vehicles/ Unmanned Aerial Vehicles (UCAVs/UAVs) to fight the current wars. The USAF has even gone through a policy shift and now is training more drone operators than fighter pilots. The versatility and diversity in terms of size, global reach, capability and performance of UAVs have found each and everyone connected with aviation interested. The USA and Israel are still the leaders in UAS technology but other countries have got substantial ongoing development programmes. What makes the UAS development programme very interesting is its breadth i.e. from micro to big airliner size wing spans, endurance from 30 minutes to days and even years (solar powered/hydrogen fuel cells), payload from a few grams to more than 1,500 kg, the operating altitude varies from near the surface to as high as 90,000 ft and even near space for hypersonic UAVs (X-51), carrier-borne operations to extend reach (X-47), from less than 50 kmph to hypersonic speeds, optionally piloted, etc. Development work on manned-unmanned teaming has a huge potential wherein a pilot will be able to command and control the payload on board a UCAV.

Some aspects of this capability have been already demonstrated between a helicopter and a number of different types of UAVs.

The utility of UAS is further highlighted by the fact that the Predators alone have already clocked more than a million hours in combat. A few military planners have even gone to the extent of calling the F-35 the last manned tactical fighter. Although the Global Hawk and Predators are flying over Iraq and Afghanistan under the control of operators in mainland USA, they do not have the freedom to fly on civil air routes. This limitation is understandable for the foreseeable future since the operator still does not have a situational awareness of the entire 360 degree sphere around it and has to contend with issues of reliable systems/ communication, tracking, and rapid command response. The Indian defence forces have been operating the Israeli Heron and Searcher UAVs for nearly a decade since the indigenous development has been slow. The 'Rustom' and 'Nishant' are under development at the Aeronautical Development Establishment (ADE) and are some distance away from induction. There is a need to leapfrog to catch up in indigenising sensors/ sensor data fusion, satellite communication, engine technology, ground control stations, automatic take-off and landing, weapon integration, etc. A range of UAS are urgently required by the defence and paramilitary forces and this demand can possibly be met by indigenous development through joining hands with some friendly foreign country/countries.

Aerospace Power and Force Multiplier Elements
Till recently, it was very common for the military planners to remain focussed on fighter/bomber aircraft and overlook the contribution made by the combat support elements towards winning a war but all this has changed thanks to the lessons learnt from the wars in the last two decades. Force multiplier systems did increase the efficiency and effectiveness of the combat force and they were particularly helpful to airborne components in terms of improving range, persistence and speedy action. Modern war needs the combat support elements to commence their operations even before a fighter aircraft gets airborne. A few examples of the combat support elements are:

- Airborne warning and control system.
- Aerial refuelling aircraft.
- Intelligence, Surveillance and Reconnaissance (ISR) and communication platforms in air and space.
- Maritime patrol aircraft.
- Electronic Warfare (EW) systems.
- Precision weapons.
- Ground/space-based radar and air defence systems.
- Network-centric environment.

The combat support elements mentioned above mainly pertain to surveillance, communication, persistence, precision weapons and networking all these systems definitely brings synergy. The importance of these combat systems has been well recognised and both the government and defence industries of major aerospace powers are driving the research to bring about revolutionary changes. As far as the platforms are concerned, saving costs through the use of militarised versions of civil aircraft as platforms, namely, tankers by Boeing and EADS, Boeing 737-800 for the P-8I/ Joint Surveillance Target Attack Radar System/ Airborne Early Warning and Control (JSTARS/AEW&C) for the Royal Australian Air Force (RAAF), Boeing 767/G-550/Saab 2000/Embraer 145 etc for AWACS/AEW, etc is the key. The integration of the Advanced Electronically Scanned Array (AESA) radar on the Airborne Warning and Control System (AWACS) and AEW&C aircraft has already been accomplished by Boeing, USA, and IAI Israel, and now the USAF is seriously considering changing the 50 year-old platform and also the old rotodome technology. Integration of the AESA radar in a fixed dome has already been accomplished in the Phalcon programme and on the Boeing 737 aircraft on the dorsal fin on top of the fuselage for Australia.

From the foregoing, it is clear that the radar is the most important sensor and that is why maximum efforts are also being made to defeat it through 'stealth' and 'electronic warfare'. Simultaneously, more research is being undertaken to make it more potent. AESA, Over the Horizon (OTH) and dual/multi-band radars hold the key to making the next generation radars detect and simultaneously target a larger number of objects on the ground as well as in the air. Space radar is the most promising area where a number of countries are carrying out research but this programme is very expensive and a constellation of these radars in space can only be maintained through collaboration between different countries. This space-based capability for ISR, radar imaging, command and control, navigation and targeting will be the game changer and that is why all the major countries are developing the capability, either independently or in collaboration. Wars in the last two decades have shown an increasing requirement of communication bandwidth for data fusion, transfer of information and networking all the users. The researchers in the USA are now developing systems to work in Advanced Extremely High Frequency (AEHF) and EHF through satellites and onboard aircraft equipment to operate in the millimetre wavelength. Increased communication bandwidth is essential for the networking of MPA, ISR, JSTARS and EW platforms to enhance effectiveness.

Where does India stand in indigenously developing radar, communication and EW systems and what is the suggested direction? The Defence Research and Development Organisation (DRDO) in India has done some D&D work in the field of AEW, AESA ground-based radar, electronic warfare systems, Electronic Intelligence (ELINT) and Commercial Intelligence (COMINT) ground and airborne systems. DRDO labs have designed systems and sub-systems in the past and utilised the limited capability to fabricate these advanced systems within the country. DRDO has displayed expertise in system integration using the indigenously designed as well as imported sub-systems. Success in airborne AEW and EW systems has been a mixed bag and DRDO must build upon it to meet the needs of the user and also keep on upgrading it by inducting the latest techniques and technologies. The Indian armed forces are individually developing their own communication networks and it is hoped that the networks will be totally compatible. The three fighting arms need to have compatible horizontal and vertical connectivity and information technology systems for their professed goal of jointness through network-centricity. No country has so far been able to test its Network-Centric Warfare (NCW) capability against a capable adversary and, hence, the success of this approach to warfare and future development is based on modelling and simulation. The communication bandwidth is also expected to get a boost with the imminent launch of a military satellite and it is hoped that through joint usage, the spirit of cooperation transcending ownership will emerge. The Indian Space Research Organisation (ISRO) has been a success story when it comes to developing satellite launch vehicles and imaging satellites for military reconnaissance/surveillance and remote sensing. India is one of the few countries, which has a well mapped out programme for peaceful use of space for navigation, communication, imaging/remote sensing and space probes for economic development. Security is one of the major issues in the cyber domain and only a joint approach to cyber security will bring confidence in one another's network.

Weapon Systems Development
Revolutionary changes are in the offing where precision weapons are concerned but real promise is expected through research for directed energy weapons. Although sometimes the discussion on the Directed Energy Weapons (DEWs) verges on science fiction but given sufficient time, these weapons may become a reality. The USA has been the trendsetter in the development of Precision Guided Munitions (PGMs) in the past and now is the undisputed leader in the development of directed energy weapons. Some other developed countries like France, Germany, UK, Israel, etc also have indigenous air-to-air and air-to-surface precision weapons. Only the USA and France have developed the Joint Direct Attack Munition (JDAM), which overcomes the practical limitations of the laser and electro-optic guided bombs. There is clear emphasis on accuracy, matched weapon selection, reduced weight of ordnance and platforms, increased survivability, and limiting collateral damage to avoid bad publicity.

Research in the use of the megawatt class airborne laser as a weapon mounted on a Boeing 747 platform against tactical ballistic missiles has achieved limited success so far. However, plasma weapons and high energy microwaves have a lot of potential to cause serious damage to unshielded electronics, with very little loss of life. These weapons may take another decade or more to be operationalised but will call for a change in the doctrine.

The Indian DRDO and Indian Ordnance Factories (OFs) have lagged behind in developing air-to-surface and air-to-air guided weapons. This is an indirect result of import and licensed manufacture of aircraft since the IAF has always purchased weapons for immediate operational capability and thereafter has not pushed for design, development and integration of indigenous weapons. Recently, DRDO successfully tested a Laser Guided Bomb (LGB) kit in January 2010 and June 2010, and is also developing a Beyond Visual Range (BVR) for the LCA and other aircraft. This is a laudable success but we must realise that LGBs were designed and developed in the Sixties by the USA, France, erstwhile USSR and later by Israel and China. India has a very long way to go in the D&D of precision guided weapons and integrating them on our airborne platforms. This success should spur us to speed up research to bridge the gap between where we are and where we need to go on precision weapon systems and, if required, jointly with other friendly countries. The research in directed energy weapons is very expensive and requires a different technical base than for the normal weapons in use today, hence, research should go on but the focus should be on more precision weapons for all airborne platforms in the near future. The Indian Air Force is the repository of knowledge on air-to-air and air-to-surface weapons and should be the stakeholder in weapons development.

Surface-to-Surface Missiles and ABMs

News of developing and testing ballistic missiles, especially by the countries those are either under sanctions or are in a state of turmoil, grabs the attention of the world community. All major powers having a huge arsenal of missiles, from short range to Intercontinental Ballistic Missiles (ICBMs) have mostly stabilised the numbers and are now busy developing effective Anti-Ballistic Missiles (ABMs). Other smaller countries have found missiles, both ballistic and cruise, very useful in overcoming asymmetry since no country has yet fielded an effective ABM system, and it helps in making the major powers also feel threatened. The US Missile Defence Agency (MDA) has introduced the concept of Network-Centric Airborne Defence Element (NCADE) to target missile launchers and even the missile itself in the boost phase. The concept involves launching boosted AIM-120, AMRAAMs from aerial platforms but the same principle can be extended to versions of the naval SM-3 with wide angle multi-spectral infrared sensors to detect the launch. China is trying to match the missile arsenals of the USA and Russia, in both numbers and capability, and has positioned a large number of medium range missiles to target Taiwan. A number of countries like North Korea, Pakistan, Iran, Saudi Arabia, etc have obtained technology to develop their own arsenals. India also needs to develop the Agni series of missiles, in both numbers and reach. The liquid fuelled Prithvi can at best be a stop-gap arrangement in a 15-year horizon.

India should be prepared to face the threat from ballistic missiles in the region, which are growing both quantitatively and qualitatively. India has already tested a surface launched ABM development programme in the endo and exo-atmospheric regions but should develop the capability similar to NCADE of the USA to counter the short range ballistic missiles, cruise missiles or even an AWACS. It is, of course, a very tall order since even the USA intends to develop the ABM system in partnership with allies but a comprehensive system is a must to counter any potent threat, given the geography of our region.

Battle Space Information and Intelligence

Aerospace power and battlefield intelligence are inseparable. The results of an air campaign will depend upon situational awareness, which in itself is dependent on availability of timely, accurate and comprehensive information about the ongoing battle and the deployed military assets of the enemy. Wars in the last two decades have shown that the USA can call upon a large number of sensors and communication systems, both airborne and space-based, for continuous surveillance at the place and time of its choosing. JSTARS, JTIDS, UAVs, AWACS, satellites, MPA, Airborne Command Post, etc are just some of the sensors/platforms, which have been used in past operations and have proved their efficacy. All major military powers have either developed sensors/platforms of their own or have obtained them from the USA and have ensured interoperability with their war-fighting systems through regular exercises. The USA is undoubtedly the leader in this technology and has been continuously upgrading the level. India has a long way to go in developing these sensors and will face an uphill task to integrate them since the systems are either being purchased or developed and need to be integrated with platforms sourced from different countries. Even integration of systems of different vintage, with some of them verging on obsolescence will cause difficulties. Except for JSTARS, the Indian Air Force has either developed or purchased the other systems/platforms and through Operational Data Link (ODL) and AFNET can achieve the connectivity and networking. A major limitation in the existing system is lack of capability to automate collation from different sources, including Human Intelligence (HUMINT), and fusion, analysis and transfer of the intelligence to the war-fighter in time. The Indian defence forces lack the capacity to handle even the existing amount of data and unless urgent steps are taken to train and equip them, the intelligence personnel will be flooded by the huge amount of data available through networking in future.

Aircraft Engines

Another key technology which must be mastered for self-reliance is the development of jet engines. One cannot become an aerospace power with dependence on imported aero engines. Aero engines are presently the preserve of a few countries and all other military powers without this capability cannot develop their own aviation industry. China is trying to develop its own jet engines to be in the same league as the USA, UK, Russia, France, Germany, etc so as to power their combat aircraft and helicopters. India has already suffered the consequences of lack of capability and, therefore, had embarked upon development of the Kaveri engine for the LCA. There has been very limited success and the only way is to persevere. It is very easy to sermonise but the goal of developing an indigenous jet engine cannot be sacrificed.

Force Restructuring

Major militaries the world over undertake defence reviews for a relook at the strategy, force restructuring to counter the changes in the region/ neighbourhood and also, in some cases, due to the faltering economic scenario. In the recent past, strategic defence reviews have been undertaken by the USA, UK, Australia, Russia and China. The USA has had to review its strategy in Iraq and Afghanistan, which has led to major changes in force employment and equipment induction. The strategic defence and security review in the UK has called for reduction of equipment, aircraft and manpower to affect 8 percent savings. Australia has carried out a review of the threats and has planned to restructure its aircraft inventory. Russia had cut down the induction of new aircraft post the Cold War and has now started ordering new aircraft but their present capability is a far cry from what it had till the Eighties. China has been scaling up its high-tech capability at the expense of manpower and has also restructured its Military Regions. The infrastructure developments in the Tibet and exercises being conducted in the Tibet region have called for major changes in deployment. One common comment on these reviews has been the lack of a new strategy/direction. It has focussed single-mindedly on justified reduction in defence expenditure and the inventory. India has not undertaken any review of the force structure so far and the changes taking place are a reaction to the induction of new equipment. There is an urgent need to undertake a periodic strategic defence review, particularly to decide upon the long-term strategy which will help in the development of infrastructure, review basing policy for aircraft, keeping in mind the induction of aircraft with global reach, and enunciation of the area of interest by the Government of India.

Conclusion

All military powers, having understood the war-winning role played by air and space platforms in the last two decades, have taken steps to build their aerospace capability but are faced with a limitation of technology and economics. Since revolutionary technology is both expensive and takes time, the emphasis has shifted to evolve the existing technology through partnership, cooperation and collaboration. There is also a shift in focus on developing technologies to fight the current war, which may have long-term implications for the USA and some other advanced countries. Unmanned aerial systems and combat support elements are receiving the maximum attention and cutting edge research in the field of directed energy weapons will change the way wars will be fought in the future. Technology development in India has seen limited success but given the impetus and a stake by the user, research can be directed to meet the user needs in the given timeframe. The buyer-seller relationship has no future for India, especially when faced with Intellectual Property Rights (IPR) issues, hence, self-reliance through joint research and technology development with friendly major foreign aerospace powers will be a win-win situation for all. There is an urgent need for institutionalising the process of periodic defence reviews so that military power is developed as part of a strategy, and is not directionless, based solely upon available resources and technology.

Desirable Mix of Platforms in the IAF: 2025

✿ N.V. TYAGI

India is a growing economy, an evolving technological giant, an important nation on the world strategic scenario. In order to sustain and enhance this status, India's armed forces form an important constituent and are increasingly being subjected to enhanced responsibilities and ever growing areas of operations. This is resulting in India's armed forces growing exponentially in capabilities and strength. The Indian Air Force (IAF) is a dynamic force, evolving with time and the need of the hour. With the changing world order and special attention to our immediate neighbours, we need to transform at an accelerated pace to maintain a strategic edge. The ongoing military expansion of China, the uncertainty in Pakistan and other situations in our neighbourhood have resulted in a new higher direction for the Indian Air Force. It is not only the numbers, but also the technological edge which we need to build up by 2025. We look forward to 2025 and we see a capable, strong, technologically advanced, well-knit and integrated Indian aerospace force. Towards this, we need to understand the factors which may affect the force planning. These are as follows:

- Indian economic growth.
- India's strategic imperatives.
- Spectrum of conflict.
- Desired capabilities.

Indian Economic Growth

India's Gross Domestic Product (GDP) is presently ranked 6th in the world and is constantly growing. The present rate of growth has been of the order of 8 to 9 percent. By 2025, India's economy will be worth US$ 3,000 billion and will be the fourth largest economy in the world. By the year 2035, economists envisage the emergence of a tripolar economic order, with India, China and the US competing for dominance over the global economy.

India's Strategic Imperatives
With expansion of Indian national interests, the geographical space and its relevance to national security has expanded. The primary area of strategic interest for the IAF would encompass our neighbouring countries, mainly China and Pakistan, and would stretch from the Malacca Strait in the east to the Gulf of Hormuz in the west, and from the Central Asian Republics in the north to the equator in the south. With the expanding area of influence and responsibility, the government has issued directions to ensure a conducive international and external environment for the unhindered economic progress and socio-political development of India, enabling it to assume its rightful role in the emerging world order. The higher directive to the three Services provides an overview of the existing security scenario and indicates a paradigm shift in our outlook and posture towards our prospective adversaries. In turn, the IAF looks forward to a few objectives:

- Build and maintain credible aerospace power to deter any conflict to ensure unhindered economic growth and social development.
- Prosecute war, if deterrence fails, and inflict unacceptable damage on the adversary.
- Build up capabilities to undertake operations in our area of concern in the short term and area of influence in the long term.

Spectrum of Conflict
War-time Roles: We need to keep in mind the exigencies which are required to be dealt with in the future. It can be a war-time or peace-time requirement for which the IAF needs to be prepared at all times. The spectrum of conflict during war-time can be as follows:

- Total war.

- Limited war.
- Low intensity conflict.
- Counter-terrorism/insurgencies.
- Nuclear war.
- Operations other than war.

Peace-time Tasks: War-time requirements are few and unpredictable, but require preparedness at all times. However, the IAF is continuously involved in various peace-time operations which are as follows:
- UN peace-keeping/peace-enforcement.
- Aid to civil power.
- Friendly military engagements.
- Humanitarian assistance.
- Disaster relief.

Capability Comparison. Military aviation, being technology oriented, has continuously been subjected to change at an ever accelerated pace. It is not just the speed, altitude and range enhancement but much more. The capabilities that the IAF had in 1960 were just a fragment of what we have today. A comparative study from 1960 to today is as follows:

Table 1

Platform / Weapon	Capability 1960	Capability Today
Fighter Weapon Load	1-2 tons	8-10 tons
ROA	1-400 km	1,000-1,500 km + with AAR
Role	Single	Multi-role and swing-role
Weapon Range	8-10 km	300 km ASM
Weapon Accuracy	20-250 m	1-3 m

Changing Employment Philosophy: With the enhanced capability and expected further enhancement in the future, the employment philosophy also needs to be expanded. We need to think in terms of enhancing our capability in a systematic manner. The IAF envisages changing the employment philosophy in the following manner:

- Planning needs to change from 'platform-based' to 'capability-based'.
- The Optical Transition Radiation (OTR)-based strike package needs to be replaced with the effect-based strike package.
- We need to evolve from platform-centric operations to net-centric operations.
- We already have multi-role capability. We now need to undertake many roles within the same missions. In other words, we need to undertake swing-role operations.

Desired Capabilities

With the changed employment philosophy, the capabilities will have to be enhanced exponentially. A completely changed outlook towards the present capabilities is required. For climbing up this ladder, we look forward to the following desired capabilities:

- We need to be able to conduct air operations in our entire area of concern.
- All weather, round-the-clock offensive and defensive operations are essential.
- Enhanced airlift and helilift with required reach is a must.
- Special operations and Out of Area Contingencies (OOAC) capability is needed.
- Network-Centric Operations (NCO) for real-time Command and Control (C^2), air battle management, mission planning and air tasking need to be incorporated.

Planning Considerations: What we need to keep in mind is that everything comes at a cost. Acquiring these capabilities is going to be a long drawn and expensive process. We need to keep a few considerations in mind while planning to achieve these desired capabilities:

- Procurement costs are very high.
- Aircraft upgrade is a viable option to ensure operational relevance.
- A mix of new and upgraded platforms with a mix of high and medium technologies has to be maintained.
- Obsolescence management of electronics and sensors needs to be of the highest order.

- Operation, maintenance and administrative infrastructure needs to be developed to support operations.
- Human Resource Development (HRD) forms an important part.

Force Structure

After identifying our imperatives, desires and considerations, we need to identify the exact capabilities which we look forward to by 2025. All the aerial platforms in terms of fighters, transport aircraft, helicopters and force enhancers have to be identified for acquiring a desirable mix of airborne platforms. A detailed study of individual platforms is required to reach this desirable mix.

Fighter Aircraft: Fighter aircraft are the main offensive force of the IAF. Presently, we have a mix of low, medium and high technology aircraft with a large number of variants available to us. Many of these are completing their calendar life also. However, the IAF is in the process of phasing out the aircraft which are completing their calendar life, extending life where technically feasible or upgrading the existing fleet and procuring new platforms. For our future fleet, a few combat capabilities have been identified:

- Long range and endurance with Air-to-Air Refuelling (AAR) capability.
- Swing role, precision attack, standoff long range weapons.
- Improved avionics and enhanced survivability.
- All weather day and night operations.
- Stealth, super cruise, internal carriage of weapons.
- Short take-off and landing run.
- Low turnaround time, easy maintenance, low operating cost.

For having these capabilities, the identified platforms for future induction for the IAF are the Su-30MKI, Light Combat Aircraft (LCA), Medium Multi-Role Combat Aircraft (MMRCA) and Fifth Generation Fighter Aircraft (FGFA). Also, we need to upgrade our present fleet of Mirage-2000, Jaguars and MiG-29. With the phase out of other aircraft, upgrade of the present fleet and induction of futuristic platforms in a phased, planned manner, we look forward to having a highly potent, agile and reliable combat fleet of aircraft.

Transport Aircraft: For optimum utilisation of these combat aircraft, we need to have an equally potent and sufficient fleet of transport aircraft. These platforms are continuously being subjected to operational and peace-time engagements as these are deployed at forward areas, as well as undertaking all peace-time missions within and outside the country. Support of this fleet is essential for efficient and time-bound deployment of our assets and forces, which may be crucial in any swift, compact futuristic combat scenario. With the requirements of OOAC, the transport fleet has a larger role to play. The capabilities desired in our transport fleet are as follows:

- We need to have aircraft across all categories, from light to very heavy.
- Long range and endurance with AAR capability is required.
- Mission adaptability in terms of load, range and configuration is needed for all platforms.
- Keeping in mind the areas of operations, Take-off (T/O) and landing from short and unprepared runways is an essential capability.
- Improved avionics and enhanced survivability in a technologically dense aviation environment and battlefield are prerequisitess.
- All weather day and night operations capability needs to be incorporated.
- Low turnaround time, easy maintenance and low operating cost are required.

Keeping these capabilities in mind, we look forward to procuring the VHETAC aircraft like the C-17 HETAC aircraft which will replace the ageing IL-76 fleet, Medium Transport Aircraft (MTA) which will be jointly produced by India and Russia and will replace the ageing workhorse An-32, light transport aircraft like the Dornier Do-228, Saras, and replacement of the Avro HS-748 and also communication aircraft like the BBJ and Embraer Emb-135. This mix of all types of transport aircraft will support and augment our operations in all possible contingencies in a big way.

Helicopters: With the agility, ability and multi-role capability, the helicopters are increasingly becoming an important facet of aerial platforms of any air force in the world. Military helicopters are continuously being deployed for operational and peace-time roles effectively. The contribution of IAF helicopters towards numerous operations has been lauded at all levels and needs no elaboration. This enhanced employability of helicopters has evolved the further need of having a much larger and potent helicopter fleet. The desired capabilities of helicopters are as follows:

- Transport and attack roles are the major roles of all helicopters. We need to have helicopters across all categories from light to very heavy for meeting all the roles and tasks.
- Long range and endurance.
- Mission adaptability in terms of load, range and configuration is needed for all helicopters.
- Improved avionics and enhanced survivability in a technologically dense aviation environment and battlefield are prerequisites.
- All weather day and night operations capability needs to be incorporated.
- Low turnaround time, easy maintenance, low operating cost are required.
- Advanced aerial delivery and extraction systems for improved reliability and efficient operations.

For these desirable capabilities, we need to have a fleet of modern Light Utility Helicopters (LUH), Medium Lift Helicopters (MLH), Heavy Lift Helicopters (HLH), communication and attack helicopters. This will be achieved by phasing out helicopters reaching life expiry, upgrading the present fleet where feasible and procuring the newer generation helicopters to maintain a healthy mix of all types of helicopters in view of our future requirements.

Force Enhancers
Modern-day battles have shown aptly the utility of force multipliers and

force enhancers. It is not just the mix of combat, transport and helicopter class of aircraft but also the fleet of force enhancers which make the difference. These assets improve the strike capabilities exponentially and stand out as the major factor towards stretching the adversary to the limit and achieving the objectives.

- **Airborne, Warning and Control System (AWACS), Airborne Early Warning and Control (AEW&C), Aerostats:** These are the eyes in the sky, which not only enhance effectiveness of our own offensive and defensive operations but also stretch the enemy Air Defence (AD) to its limits.
- **FRA:** Flight Refuelling Aircraft (FRA) enhance the range, endurance and load carrying capacity of combat aircraft enormously. The combat aircraft have achieved global reach with the help of FRA.
- **Special Operations Aircraft:** Special operations have become an integral part of modern-day warfare of all types. Innumerable examples exist which highlight the special operations capabilities of the armed forces, especially the air force. The IAF is acquiring the C-130J-30 which is best suited for special operations.
- **UAV and UCAV:** Utility of Unmanned Aerial Vehicles (UAVs) and Unmanned Combat Aerial Vehicles (UCAVs) has been appropriately demonstrated in various modern operations the world over. Besides, safety of human life, it has enhanced the utility of these platforms manifold. With stealth capability, these platforms can prove to be of enormous advantage in various roles. UCAVs with armed UAVs will provide the required safety, surprise, shock and accuracy of strike and provide essential lethal power to strike capability.
- **Reconnaissance and Surveillance:** Maximum information about the adversary is essential for optimally deploying own forces. Adequate reconnaissance and surveillance capability can prove to be a very potent force enhancer in today's conflict situation.
- **Net-Centric Operations:** It is essential for a commander to have real-time battlefield information in order to preclude any fog of war, any doubts about the optimisation of deployed forces. Net-centricity has

become essential in modern-day warfare to enhance the efficiency and capability of the commander and the air warriors engaged in the battle.

These force enhancers are being acquired and there is a need to further increase such procurements in a planned and phased manner and have a well structured fleet of all force enhancers in the desired numbers.

Training

Training is an extremely important facet of any air force and can prove to be the decisive factor in proving its capability and strength. No platform is good enough without well orchestrated, disciplined and focussed initial and continuation training in all the systems, and orientation towards the ethos and values of the Service. Accordingly, training is given a very important role in the IAF. All the basic, advanced and continuity training establishments are undertaking their tasks with utmost sincerity and are instrumental in grooming our operators and leaders. Training platforms are equally important in grooming the operators towards optimum utilisation of these assets. The trainer aircraft for the IAF that need to be procured for future requirements are as follows:

- Basic trainers for replacing the HPT-32.
- Intermediate trainer like the IJT.
- Advanced trainers like:
  - Hawk for fighter training.
  - Dornier Do-228 for transport training.
  - Light utility helicopter for helicopter training.

Budgetary Support

In the light of the existing scenario and perception for the future, the need to optimise existing resources and constantly upgrade in consistence with an emerging India cannot be overemphasised. This indeed is a humongous task and will require huge capital inputs for maintenance as well as for upgradation. The government is indeed aware of this reality and its supportive role is amply reflected in the overall allocations for defence and the IAF in particular over the years.

Conclusion

India has emerged as a great regional power and is aspiring to become a major player in world affairs in the years to come. Accordingly, the challenges for the IAF are increasing, with the emergence of multi-dimensional and multi-front threats. The IAF inventory is a mix of old and new generation aircraft. The IAF is in the process of modernising its combat fleet by upgrades as well as procurement of new platforms in addition to force enhancers. The IAF is also rapidly progressing towards preparing for complete network-centric warfare. Integration of all weapon systems to achieve network-centricity is an important facet of modernisation and the IAF is making rapid progress in this field as well. However, the important factor is that all acquisitions have to be well planned and in a phased manner. Timely acquisition of new platforms and upgradation of the existing fleet is essential to maintain us as battleworthy and help us achieve our aims towards modernisation by 2025. There is a need for adequate and continued budgetary support. An important strategic requirement is indigenisation of defence production and our own Research and Development (R&D), leading to self-reliance in defence production. A strong defence R&D and defence industrial base will ensure building the required fleet of platforms and unhindered supply of essential supplies and stores for the same. Also, adequate maintenance and administrative infrastructure and budgetary support are essential to support this force level.

We are a different force from that of the 1960s or even the 1990s, and we will be different in 2025. Adequate impetus is being given towards the planning of force structure and major steps are being taken towards building a potent, lethal, agile, well connected and powerful Air Force. We look forward to a well balanced, complete Air Force in all respects, with a mix of all aerial platforms, with desirable features and facets.

Major Hurdles in Force Modernisation and Indigenisation

PART I : DEFENCE PROCUREMENT PROCEDURE (DPP)

The armed forces' acquisition proposal is initiated by individual Service Headquarters (SHQ) and forwarded to HQ Integrated Defence Staff (IDS). Simultaneously, copies of it are forwarded to the Administrative, Finance, Defence Production and R&D wings of the Ministry of Defence (MoD). After parallel examination of the case, a meeting is convened of the Services Capital Acquisition Plan Categorisation Committee (SCAPCC). All the stakeholders are invited to this meeting and necessary clarifications are provided by the concerned SHQ regarding various aspects of quantitative and qualitative requirements, commonality and interoperability and the recommended category of the scheme. The Defence Procurement Procedure (DPP) requires a capital acquisition proposal/scheme to be processed under one of the five defined categories. After detailed examination at the SCAPCC, the cases are put up to the higher categorisation committee (SCAPCHC) for according Acceptance of Necessity (AON) for the final category of cases falling within the delegated powers of the SHQ and to make final recommendations for approval by the Defence Procurement Board (DPB) or Defence Acquisition Council (DAC), as applicable, for cases with higher cash outlays.[1]

At the time of forwarding any acquisition proposal to the MoD, the primary concern of the SHQ is to ensure that the required defence capability would be acquired without any compromises and within the desired timeframe. The category which would ensure this objective would be the obvious choice from the various categorisation options provided in the DPP. However, a number of considerations are gone into before the final choice is made for various capital acquisition schemes. This paper examines the user's dilemma/considerations for recommending categories and has given examples of mainly Air Force related projects based on the author's personal experience. The experiences of the other two Services are expected to be similar.

First of all, I would like to dispel a popular myth that the SHQ want only imported top of the line weapon systems. Having spent the better part of my Service career in various Indian Air Force (IAF) Establishments and Directorates at Air HQ connected with capital acquisition, flight testing and evaluation, I can categorically state that the reality is far from it. The SHQ are fully conscious of the axiom; "No nation can achieve great power status on bought out weapon systems and second-hand military technology." They are also fully aware of the perils of imported weapon systems. The buyer may have all the money but he cannot decide what technology he gets. It is the seller who decides what technology to release. In the Cold War era, the buyer's "bloc" affiliation and geo-strategic considerations invariably decided the level of technology to be released to him. For a non-aligned nation like India, more often than not, technology verging on obsolescence was released. The cutting edge technologies were reserved by the superpowers for themselves or their close allies. After the 1962 War with China, India was promised a large amount of military aid by the US. However, when it came to specific equipment, the buyer had no say. India wanted to buy F-104s but the US government decided to release only F-100s, whereas F-104s had been given to the next door neighbour, Pakistan. That is what appears to have prompted India to seek the MiG-21s and the follo- on weapon systems from the then Soviet Union. Even when state-of-the-art technology is offered, it may come with unacceptable strings attached. Many a times, the seller puts severe restrictions on the usage of the weapon system itself. Not only that, many countries have very intrusive end use monitoring regimes which may not be acceptable to the buyer.

Generally, the bought out equipment is optimised for the operating environment and population percentile prevailing in the country of origin which may not be suitable for our diverse and somewhat extreme operating conditions prevailing in the coastal areas, deserts of Rajasthan, tropical jungles of the northeast and mountainous regions of the Himalayas. The buyer is also vulnerable to sanctions and denial regimes for any act which is perceived as being against the interests of the seller. Indian readers would readily recall the embargo on the sale of military equipment, including spares, imposed on India by some Western countries in the wake of the 1965 and 1971 Wars and also various kinds of sanctions imposed in the wake of the 1974 and 1998 nuclear tests. The economic woes of the Western world and intense competition in the global arms market may have reduced the chances of recurrence of such measures, but they do have an important lesson for us.

Apart from the above contingencies, the buyer of an imported weapon system is fully dependent on the foreign Original Equipment Manufacturer (OEM) for the entire technical life of the weapon system for various activities like logistic support, major repairs and overhaul, obsolescence management and design support for flight safety related issues and for periodic upgrades which are vital for sustaining the required capability at the desired level of readiness and operational relevance under changed threat environments. In fact, once a weapon system has been imported, the buyer becomes a captive customer of the foreign OEM for the entire technical life of the weapon system. The OEM can demand any price and the buyer has to pay if he wishes to use the bought out system. Even then, the foreign OEMs are reluctant to commit to lifelong Performance-Based Logistic (PBL) support. Thus, serviceability level or combat readiness of the bought out fleet can never be taken for granted and will depend on the goodwill of the seller.

Looking at the threat environment, India is located in perhaps the most hostile neighbourhood in the world. She is faced with two nuclear armed neighbours who continue to occupy large tracts of her territory. Innumerable rounds of talks have been held with both the neighbours but the boundary disputes remain unresolved. Some of them are even providing covert support to terrorism and insurgency in India. Cross-border terrorism appears to have become foreign policy tool with one of them. Revelations in the wake of the 26/11 attack in Mumbai bear testimony to that. On the maritime front, India has to protect a large coast line and its vast Exclusive Economic Zone (EEZ). India's import dependence for energy resources and other raw materials and imperatives of global trade require that the sea lanes of communication be kept free from interference as they pass through piracy infested areas and are vulnerable to hostile interference. India has a very large diaspora, spread across the globe. As recent events in the Middle East have shown, India will have to come to their aid in case of any trouble sparking off in the countries of their residence. Besides these, there are many other national interests for which the armed forces are required to be ready to act at very short notice. These responsibilities demand that the Indian armed forces maintain a very high level of all round military preparedness to meet any eventuality at short notice. However, our archaic bureaucratic procedures have proved unequal to the task, leading to large scale obsolescence and deficiencies in force levels. Faced with this reality, the SHQ can certainly not be faulted for wanting timely acquisition of capabilities which would match the weapon systems already in the inventory of the potential adversaries. It is with this backdrop that one needs to look at the user's dilemma in recommending the category for various acquisition schemes.

DPP 2011 permits categorisation of an acquisition scheme under the following five categories:

- **Buy**
  i. **Buy Indian:** Outright purchase from Indian vendors only. Hence, the Request for Proposal (RFP) is issued only to the Indian vendors. With the current state of the Indian defence industry, largely the common user items fall in this category. However, in case the system is being integrated by an Indian vendor, the indigenous content must be at least 30 percent.
  ii. **Buy Global:** Outright purchase from global vendors (including Indian vendors).

- **Make:** For systems to be designed, developed and produced in India.
  i. **Strategic/Complex and Security Sensitive Systems:** These are required to be funded and managed by the Defence Research and Development Organisation (DRDO), using the DRDO procedure, with oversight by the Defence R&D Board.
  ii. **High Technology Complex Systems:** These are permitted to be undertaken by Defence Public Sector Undertakings (DPSUs)/ Ordnance Factory Board (OFB)/Raksha Udyog Ratnas (RURs)/ Indian industry consortia on a level playing field and shared development cost basis.
- **Buy and Make:** For outright purchase from a foreign vendor of limited quantity, followed by licensed production in India.
- **Buy and Make (Indian):** For procurements from Indian vendors or Indian joint venture companies having production arrangements with the foreign OEM by licensed production. Such systems must have at least 50 percent indigenous content on cost basis.
- **Under Inter-Government Agreement:** Para 71 of DPP 2011 provides for procurements from friendly foreign countries. These would not follow the standard procurement procedure but a mutually agreed one between the two countries.

Once the RFP is issued under the 'Buy' category, the SHQ are reasonably sure of getting the desired capability in approximately three years. However, there are some problem areas which the SHQ need to take into account before recommending this category. The 'Buy Global' recommendation invites the most intense scrutiny at all stages. At the AON stage, detailed justification needs to be given for the quantities required as well as the qualitative requirements of not only the main equipment but also of the support systems, infrastructure and training requirements, etc. During the Categorisation Committee meetings, R&D representatives resist this category and want the system to be developed indigenously. The DPSUs, on the other hand, want to supply it themselves, as Indian integrators of the system by aligning with one of the global majors. If the scheme passes unscathed, all the problems given under the perils of bought out weapon systems (paras 4 and 5 above) still remain, including the release of the required technologies by the OEM's parent countries. There is also an apprehension of a single vendor situation developing during the procurement process, which may require reissue of RFP.[2] Even after crossing these hurdles, any complaint from an unsuccessful bidder or any other party can cause serious delays in the procurement timeframe. Once that happens, no one in the Ministry of Defence (MoD) wants to touch such a case, lest he be accused of undue haste or bias or some other wrongdoing. The wait for the 'all clear' signal may stretch to years. To avoid inordinate delays, SHQ are even informally advised to take up cancellation of the present RFP and reissue of a fresh one. There may also be occasions which require some deviation from the provisions of the DPP—here too the procurement process may face inordinate delays. Every deviation has to be justified to the DPB and if it is convinced, the case is submitted with DPB recommendations for approval by the Raksha Mantri (RM). The remedy perhaps lies in an independent oversight of the entire procurement process by an empowered regulatory authority— say an Ombudsman for defence acquisition, who should be directly under the RM, outside the normal bureaucratic set-up of the MoD. A prompt independent investigation by him would quickly establish the bona fides of the complaint. In case no malpractice or undue favour to any party is found, the complaint would be dismissed and the go-ahead given to resume the procurement process in a time-bound manner. Only those cases, where a malpractice has been detected, would be referred to the Central Vigilance Commission/Central Bureau of Investigation (CVC/CBI) for further investigation and prosecution where warranted. Similarly, the bona fides of the request for deviation can be established without any delay and if justified, the go-ahead given for the deviation. Such an oversight would ensure better accountability of personnel and even organisations involved in the procurement process and ensure time-bound completion of various activities.

Traditionally, 'Make' projects have been executed by DRDO or DPSUs. Recently, DRDO and DPSUs have also been venturing into joint development projects in collaboration with foreign OEMs. The DPP also provides for major private sector entities with RUR or 'Champion' classification to undertake such projects on cost sharing basis.[3] A closer examination of 'Make' projects being executed or proposed to be executed by various agencies would give a better appreciation of the user's dilemma in considering this category:

- DRDO projects have generally been marred by time and cost overruns and invariably there is performance shortfall vis-à-vis the Services Qualitative Requirements (SQRs). Reliability and maintainability have also not been receiving the attention they deserve during the design stage. Transfer of technology to the production agencies has also not been smooth. Thus, user satisfaction with the end product, as a complete system, has been rather low. The warranty service and product support have also suffered because of the lack of a single window approach. The examples are numerous but I will just the cite IAF's less than satisfactory experience in the induction of the Prithvi missile and Lakshya Pilotless Target Aircraft (PTA).

- The expertise of DPSUs is mainly in licensed manufacture. However, they have also undertaken several indigenous development projects but mainly of low technology products. Whenever they attempted development of medium or high technology products, they had to have hand-holding by a foreign collaborator, e.g. the Messerschmitt-Bolkow-Blohm (MBB) for the Advanced Light Helicopter (ALH), and earlier, Dr Kurt Tank and his design team for the Marut project. In any case, all the DPSU projects have suffered from the problems characterised for the DRDO projects, i.e. time and cost overruns, performance shortfall and low user satisfaction owing to poor reliability, maintainability and also poor product support.

- DRDO has also undertaken several joint development projects. While there has been fair success in somewhat smaller projects, e.g. the Brahmos and Electronic Warfare (EW) systems, the indigenous content in them has been rather low. A number of bigger joint development projects with DRDO and DPSUs are on the anvil, e.g. the Fifth Generation Fighter Aircraft (FGFA), Medium Transport

Aircraft (MTA), Medium Range Surface-to-Air Missile (MRSAM), etc. The jury is still out, and only time will tell how they fare.

- Private sector participation in 'Make' projects has largely been limited to them acting as sub-vendors to DRDO or DPSUs. However, private sector entities have not been able to independently undertake large 'Make' projects on a cost sharing basis, as provided for in the DPP. The primary reason for that is that the first condition stipulated in the DPP for their participation, i.e. the RUR/Champion classification, has still not been fulfilled. Over five years have lapsed since it was first incorporated in the DPP and nothing has been done. It appears that this exercise cannot be left to the Department of Defence Production. There seem to be too many vested interests preventing implementation of this provision. It can only be enforced by the Ombudsman (as amplified above).

The dilemma faced by the SHQ is that while a project with 'Make' recommendation would go like a shot through the categorisation and approval processes, it would have long-term implications for the force levels. There is no guarantee that they would get the combat capability that they require. Also, the development timeframe and the final price tag may be quite different from what was originally envisaged. Even then, one may have to contend with a much lower level of reliability, maintainability and product support, which directly translates into lower combat readiness level. This perhaps explains the approach adopted by the Air Force of accepting the indigenously developed products in support and training roles as well as in less demanding combat environments, even if they fail to meet the IAF requirements in full, while insisting on full compliance with the Air Staff Requirements for the front line equipment. Notable examples of this approach are acceptance of the indigenous Tejas Light Combat Aircraft (LCA), Akash SAM, indigenous Airborne Early Warning (AEW) project, ALH and Intermediate Jet Trainer (IJT) for less demanding combat support roles and training, while insisting on full Air Staff Requirements (ASR) compliance for Multi-Medium Multi-Role Combat Aircraft (MMRCA), MRSAM, AWACS, etc for frontline requirements,.

'Buy and Make' projects are progressed by the MoD in a manner similar to the 'Buy' projects, with the addition of Transfer of Technology (ToT) requirements in the RFP, as specified by the DPSU nominated for licensed production.[4] Therefore, SQR compliance by the selected option is assured. The main/umbrella contract, covering the overall framework, direct supply component, support equipment and training of operators, etc. is concluded by the MoD. Simultaneously, the ToT and licensed production arrangements are negotiated by the nominated DPSU/OFB under the aegis of the Department of Defence Production. Invariably, phased production is undertaken, starting from a few units in the fully assembled stage, followed by some from semi-knocked down and completely knocked down kit stages and, finally, the raw material stage. Delivery schedules for supply of these kits, raw material, jigs and fixtures, production processes, documentation and the associated infrastructure are finalised, together with arrangements for training of various categories of personnel. Often ToT arrangements for Maintenance, Repair, Overhaul (MRO) activities are also finalised at this stage itself or an enabling provision for the same is made.

The SHQ are faced with the dilemma that while SQR compliance is ensured in this option, the DPSU work culture cannot be wished away, with attendant problems of poor product support and low reliability and maintainability of locally produced systems. Also, it is seen that the bulk of the ToT contracted is mainly for one-time front end activities like airframe fabrication rather than for production of fast moving spares and lower technical life sub-systems and aggregates which require frequent replacement for lifelong exploitation. This appears to suit the DPSUs as well as the OEMs. The DPSUs are happy doing more glamorous front end activities and the OEMs are happy as this arrangement ensures the user's life-time dependence on them. The most commonly used excuse is that sub-systems and aggregates are proprietary items of their sub-vendors who are not under their control, and ToT will have to be separately contracted with them. Thus, despite licensed production by the designated DPSU, the user continues to be dependent on the OEM for logistic support of a very large number of items, ROH of major aggregates and sub-systems and obsolescence management, etc. This needs to be corrected by the SHQ by insisting on inclusion of ToT for short life aggregates and frequently required components and spares. This could even be a part of the offset package. During the exploitation of a weapon system, unforeseen problems crop up from time to time and some of them may even require design fixes. Similarly, obsolescence of various computer-based systems requires periodic modifications and upgrades, to maintain operational relevance of the weapon system under a changed threat environment. Since the ToT for licensed production does not involve design related 'know-how' and 'know-why', design support for various flight safety related issues and periodic modifications and upgrades continues to be sought from the OEM. Often, the foreign OEMs charge exorbitant prices for it on one pretext or the other. The MiG-29 and Mirage 2000 upgrade projects are classical examples.

It was hoped that the defence offsets would catalyse the development of ancillary industry which would take on the back end activities like production of spares and short life aggregates and their repair and overhaul. However, the *laissez faire* approach adopted in the implementation of defence offsets has belied this hope and no ancillary industry worth its name has come up and taken on these tasks. Only a dedicated Defence Offset Management organisation with ample representation of users and other stakeholders can play a proactive role in directing offsets into the desired areas to promote ancillary industry as well as to obtain critical defence technologies. The scope of defence offsets could then be enhanced significantly to include creation of infrastructure for training, comprehensive logistic management, including MRO. The period of offset banking also needs to be increased and even offset trading should be permitted in due course. This organisation could formulate a system of multipliers for evaluation of technology offered, and closely monitor faithful implementation of defence offset obligations and their banking and trading (when permitted).

A major difference between the 'Buy and Make' (Indian) and the 'Buy and Make' projects is that in this category the choice of the foreign manufacturer, ToT and production arrangements are left to the Indian vendor provided he absorbs critical technologies and he competes against other Indian vendors based on their project proposals, jointly prepared with the help of selected foreign partners. Other procedural differences are that the AON is obtained through a Capability Definition Document (CDD) instead of a Statement of Case. Likely Indian vendors are identified by SHQ through the Request for Information (RFI) and the approved CDD is floated to the identified vendors. Vendors are then required to submit a Detailed Project Proposal giving details of the foreign partner, development and production roadmap with work share, range and depth of technology and ToT details, indicating absorption of critical technologies, 50 percent of which should be in Categories I & II specified in Appendix L to Schedule I of the DPP. These proposals are examined by a Project Appraisal Committee constituted by the Acquisition Wing and those found acceptable are shortlisted. Thereafter, RFPs are firmed up and issued to the short-listed vendors. Further processing of these projects is as per the procedure for the 'Buy and Make' category.[5]

Depending upon the complexity of the case, the above additional steps for this category could take one to two years. Even then, the project could end up with a DPSU. Thus, the SHQ have to ponder over whether this delay in the procurement process is really worth it. The temptation would be to opt for the 'Buy and Make' category instead. I personally prefer this category as this is a very progressive step, in line with the practices followed by even the advanced countries. If implemented forcefully, this can be a major catalyst in the broadening of the defence industrial base in India and unleash the true potential of the private sector. Therefore, this category should be encouraged for all the schemes where numbers justify licensed production in India. The 'Buy and Make' category in which only a DPSU is nominated for production should be reserved only for very large strategically important schemes like the combat aircraft or warship or main battle tank, etc. To avoid frivolous players vitiating the process, the private sector entities need to be segregated according to their product range and classified as per their production capacity and financial strength, into Tier I, Tier II and Tier III. RFIs and RFPs for various schemes could be accordingly issued to the appropriate entities. This task of classification of private sector entities should also be entrusted to the Ombudsman for the reasons elaborated above. After, say, ten years, when the private sector has also achieved the same degree of proficiency and capacities as the DPSUs, both the categories should be merged into one—'Buy and Make (Indian)'. A high degree of competition generated by this approach will not only ensure better customer satisfaction and life-time performance-based logistic support for the armed forces but also ensure much better technology absorption, in-house R&D and innovation and, thereby, a much higher level of self-reliance. It would also ensure rapid proliferation of the ancillary industry for aerospace components as well as MRO, as seen for the automobile sector. To cut down delays, some simplification of the procedure with parallel processing would be necessary.

The provision of procurements under the Inter-Governmental Agreement (IGA)[6] has been the most preferred option for the SHQ to fill critical capability gaps in the earliest possible timeframe and with the least controversies, especially when the quantities required are small. Even the bureaucracy seems to like it as allegations of wrongdoing or chances of a 'witch hunt' after a change of regime are the least. However, the main difficulty is in convincing the powers-that-be that this is the best option, as it entails a single vendor situation with little transparency in the pricing mechanism. Initially, this arrangement worked wonders with the Soviet Union and its 'friendship' prices. Later, this arrangement continued with the Russians sans the 'friendship' prices. In fact, the Soviet 'friendship' prices have recently given way to some very unfriendly price escalations by the Russians, as seen in cases like the *Admiral Gorshkov* acquisition for the Navy and MiG-29 upgrade for the Air Force. Of late, the United States of America has joined the party with a flurry of acquisitions from them under their Foreign Military Sales (FMS) programme, e.g. C-130J, EW/communication systems for the VVIP aircraft, etc.

To conclude, the imperatives of high military preparedness and uncertainties of indigenous development are the primary reasons for the user to opt for a category which will ensure acquisition of the desired capability, without any dilution and in the shortest possible time. Thus, where the numbers are small, the 'Buy' category under IGA, is the preferred option, followed by the 'Buy Global'/'Buy Indian'. When the numbers are large enough to justify licensed production, the preferred option becomes 'Buy and Make'. Despite licensed production, lifelong dependence on the OEMs has continued unabated due to misplaced priorities for ToT and *'laissez faire'* in implementation of defence offsets. The 'Buy and Make (Indian)' category entails a much longer procurement timeframe due to the additional requirement of preparing a detailed project proposal prior to even the issue of RFP, thus, it has not found favour with the SHQ. However, if implemented forcefully, it has the potential to revolutionise the defence industrial base. Uncertainties of SQR compliance, development timeframes and costs render the 'Make' option the least preferred. No wonder, even six decades after independence, India is yet to cross the 30 percent mark for indigenous military equipment. The challenge lies in reversing the present order of preference to 'Make', 'Buy and Make (Indian)' and last preference for the 'Buy' option, so that the ratio of 30:70 can be changed in favour of indigenous equipment and our combat readiness does not remain mortgaged to the goodwill of foreign OEMs. For this to happen, indigenous development agencies will have to become far more accountable and responsive to the user requirements. Also, certain organisational and procedural changes, identified in the paper, would be necessary.

PART II: STAFF QUALITATIVE REQUIREMENTS (SQRS)

In the name of probity and transparency, the Defence Procurement Procedure (DPP) has been made very cumbersome and time consuming. By its own stipulation, the time taken for an acquisition under ideal circumstances is two to three years after the acceptance of necessity is accorded by the Defence Acquisition Committee (DAC). Practically speaking, the time taken for various steps is much more than stipulated. Various actions required to be completed at SHQ and HQ IDS before accord of AON can easily take up to two years. Thus, even for a simple system, from the time the operational necessity is felt to the time its contract is concluded, it would take about five years, and for complex systems, there is no upper limit. The AJT took exactly 20 years from requirement formulation in 1984 to contract conclusion in 2004. Similarly, the requirement for the MMRCA was felt in 1998-99, the AON was accorded in 2001, L1 was announced at the end of FY 2011-12 and if all goes well, the contract would be concluded in 2012-13. Under these circumstances, the only way the SHQ can minimise the procurement timeframe is by completing various activities assigned to them in a professional and proactive manner.

The most important activity by the SHQ in the acquisition process is the formulation of their Staff Qualitative Requirements (SQRs). In the Army, these are known as General Staff Qualitative Requirements (GSQRs), Naval Staff Requirements (NSRs) in the Navy, and Air Staff Requirements (ASRs) in the Air Force and these are issued by the respective SHQ. For equipment common to two or more Services, these are formulated under the aegis of HQ IDS and are known as Joint Staff Qualitative Requirements (JSQRs). Unrealistic or poorly drafted SQRs can lead to a single vendor situation and, in some cases, even disqualification of all the contenders. The bedrock of DPP is to create maximum competition so as to achieve maximum economy. Therefore, a single vendor situation before the field evaluation stage necessitates cancellation of the RFP and reissue of a fresh one. For that, the concerned SHQ has to face significant embarrassment by having to give an explanation for the lapse and then obtain approval for the issue of a fresh RFP at an appropriate forum in the MoD, in the presence of the Service Chief/Vice Chief. In the case of indigenous development, unrealistic requirements can lead to not only time and cost overruns but may even require short closure of a project due to serious shortfall from specified performance parameters. In either case, the ultimate loser is the user who has to suffer the consequences of degraded capability for extended periods.

It is generally accepted that a user knows best what he wants. This principle has also been recognised in the DPP and the responsibility of formulating SQRs has been entrusted to individual SHQ. However, a wide range of factors influences the definition of required capability or final choice of weapon system. The three most important factors which need to be taken into consideration are the threat environment, technologies available and affordability. The first is a given, arising out of the geostrategic environment, relations with immediate neighbours and national interests and aspirations. The last is defined by the government in the form of budgetary support for the current year and an indication of the likely availability in future, based upon which annual and long-term perspective plans are made. Thus, authentic and indepth knowledge of the technologies available becomes crucial for the definition of required capability in the form of realistic SQRs. It may sound simple but defence deals, the latest developments in the various types of weapon systems and the emerging military or dual use technologies are shrouded in secrecy. What is published in the magazines and journals or posted on the internet are articles and snippets based on generalised or deliberately leaked information. *Jane's* defence related publications are considered most authentic. Even in these, unclassified information of a general nature is provided. Another source of information comprises the OEMs and their agents. They regularly bombard the SHQ with a large number of glossies and brochures and offer unsolicited briefings and presentations about their equipment. These are for sales promotion and make tall claims about their products, while carefully hiding shortcomings or technological limitations or impending obsolescence. Often, the systems offered by them or technologies employed in these systems are obsolescent. The state-of-the-art or emerging technologies are zealously guarded or denied by them. Only after an obsolescent system has been bought are the later models employing contemporary technologies revealed or offered. The depicted capabilities are normally under ideal conditions. At times, it is seen that OEMs from South Africa, Israel and some East European countries even advertise for weapon systems and technologies which may only be under development or at a conceptual stage, awaiting a potential buyer to fund their development. Also, there is a large difference between the unsubstantiated claims put in the glossies and the guaranteed performance required under user defined operating conditions, to be demonstrated during field evaluation, and the reliability and maintainability levels to be specified in the contract, with stiff penalties for non-compliance. Thus, there are many pitfalls in the formulation of SQRs based on such ambiguous sources of information.

Availability of technology is another aspect which needs to be taken into account while formulating the SQRs. The technology may have been developed but if the seller is not willing to release it to the user, it is of no use. As brought out in Part I, cutting edge technologies are often denied to the developing countries or non-aligned nations like India. Even when state-of-the-art technology is offered, it may come with unacceptable strings attached. Many a times, the seller puts severe restrictions on the use of the weapon system itself. Not only that, many advanced countries have very intrusive end use monitoring regimes which may not be acceptable to the buyer. Thus, technologies and weapon systems developed by such countries have to be considered not available. In today's globalised world, we often see mergers and acquisitions and cross-holding of shares by various multinational companies. Products of a company located in a country practising technology denial or its subsidiaries in other countries are similarly not available. In fact, one needs to identify substitutes for even components and aggregates of such companies fitted on third country systems. A classical example of this was the need to identify and fit substitutes for American origin components on the Hawk, as the US had imposed sanctions on India in the wake of our nuclear tests, and we had to pay a sum of over Pounds Sterling 30 million to BAE Systems as integration cost for the substitutes.

India has one of the most varied and demanding operating environments comprising a highly corrosive saline and humid atmosphere in the coastal areas, extremely high temperatures in the western sector, dense tropical forests in the east, and high mountainous terrain in the north where the temperatures can dip down to -30 to -40°C in winters and extremely 'hot and high' conditions prevail during the summer. The laws of physics dictate that performance levels, in terms of system accuracies, engine output, aerodynamic efficiencies, etc, are much degraded in the rarefied atmosphere of the Himalayas. Similarly, the cooling requirements for crew comfort may not be achievable in the very high temperatures of the Rajasthan desert, rendering a system unusable in the peak of summer. Also, reliability and maintainability levels could be much lower at extreme temperatures and in saline and humid atmospheres. In addition, India's population is varied in terms of body measurements. Thus, the weapon systems would not only need to operate over a very wide range of climatic and topographical conditions but would also need to be ergonomically adjustable for a very wide range of the Indian population percentile. Therefore, a technology scan based on published literature or glossies supplied by the OEM would not be adequate to formulate realistic SQRs. It would need to be based on authentic information supplied by the OEM in response to a Request for Information (RFI) or test reports from the test centres of the country of origin or other users, and take into account availability as well as performance levels moderated for our operating environment.

Obtaining various test reports and their detailed analyses to determine the maturity levels of various technologies and their application in various weapon systems is a highly specialised activity. Dedicated scientists and engineers, with detailed analytical and data archival and retrieval infrastructure, are needed for this task. Unfortunately, the Army and Air Force do not have any organic design and development capability[7]. Hence, they are severely handicapped in obtaining/developing an authentic data bank of cutting edge and emerging technologies, their likely application and availability. Perhaps recognising this limitation, the DPP stipulates that the draft SQRs are vetted by the Staff Equipment Policy Committee (SEPC), comprising members from the user and maintenance directorates, MoD, MoD (Fin), DRDO, Certification, Standardisation, QA agencies, DPSU concerned, Department of Defence Production, etc. It is hoped that all the wise men from diverse fields would critically examine the draft SQRs and remove all the anomalies. After clearance by the SEPC, the GSQRs are formally approved by the designated Principal Staff Officer (PSO) at the SHQ and cleared for inclusion in the Request for Proposal (RFP) without any further scrutiny. At a macro level, this arrangement appears to be perfect, however, the devil is in detail. The reality is that half the members of the SEPC are non-technical, looking at procedural and financial aspects. The others have knowledge/interest in limited niche areas. As is typical of the bureaucracy, the Director level appointments are members of such middle level bodies. However, the Director is a very busy person and is required to attend to many urgent bushfires. Membership of this committee is an additional 'burden' for him, with no direct accountability for its decisions. Invariably, an unconnected substitute is detailed at the last moment to represent the Director. The substitute has little to contribute to the subject under discussion and normally confines himself to the part concerning his department but occasionally he comes out with misleading or motivated suggestions which may require significant time and effort to undo.

Different SHQ follow different models for formulating SQRs. However, the common approach is that the procurement directorate asks the specialist directorate to forward the draft SQRs along with the SOC for the scheme, with maintenance related QRs being sought from the concerned maintenance directorate. They, in turn, with the help of various field formations/training centres or specialised establishments, prepare the draft SQRs. Unfortunately, the staff at the user directorates or field formations/training centres has little expertise in procurement procedures. The information available with them is largely based on the journals/internet or hearsay. They are not even in direct communication with foreign agencies or our AAs/DAs. There is also a tendency by the staff to demand 'a little more', thinking that the system would come into service only after five to ten years and the state-of-the-art would have moved on. Therefore, they tend to list the best features they have read or heard about, without realising that such a hybrid system may just not exist. An interesting example of this was the draft ASR for survey and target towing aircraft presented to me in 2003, prior to submission to the SEPC (known as the ASR Committee in the Air Force). The draft ASR had been formulated taking inputs from the specialist agencies responsible for the various tasks it was required to perform. While the document was comprehensive, some of the requirements in terms of performance parameters and space allocation in the cabin and baggage hold, etc did not appear to be realistic. On query, the JDs and DDs rattled off the names of different aircraft on which these requirements had been complied. However, when asked for a single aircraft on which all the requirements could be complied, there was no answer as they had picked the best features of various aircraft in the fray. The draft ASR had to be sent back, asking them to reformulate it in such a way that it could be complied in full by at least three existing aircraft in the world market.

Invariably, innovative tasks like the SQR formulation are given to the bright and ambitious officers. Bright as they are, they are quick to find out the preference of the boss. The requirements are thereafter 'tweaked' appropriately. Sometimes, this may also happen on the direct orders of the brass. An interesting example of this is the ASR for the much talked about MMRCA. Impressed by the Mirage 2000 performance in the Kargil conflict, the IAF put up a requirement for inducting 126 Mirage 2000 multi-role combat aircraft. However, the then Defence Minister approved the requirement of 126 combat aircraft but annotated that the choice of the aircraft was to be determined as per the laid down procedure. The IAF tried hard to convince the MoD that the Mirage 2000 was already in our inventory and should be procured under the DPP provisions of "more of the same". When it did not succeed, an attempt was also made to tailor the ASR to suit the preferred aircraft. That is when the term 'medium' was added to the MRCA. It became a classical case of the user not knowing what was best for him. If he had his way, he would have ended up inducting technology of the 1980s in the second and third decades of the 21st century. However, better counsel prevailed and a broad-based ASR was thereafter prepared with clear annotation of current technologies and selection of L1 on the basis of cost of ownership for a defined usage (a variant of life cycle cost).

As regards SQRs for indigenous Design and Development (D&D), the main players are the DRDO and DPSUs. As brought out in Part I[8], the private sector has been effectively kept out of it by vested interests, despite a novel procedure set out for its participation in the DPP. It is well known that the DRDO and DPSUs, in their exuberance to get the project, lead the user to believe that the SQRs will be met by them in full in whatever timeframe the user wants, with total disregard to their own technological limitations and past record. In their Feasibility/Project Definition Reports (FR/PDRs) too, they make very unrealistic/optimistic projections in terms of development timeframes as well as cost estimates to achieve the SQRs. Invariably, the time and cost estimates are exceeded by large margins and concessions are sought to SQRs for shortfalls in many areas. At times, the shortfalls are so acute or in such critical areas that the project has to be foreclosed. Thus, the user must make critical assessment of the capabilities of the development agencies and their design and development related tie-ups, fall back options, etc. The ultimate objective of any development process is to efficiently produce the desired system in the required quantities for induction and to sustain it at the specified level of combat efficiency for the defined period of usage. Therefore, the production agency for DRDO projects must be identified at the very outset and the PDR should be prepared by them jointly, with clear identification of responsibilities for conversion of design drawings into production processes and drawings, warranty obligations, time-bound delivery of product support, design support, obsolescence management, upgrades etc. Thereafter, a collaborative approach needs to be adopted between the user, developer and the production agency with joint design reviews at critical milestones/timeframes. These aspects need to be specified in the SQRs, along with a provision to foreclose the project if the development agency is unable to meet the specified design objectives within the defined timeframes. This would also act as a deterrent against the development agencies making overambitious projections of their capabilities and development timeframes. The SQRs should normally provide for spiral development for complex projects, with base line/proto-type models, based on the existing major sub-systems and technologies, and clearly defined incremental improvements required thereafter in succeeding production batches/blocks, e.g. block-wise improvements in the F-16 and MiG-21 family of aircraft.

It is generally seen that in the 'Buy and Make' projects, there is a reluctance on the part of OEMs to arrange ToT for the bulk of fast moving and short technical life components and aggregates, which are essential for long-term sustenance of the acquired weapon system[10]. The normal excuse offered is that these are vendor supplied items and that they have no control over them. The DPSUs are also happy in obtaining

ToT for more glamorous front end one-time activities such as fabrication of airframes and major sub-assemblies, instead of getting bogged down in protracted negotiations with a large number of OEMs of fast moving and short technical life components and aggregates. The user needs to safeguard his long-term interests of product support and obsolescence management by including the ToT requirement for such items in the SQRs for the 'Buy and Make' projects. Once included in the SQR, there is no escape for the OEM or the DPSU. As and when the DPP permits, these could be included as offsets required to facilitate development of ancillary industry.

The DPP stipulates that only essential requirements are to be included in the SQRs and non-compliance with any requirement would automatically disqualify the system on offer. Therefore the SQRs must be simple, realistic and broad based. In other words, they must be qualitative in nature and define minimum operational needs. The quantitative requirements should be as few as possible, without which the system will be totally unacceptable. While they must specify the operating environment and percentiles, any temptation to add any other unnecessary details to the SQRs must be resisted. The quantitative requirements must be based on authentic information, duly moderated for our operating environment, as these would need to be demonstrated during field trials in India. Such authentic information about a weapon system can only be supplied by the manufacturer or the user service in the country of origin. It is for this reason that the recent revision of the DPP has made it mandatory to issue an RFI to all the known manufacturers of the desired systems prior to formulation of SQRs. The RFI would need to give the intent for acquisition, broad requirements and seek detailed information on their systems, as applicable under Indian operating conditions. To ensure authenticity of information and to weed out non-serious and undesirable vendors, the RFIs should contain a cautionary note that any shortfall from the claimed performance could lead to disqualification of the vendor. All ambiguities in the vendors' responses must be clarified through detailed briefings by the vendor teams and written confirmation obtained for all amendments and amplifications.

The UK's Acquisition Policy consciously recognises that 'best is the enemy of very good '. After all, only one system can be the best and any attempt to acquire only the best would automatically lead to a single vendor situation. Thus, it would be self-defeating to aim for the best as it would thwart the ongoing procurement process besides causing embarrassment to the SHQ concerned to get approval for the issue of a fresh RFP. Even for indigenous development, it needs to be recognised that any incremental improvement in performance beyond the existing state-of-the-art comes with significant increase in cost and a large measure of uncertainty. Our young, bright and ambitious officers need to be made aware of this prior to being given the task of formulating SQRs. Also, after they have formulated the SQRs, they need to be tasked to show compliance in full by at least three options based on the authentic information obtained through the RFIs.

Speaking for the armed forces, their primary objective is to fight and win wars. Thus, the grooming of their officer cadres is focussed on leadership and combat related functions of the various arms and Services. There are so many criteria for command and staff appointments and career courses for an up and coming officer, that each appointment at mid and senior levels is compressed to barely 18 to 24 months. Yet, it is necessary for the best and the brightest to be exposed to procurement related appointments so that as PSOs and Commander-in-Chief (C-in-C) they understand the intricacies and manage these processes proficiently. However, there being no structured training for acquisition processes, most of their tenure in such appointments goes in learning from their mistakes. Thus, training capsules, covering procurement related procedures and organisational structures in individual SHQ, HQ IDS and MoD, need to be designed for officers at various levels posted to the SHQ and MoD for such assignments. These should be conducted preferably every month at Delhi so that all the newly posted officers at the various SHQ and MoD can attend them with least resistance. This would ensure full effectiveness of such officers from the very beginning of their tenure. It is heartening that the MoD is considering setting up an Acquisition Institute for this purpose.

The SHQ need to recognise that formulation of SQRs is a multi-disciplinary activity requiring inputs from a large number of agencies associated in the operation, maintenance, training and other support activities associated with the desired capability. Also that all the serving officers are busy with their allocated duties and formulation of SQRs is an additional burden on them. Therefore, the current approach prevalent in various SHQ of asking every agency to give its inputs, to be compiled into one by a coordinator, would not work. For a realistic and cohesive SQR to be formulated, a dedicated multi-disciplinary team needs to be constituted, drawing experts from these agencies, and formally tasked to formulate first the RFI, followed by analysis of responses and, finally, the preparation of the draft SQR. As we have seen, young ambitious officers are known to blindly follow the orders of the boss, even if the order is biased. Therefore, there is a need for independent validation of the draft SQRs before they are put up to the SEPC for clearance. For meaningful independent validation of SQRs, once again, a multi-disciplinary team would be needed, with members having domain expertise but outside the control of the uniformed brass and other agencies with vested interest in the project. For this, the services of recently retired officers with the required domain knowledge and expertise could be used.

In conclusion, it can be said that formulation of SQRs is the most crucial activity in the acquisition process. Clear definition of minimum operational needs, based on authentic information of the available technology options, would ensure timely acquisition of the desired capability at a most economical price. This paper has identified the major lacunae in the present practices followed by various SHQ in SQR formulation and gone on to suggest remedial measures to overcome these. By following these simple suggestions, the armed forces can contribute immensely in making realistic SQRs and ensuring that no procurement or indigenous development process is thwarted due to unrealistic SQRs.

Notes

1. Paras 4 - 20 of DPP 2011 for 'Buy' and 'Buy and Make' procedures.
2. Para 36, p. 13 of DPP 2011
3. Para 3, p. 149 of DPP 2011, 'Make' procedure.
4. Para 27, p. 10 of DPP 2011.
5. Para 25a, p. 9 of DPP 2011.
6. Para 71, p. 21 of DPP 2011
7. The need for 'Organic D&D Capability in the IAF' has been covered in detail in a separate paper in the book.
8. Paras 9 - 12 of Part I.
9. Para 12 of Part I refers to this.

Force Modernisation:
Indigenous Focus

✿ A.K. NAGALIA

The last two decades have seen the Indian economy taking rapid strides. Today, it is the third largest economy in the world and is on the threshold of double digit growth. However, India is an energy deficient country and has a vital interest in maintaining stability in the oil producing countries. As its manufacturing industry grows, its dependence on shipping for import of raw materials and export of finished goods will increase. It, therefore, has a vital interest in keeping the Sea Lanes of Communication (SLOCs) open and free from interference by pirates and other non-state actors. With rapid economic growth, India's stature in the global community has also gone up significantly and other countries look at it as an important actor in the stability of the Asia-Pacific region. It is also aspiring to be a permanent member of the UN Security Council. In fact, most countries, including the USA, have endorsed this.

South Asia is considered one of the most unstable regions in the world. India has already fought several wars with Pakistan and China on boundary disputes. Both have laid claims to large tracts of Indian territory and, in fact, these continue to be under their occupation. Relations with other smaller neighbours are at best uneasy. In the wake of this, India has to manage its relations with the immediate neighbours and adequately respond to the unrest developing in the extended neighbourhood from Strait of Hormuz to the Strait of Malacca. Internally too, India faces insurgencies in Kashmir and the northeast, and Maoist movements in the central regions. India also has a very large diaspora spread across the globe from New Zealand in the east to the American continent in the west. In times of need, they look up to India to intervene on their behalf or if the situation so demands, to evacuate them from the trouble spot. History has taught us that no country has been able to maintain growth and achieve supremacy without intrinsic military strength. Therefore, capabilities have to be built across the entire spectrum of conflict, covering not only aerospace but cyberspace too.

Technology has always had a decisive impact on the outcome of war, whether it was the discovery of gun powder in the early days or nuclear weapons during the closing stages of World War II. In today's world of rapid advancements in technology, obsolescence is a major problem for operational planners. Here, we are faced with a paradox. On the one hand, advancements in metallurgy and production processes have significantly improved fatigue tolerances and the technical life of various platforms. On the other hand, various onboard systems like sensors, communications, radars, displays and monitoring and control systems are Information Technology (IT) intensive. Therefore, they follow Moore's Law, which states that the processing power of a given size of computing device doubles every two years. Therefore, upgradability has to be built into the weapon system at the design stage itself, e.g. modular designs or open system architecture. However, for imported equipment, the user is at the mercy of the foreign Original Equipment Manufacture (OEM) for upgrade or replacement. In our case, the situation is indeed bad, as the bulk of our combat assets and support systems are imported and are verging on obsolescence. We have to depend on foreign OEMs for their upgrade or replacement for the foreseeable future.

'Force modernisation' is a continuous process: while its direction is technology dependent, the quantum would depend on availability of resources and the threat environment faced by a nation. Since there is no permanent friend or enemy and intentions can change overnight, it is incumbent to take steps to match the capabilities of the neighbours and others likely to become competitive. Keeping in mind our regional and global aspirations, we must have expeditionary capability, complemented by space-based assets and must adequately cover the emerging dimension of cyber warfare. A study of our own existing inventory which is based on decades old technology, degraded over a period of time, immediately drives home the crying need to modernise the equipment through either replacement or upgrade.

Taking advantage of the US vulnerabilities in Afghanistan, Pakistan has been steadily modernising its armed forces, especially the Pakistan Air Force (PAF). It has upgraded its existing F-16 fleet as well as sought a fresh supply of F-16s. The F-16 upgrade kit includes modern sensors, advanced Electronic Warfare (EW) suite, Night Vision Goggles (NVG) compatible cockpit, Beyond Visual Range (BVR) and precision strike capabilities. In addition, Pakistan is also undertaking joint development of the J-17 aircraft with China and there is also a possibility of the sale of the J-10 by China. With the induction of BVR and already acquired SAAB Airborne Early Warning and Control (AEW&C) system, the Pakistan Air Force has considerably eroded the Indian Air Force (IAF) superiority and both the air forces will be almost at par. Pakistan is also continuing with its policy of fomenting internal trouble with the help of *jihadi* militants. Also, it has been frequently flashing the nuclear card. The need to modernise obsolescent IAF combat assets is, therefore, all the more urgent.

China has been steadily developing infrastructure in the Tibetan region and is working towards transforming its military force and to build its capabilities. It appears to be focussed on developing capability for anti-access and area denial, keeping in mind the US commitment to defend Taiwan in case of an attack by Mainland China. China continues to follow the policy of encircling India – also called "String of Pearls". The investment in defence Research and Develpment (R&D) by China is huge when compared to the amount spent by India. It has been variously put as $30 billion vis-à-vis India's $2 billion. Even the Prime Minister (PM) acknowledged this recently, and called for much greater investment in R&D in various fields. The Chinese defence industry has also come of age. It is no longer content with copying the Russian designs. Backed by the extensive state owned defence R&D organisation, it is undertaking *de novo* design and development of combat aircraft like the J-10 and J-17 and has a flourishing export market to achieve economies of scale.

It is no secret that the IAF is facing deficiencies to the tune of 20-25 percent in government authorised force levels. Out of the existing inventory too, only 20-25 percent assets can be called contemporary. About 30-35 percent of them are in mid-life, in various stages of upgrade, and the rest are verging on obsolescence, awaiting replacement. This is not all: an overwhelming majority of our combat assets and support systems is imported (including licensed produced items) with the bulk from Russia. Thus, we have to depend on foreign OEMs for their sustenance, upgrade and/or replacement for the foreseeable future. We have very little to show by way of indigenous R&D, and the defence industry is largely restricted to a handful of Defence Public Sector Units (DPSUs) and Ordnance Factories (OFs). Also, the bureaucratic approach of the Defence Research and Development Organisation (DRDO) and the public sector work culture of DPSUs do not give much hope for the future

In Financial Year (FY) 2011-12, a budget of Rs 1,64,415 crore was allocated to the Ministry of Defence (MoD) (1.83 percent of India's GDP), with Rs 69,199 crore earmarked for capital acquisitions. In his budget speech, the Finance Minister also mentioned that the government had accepted the recommendation of the Thirteenth Finance Commission that defence allocation should increase at the rate of 8.33 percent per annum. However, in terms of GDP, this translates into a progressive reduction to 1.76 percent by FY 2014-15, well below the normally accepted optimum level of 3 percent of GDP. This year, the IAF share amounted to Rs 46,152 crore (28 percent of the defence budget) with Rs 30,224 crore earmarked for modernisation. The IAF, being a capital intensive Service, has a much higher modernisation budget, amounting to over 65 percent of the IAF budget or 44 percent of the entire defence modernisation budget. But the reality is that even this allocation would barely meet the requirement of replacements to combat obsolescence and not make good existing deficiencies for which special allocation outside the normal budget will have to be made. What is even more worrisome is the inability of the MoD to gainfully spend the allocated budget. Year after year, large sums of money from the modernisation budget are being returned unspent. In the last decade alone, the MoD has surrendered over Rs 50,000 crore.

Modernisation entails infusion of contemporary technologies which may have long gestation periods and require large capital outlays. Therefore, the process commences with a detailed study carried out to define capabilities required to meet the operational tasks of the future, covering the next two to three decades and the likely budgetary support required. Modernisation may require either replacement of the obsolete equipment through fresh acquisition or upgrade of existing assets. In either case, it has to be processed as capital acquisition, the Bible for which is the Defence Procurement Procedure (DPP). Currently, DPP 2011 is in force. It defines that these requirements, based on their launch date, are split into the long, medium and short terms. The requirements covering the period of next 15 years are compiled in the form of a Long-Term Integrated Perspective Plan (LTIPP), divided into three 5-year plan periods called Services Capital Acquisition Plans (SCAPs). From the individual Service plans received from the three Services, the integrated LTIPP and SCAP are prepared by Headquarters (HQ) Integrated Defence Staff (IDS) and submitted to the MoD for in principle approval. From the current SCAP, the Annual Acquisition Plan (AAP) is culled out, which is a rolling plan and covers a period of two years, and in the case of some long gestation period schemes, it may stretch to even three years or more.

A major objective of a developing country, starting from a very low industrial base, is to promote self-reliance in sourcing of various weapon and support systems. However, as brought out above, India also faces a very grave threat environment because of which choices were not easy. While maintaining contemporary war-fighting capability, it had to establish de novo a military industrial complex and embark on the path of self-reliance. Under these circumstances, the Air Force had to find an optimum product and technology mix for outright imports, licensed production and indigenous development, so as to achieve a very high degree of self-reliance, without compromising immediate operational imperatives. Keeping these objectives in mind, Air HQ appears to have adopted the judicious approach of accepting indigenously developed products in support and training roles as well as in a less demanding combat environment, even if they fail to meet the Air Staff Requirements (ASRs) in full, while insisting on full ASR compliance for the frontline combat assets, and it formulates its acquisition proposals accordingly.

Proposals for acquisition are sent to HQ IDS in the form of SOCs for categorisation and Acceptance Of Necessity (AON). Thereafter these are discussed in detail in the categorisation committees for completeness of the proposal, necessity, quantity vetting and categorisation and the scheme is recommended for approval by the Defence Procurement Board (DPB) or Defence Acquisition Council (DAC), as applicable. After approval these are placed in the AAP and the procurement process is initiated. The acquisition process for approved schemes involves the following stages:

- Solicitation of offers or issue of Request for Proposal (RFP) - (1.5m)*.
- Evaluation of technical offers by the Technical Evaluation Committee (TEC) – (9m)*.
- Field Evaluation – (15-21m)*.
- Staff Evaluation – (16-22m)*.
- Oversight by Technical Oversight Committee (TOC) for Acquisitions above Rs 300 crore – (17-23m)*.
- Commercial negotiations by the Contract Negotiation Committee (CNC) – (21-29m)*.
- Approval of the Competent Financial Authority (CFA – MoD/MoF/ CCS) – (22-33m)*.
- Award of contract / Supply Order (SO) – (23-34m)*.

* Cumulative time taken after AON is accorded.

The above arduous journey of an acquisition proposal faces many challenges and hurdles, the foremost being the formulation of ASRs. This aspect and other major challenges and hurdles which stem from various provisions in the DPP have been dealt with in detail in a separate paper titled, "Major Hurdles to Force Modernisation and Indigenisation". Other major challenges which need to be contended with are briefly covered below:

- In the past, we experimented with sourcing avionics, sensors and Electronic Warfare (EW) equipment from different vendors in different countries, to be integrated in the Russian platforms. It led to enormous logistic problems and delays, beside disputes arising out of integration problems caused by differences in design standards and interface philosophies. This aspect needs to be addressed in the RFP stage itself, with clear demarcation of responsibilities of various parties involved. In addition, vendors must commit to provide design support for integration requirements in the future.

- The CNC is required to determine reasonable and fair cost of equipment, especially under a single vendor situation and/or where difference in the original cost estimate of the scheme and the actual proposal is very large. This is a highly complex and arduous task and can hold up the commencement of commercial negotiations. Thus, original cost projection should be carefully prepared, based on the Request for Information (RFI) rather than glossies or the internet.

- Field evaluation is another area which falls within the user domain and can lead to major delays, even jeopardising the procurement process. Considering the diverse operating environment and terrain prevailing in India, the test schedule for the equipment needs to be drawn up very carefully so that it covers all the vital parameters without causing too much delay. Also, there may be a requirement for certain tests to be carried out in the OEM's facilities due to non-availability of the required test infrastructure in India or impracticality of transporting the trial equipment to India. To avoid unnecessary delays in obtaining approvals at a later stage, such cases need to be identified at the RFP stage itself and the need for it incorporated therein. While the user is given the charge of the field evaluation, a number of other agencies are required to be associated with it, e.g. Director General Quality Assurance, (DGQA), Centre for Military Airworthiness Certification (CEMILAC), DRDO, DPSUs, etc. There is a need to closely coordinate various tests with them to avoid delays. Representatives of such agencies may at times have diverse/ motivated views, which need to be resolved quickly so that they do not cast aspersions on the suitability of the option despite it meeting all the ASRs.

- Since 2005, a minimum of 30 percent offsets has been mandated in all projects worth more than Rs. 300 crore. The DPP calls for offset proposals to be submitted in three stages: firstly, an undertaking along with the proposal for the main scheme, and a little later, a technical proposal giving an outline of the offsets planned and, finally, a detailed commercial proposal. The former is processed parallel to the technical/field evaluation and the latter parallel to the CNC. If the offset offer of the L1 vendor has some anomaly, it would need to be amended by him before the main contract is concluded and this can cause delays.

As in the past, following the above procedure, the IAF will continue to procure various urgently needed combat assets from various sources across the globe. However, that would not decrease its dependence on imports. Even after six decades of dedicated efforts in building indigenous capabilities, only a few combat assets and support systems are indigenously produced. Many of these are produced under licence by DPSUs. This state of affairs needs to be reversed and the path to self-reliance adopted in greater earnest. The canvas is very vast and we need to ponder over what can be taken up for indigenous development in different disciplines. First the combat aircraft. After 27 years of painstaking effort, the Light Combat Aircraft (LCA)/Tejas programme is beginning to bear fruit. In January 2011, it was accorded Initial Operational Clearance (IOC) and cleared for induction into service. It is hoped that Final Operational Clearance (FOC) status will be achieved soon, with a more powerful engine and full suite of sensors, weapons and EW equipment so that it complies with the ASR. We need to launch the follow-on MCA programme at the earliest so that the expertise gained in this vital field is not allowed to wither away. Although we have joined hands with Russia in their venture for developing the Fifth Generation Fighter Aircraft (FGFA), because of our late entry, Russia has already developed 90 percent of the technologies relating to the airframe and aero-engines. India will, therefore, have to rest content with mainly the development and integration of avionics, sensors, weapons and EW systems. However, we must insist on having access to core technologies for super cruise, stealth and super manoeuvrability. The Unmanned Aerial Vehicles (UAVs) have already proven their efficacy in Iraq and Afghanistan. Much larger Unmanned Combat Aerial Systems (UCAS) are expected to play a more dominant role in future and, hence, a number of development programmes are going on in different parts of the world. Our own UAS programme covers a very small spectrum of it, micro/mini to High Altitude Long Endurance/Medium Altitude Long Endurance (HALE/MALE). We need to leapfrog in this fast emerging field. The need for persistence has also been recognised and we also need to undertake development of the airship-based surveillance system. In the not too distant future, hypersonic platforms will dominate the near space. This is another area that we need to focus on and develop leading technologies.

India has traditionally imported transport aircraft for the Air Force as well as the aviation industry, except the licensed production of the HS 748 and Dornier 228. In a departure from the past, Hindustan Aironautics Limited (HAL) is embarking on joint development of a Medium Transport Aircraft (MTA) along with the Russians for meeting the IAF and Russian Air Force requirements. Upon successful development, this platform should be further exploited for various ancillary applications like Airborne Early Warning (AEW), Flight Refuelling Aircraft (FRA), survey, MR, etc. In the civil aviation sector, National Aerospace Laboratories (NAL) is developing the Saras in the 15-20 passenger range, and a regional jet (as yet unnamed) in the 50-90 passenger range. For larger aircraft, once again, a collaborative approach would be desirable. Based on the confidence gained through the development of the Dhruv helicopter, HAL is already undertaking development of a Light Combat Helicopter (LCH) and another Light Utility Helicopter is on the drawing board. It is also venturing on a 10 ton class Multi-Role Helicopter (MRH). With India's diverse and inhospitable terrain and poor infrastructure, especially in its frontiers, the requirement of helicopters for the military as well as civil sectors is bound to increase exponentially in the coming years.

These programmes, therefore, need to be accelerated. Where required, design collaboration should be sought so that these programmes can be completed in a time-bound manner.

Aero-engines comprise been a weak area and unless we are able to develop engines in various categories to fulfil our needs, we will remain dependent on others. The Gas Turbine Research Establishment's (GTRE's) overambitious project hopping has led us nowhere. In future, we need to restrict our R&D efforts to realistic and realisable projects. Design collaboration for the development of the Kaveri engine needs to be progressed in a time-bound manner, with proper accountability for all involved. Upon successful development of the Kaveri, its core engine, the Kabini, can be further developed for application in Unmanned Aerial Vehicles (UAVs), helicopters and small transport aircraft. HAL's success in developing ultra small engines for application on the Lakshya and for the Joint Strike Fighter (JSF) needs to be exploited further to develop a family of small jet turbines for futuristic needs.

India's missile development programme has indeed done us proud, with notable success in the development of the Prithvi and Agni families of Surface-to-Surface Missiles (SSMs). The success of the Prithvi Air Defence (PAD) and the subsequent interceptor missile has been encouraging and its further development into a credible Ballistic Missile Defence (BMD), along with associated long range detection and control radars holds the key towards credible deterrence, especially in view of our 'No First Use' policy. Synergistic deployment of BMD, alongside the existing AD network comprising the ground-based and airborne radar network, Surface-to-Air Missiles (SAMs) and manned interceptors, with fully integrated command and control is necessary to ensure seamless protection against intruding aircraft and missiles. The responsibility for this integrated defence of our air and space should naturally be that of the IAF. Despite some early setbacks, DRDO's SAM development programme is now on track. The Akash system is entering service shortly. The MR SAM system is under development in collaboration with foreign vendors. Similarly, the supersonic cruise missile Brahmos, an Indo-

Russian joint venture, needs to be equipped with state-of-the-art sensors and guidance system for giving it sub-metre accuracy. Development of the Astra Air-to-Air Missile (AAM) also needs to be accelerated to reduce our dependence on foreign weapon suppliers in this vital area.

So far, we have been able to develop only dumb air-to-ground weapons and fuses. Our attempts to develop cluster bombs and runway denial weapons also did not bear fruit. Precision strike capability is no longer a force multiplier but an operational necessity. With minute to minute coverage of operations by the electronic media, any collateral damage to nearby civilian property or civilian casualties brings about an immediate adverse reaction and can seriously undermine the morale of forces. Therefore, this capability has become inevitable and needs to be looked at as a system of systems, comprising Precision Guided Munitions (PGMs), aircraft, sustained surveillance, targeting and net-centricity, etc. Various elements involved in it need to be developed in parallel. We have been attempting to develop Laser Guided Bomb (LGB) kits for some time and I hope that we succeed in it soon and further exploit these for development of the Joint Direct Attack Munition (JDAM) kind of weapons using integrated GPS/laser guidance. Only 'leap frogging' with a focussed approach will help develop key technologies associated with precision attack capability. Directed Energy Weapons (DEWs), using electro-magnetic or laser beams are the weapons of the future. DEWs have the advantage of multiple target engagements , with rapid retargeting. The laser weapons are extremely precise and can even intercept ballistic missiles. While their development process is very complex and expensive, there is no escape from it.

In modern warfare, combat support systems like the Airborne Warning and Control System (AWACS), aerial refuelling, surveillance radars for both ground and aerostat applications, net centricity, a range of EW and Electronic Support Measure (ESM) equipment, etc, earlier known as force multipliers, have become essential elements of a contemporary air force. Therefore, the IAF has rightly shifted its focus to acquiring such systems and many of them are in the pipeline. These inductions will provide immediate capability but will not serve the purpose of self-reliance unless technologies are developed simultaneously and the future upgrades/replacements of these systems are done with indigenous elements. In this connection, development of the Integrated Air Command and Control System (IACCS) by the IAF and AEW&C by the DRDO are noteworthy. Integration of all ground-based radars, aerostats, airborne sensors and combat aircraft through secure data link with multiple levels of redundancy is the next step to achieve network-centricity for future warfare. The amount of information flow required for network-centricity is really mind boggling and this is only going to increase in the future. Therefore, an adequate level of redundancy, in terms of channels as well as bandwidth, needs to be built into the systems.

Control of information has, and will continue to be, a central component of military operations. With an ever increasing reliance on flow of information through cyber space and accepting the tenets of net-centric warfare, the vulnerabilities have also increased in this domain. Two recent developments have clearly demonstrated that this is the new domain where wars will be conducted in the future by states as well as non-state actors. In the first instance, the injection of the 'Stuxnet' worm for attacking Iranian nuclear installations, the first institutional manifestation of cyber warfare by a state. This is suspected to have been developed jointly by the USA and Israel and has disabled an undisclosed number of Iranian centrifuges used for uranium enrichment. It has also shown that a cyber attack can create tactical, operational and strategic effects at little cost and with relative impunity. The prowess of non-state actors was visible in the Wiki Leaks and its aftermath wherein a large scale assault was launched by a 'anonymous group of *hacktivists*' on businesses opposed to Wiki Leaks. These have demonstrated that non-military establishments are no less vulnerable to information warfare as also the helplessness of the state to even trace them, much less counter-attack them. The byte size weapon can easily go undetected past the most sophisticated firewalls in nanoseconds.

China has already stated its aim to attack the soft ribs of the powerful adversary and to prepare for a war in the backdrop of what it calls, '*informationalization*'. The People's Liberation Army (PLA) has also established the first 'Information Security Base', which is expected to mushroom into a dedicated Cyber Command in due course. The USA, on the other hand, has already created a dedicated Cyber Command under its Strategic Command for cyber warfare. This was reported to have achieved full operational capability in October 2010. India, the so-called Information Technology (IT) superpower, too needs to take appropriate measures, at the national as well as local levels. The IAF, in particular, needs to recognise that with ever increasing networking of its ground-based and airborne assets, its vulnerability to cyber attacks has also increased exponentially, and it needs to take the lead in this emerging field of warfare.

Space-based assets touch every aspect of modern warfare. India, with its widely dispersed diaspora and global aspirations, needs to lay greater emphasis on its military space programme. Although the IAF is late in realising the potential of space-based surveillance systems, nevertheless, the plans to launch a dedicated satellite is good news. Both, sustained surveillance and global communications are essential for net-centricity and expeditionary capability. This has been amply demonstrated during the Chechen War in 1999 and the more recent Gulf Wars. A networked precision strike to incapacitate terrorists and their camps will be possible by judicious fusion of Human Intelligence (HUMINT) with information from a large number of sensors, including space-based sensors.

Force modernisation has two facets viz, equipment and personnel. It is easy to visualise the weapon systems requirement since this aspect is always given prominence but the aspect of organisational restructuring, Human Resource Development (HRD) and grooming of the next generation of leaders does not get the required focus. Both the facets of modernisation must develop simultaneously to avoid the traditional mistake of fighting the next war using techniques/concepts perfected in the last war. Both are interdependent and need simultaneous attention for a smooth induction and '*operationalisation*' of new equipment. Some of the new systems demand a sea-change in operational philosophy and work culture. The Air Force will have to get over its aversion to simulators and assign much greater importance to the simulation and gaming techniques in the operational training and leadership grooming curricula and proficiency evaluation systems. A host of individual system simulators, networked multiple system simulators and scenario development and gaming simulators need to be established. New operational philosophies and concepts can be evolved only through judicious use of these. We also need to integrate cyber warfare in our operational mould as this is going to be omnipresent, blurring the distinction between peace and war. Experience shows that the most outstanding cyber warriors are jean toting rebellious teenagers or twenty somethings. It is difficult to visualise them being 'strait-jacketed' in the Service uniform or hierarchy. How can the Air Force use them effectively? It throws open new challenges to our so-called time-tested 'P Staff' policies.

To conclude, force modernisation is a continuous but well planned activity. It is both technology and resource dependent. Today, the Indian Air Force is plagued with obsolescence and deficiencies in its combat force levels. It no longer enjoys a decisive edge over the likely adversaries, who are focussed on modernising/building up their air power. Also, the Indian Air Force continues to rely on imported combat assets and support systems, a few of which are produced under licence by the DPSUs. This state of affairs needs to be reversed and the path to self-reliance adopted by user driven and user led Design and Development (D&D) projects. The requirements are very large and across the spectrum. We have to prioritise and progress various D&D projects, with the intent to increase self-reliance. The huge potential of the private sector also needs to be harnessed if the indigenisation process has to be furthered. Our modernisation process must also include the human element. Our archaic training curricula and personnel policies need to give way to modern simulation-based training curricula and scientific HRD policies for grooming the next generation of leaders.

Ignoring Organic R&D in the IAF and its Consequences

○ A.K. NAGALIA

Introduction

The Indian Air Force (IAF) prides itself in being the fourth largest Air Force in the world. In the last decade, it has been rubbing shoulders with the very best in the world, in various bilateral and multilateral exercises held in India and abroad. The IAF pilots have earned kudos from the various air forces they have exercised with and have been rated among the very best. The IAF has come out with flying colours in the 'Red Flag' exercise held in 2008 in the Nevada Desert of the USA, both in the air as well as ground operations. It has fully operational high end force multipliers like Airborne Warning and Control System (AWACS) and Flight Refuelling Aircraft. (FRA) to support its operations in any theatre of war.

One can indeed be proud of the above achievements. However, are these enough for the IAF to rest on its laurels? It has the unenviable task of defending the country against two nuclear armed potential adversaries. Both are in the process of rapidly expanding and modernising their armed forces, especially the aerospace assets. They are also in close alliance with each other and have made no secret of their intentions against India. the IAF, on the other hand, finds itself deficient of nearly 25 percent of its combat assets and support systems, both airborne as well as ground-based. Also, barring the Su-30MKI fleet and the limited number of recently acquired/contracted weapon systems, all other airborne and ground-based assets in the inventory of the IAF are verging on varying degrees of obsolescence. Despite having produced under licence and operated the MiG-21 variants for over three decades, we had to go back to the Russians for its avionics upgrade. The same is the story for the MiG-29 and Mirage 2000 upgrades. Even after six decades of independence, we have to depend on foreign sources to not only make good the deficiencies in the combat assets but for fighting obsolescence as well. How have we allowed such a situation to develop? Have we forgotten the axiom, "No nation has attained great power status on bought out weapon systems and second-hand military technology"? Are only the bureaucrats at South Block, Defence Public Sector Undertaking (DPSUs) and Defence Research and Development Organisation (DRDO) to blame for this state of affairs? Has there been any contribution of the IAF itself in it? Let us examine the latter.

Need For Organic D&D Capability in the Air Force
It is universally accepted that a user knows best what he wants. However, there is a wide range of factors to influence his choice. The most obvious and desirable factors which need to be taken into consideration are the threat environment and desire to improve self-reliance in sourcing and sustaining the desired capabilities. Not so obvious factors are the numerous agents or lobbyists of various global arms merchants trying to push through their products. Ingenious methods are employed by them to influence the user's choice. The most innocuous ones are sleek glossies and unsolicited presentations making tall claims about their products, while carefully hiding shortcomings or technological limitations or impending obsolescence. The more enterprising adopt devious methods like employing gullible politicians or bureaucrats or senior service officers to influence the choice of decision-makers in various garbs. Often, the systems offered by them or technologies employed in these systems are obsolescent. The state-of-the-art or emerging technologies are zealously guarded or denied by them. Only after an obsolescent system is bought are the later models, employing contemporary technologies, revealed or offered. Since the imported equipment needs to be well proven, it is normally procured halfway in its life-cycle with the parent country or in some cases even later. Thus, the parent country support is likely to be

available only for a small part of its intended period of utilisation by the buyer. Thus, the buyer needs to safeguard his interest by getting critical design data or 'know-how', as a part of the initial acquisition, to be able to undertake periodic upgrades and manage obsolescence related hurdles. For gainful utilisation of the design data so obtained, the user needs to have organic Design and Development (D&D) capability.

Organic D&D capability in an air force provides a ready set-up, comprising suitably qualified designers and engineers in various disciplines, the necessary laboratories and associated infrastructure, for the following functions associated with optimising selection, induction and life-time exploitation of various imported systems in the most efficient manner:

- Technical appreciation of various technology options available in the global market and identification of the most optimum.
- Assistance in evolving realistic Air Staff Requirement (ASRs) which will ensure multiple choices and fair competition to achieve an optimum balance between operational capability and economy.
- To be the repository of design data and 'know-how/know-why' of various operational systems in the inventory of the air force.
- Evolve in-house solutions to various emerging threats by using the best available technology options.
- Evolve various periodic upgrade/modernisation packages to maintain operational relevance through the entire life-cycle of a weapon system.
- Obsolescence management to avoid disruptions in the supply chain.
- Provide a pool of experts to manage various outright purchase projects through various phases of acquisition, induction and life time exploitation, i.e. 'cradle to grave' approach.

A major objective of a prudent air force is to promote self-reliance in sourcing and life-time exploitation of various weapon and support systems in its inventory. For a country like India, which started from a very low industrial base but faced a very grave threat environment, the choices were not easy. While maintaining contemporary war-fighting capability, it had to establish *de novo* a military industrial complex and embark on the path of self-reliance. Under these circumstances, organic D&D capability plays a crucial role in ensuring that the Air Force finds an optimum product and technology mix for outright imports, licensed production and indigenous development. To be able to eventually achieve a very high degree of self-reliance in a reasonably short time, the organic D&D capability has to perform the following functions:

- Concept development and proving.
- Technical appreciation of various design options.
- Assist in evolving realistic ASRs for progressive compliance during the development cycle.
- Assist the design staff of the nominated D&D agency in interpreting the ASR and provide other user related inputs during the detailed design phase.
- Provide a pool of experts to manage complex D&D projects and allied activities.

Historical Background

At the dawn of independence, the country had a very low industrial base, with practically no defence industry. By way of aeronautical industry, there was a small factory in Bangalore, set up by Seth Hirachand Walchand in 1940, which was later nationalised and is now known as Hindustan Aeronautics Limited (HAL). Out of the three Services, the Air Force has always been most technology intensive, followed by the Navy. Know-how about military aviation in the country existed only in the Air Force. All the technical functions like formulation of technical specifications for futuristic requirements, modifications, inspection/testing, acceptance, etc. were being carried out by the Services themselves.

While the Navy decided to keep the warship design, certification and inspection functions with itself, the Air Force decided not to have an organic D&D capability, despite there being no other agency having expertise in this highly specialised field. The IAF's decision to give up design certification and quality assurance/inspection during production and acceptance functions, which are usually the prerogative of the user, was indeed inexplicable. The DRDO and Department of Defence Production gratefully accepted the opportunity and promptly set up Resident Engineers and Resident Inspectors at DPSUs, who were controlled by D Aero and DTD&P (Air), predecessor organisations to the present day Centre for Military Airworthiness Certification (CEMILAC) and Directorate General of Aeronautical Quality Assurance (DGAQA) respectively. Not only that, the Air Force also supplied them the expertise in these fields by parting with some of its highly qualified and experienced engineers and other technical staff. The Air Force was now left with General Duty Pilots and Maintenance Engineers and technicians, supported by small complements of administrative logistic and other support staff. It no longer had the expertise to respond to various emerging threats by evolving in-house solutions using the best available technology option, integration of innovative solutions on various fleets, in service upgrades, inspection and certification related activities. Whenever even a simple integration task had to be done, an *ad hoc* team was constituted by Air Headquarters (HQ) for the specific task and dissolved after completion of the task, without the organisation being wiser of the experience gained. Alternatively, it was given to HAL to manage it.

Impact of Ignoring Organic D & D Capability

HF-24 Marut Development
In the mid-1950s, the IAF issued an ASR for the indigenous development of a supersonic Multi-Role Combat Aircraft (MRCA). Its performance attributes included a ceiling of 60,000 ft, speed of Mach 2, interception capability at various altitudes, and low level ground attack with a radius of action of 500 miles (805 km). Dr Kurt Tank and his team of 18 engineers were invited to work at HAL to develop such an aircraft in India. The team arrived in India in 1956 and set about converting the ASR into an aircraft, designated HF–24, which was later christened 'Marut'. The aircraft was designed around Bristol Siddeley's twin Orpheus BO-12 engine configuration. The BO-12 was being designed as 8,170 lb

thrust after burning engine, against a British government requirement. Unfortunately, the British requirement for such an engine was dropped and the Government of India (GoI) refused to underwrite the remaining developmental expenditure of Pounds Sterling 3 million. (Also mentioned as Pounds Sterling one million by some old timers involved in its D&D activities.) It was decided that as an interim measure, the development and initial production of the Marut would be continued with the Orpheus 703 engine, which was under licensed production in India for the Gnat programme, while a frantic search was launched to find a suitable engine to realise its full potential. The Egyptians were developing the E-300 engine of similar specifications with the help of a German design team around the same time. It was decided to join hands with them. In fact, one aircraft was positioned there and modified and flown with this engine. However, in the wake of the 1967 Arab-Israeli War, this project was foreclosed. Thus, a suitable engine for the supersonic Marut was never found. Even the transonic Marut in pure ground attack configuration had to be prematurely phased out in the late Seventies due to poor reliability and maintainability. Those of us who have flown this aircraft, still swear by its pleasant handling and superb acceleration characteristics and are unanimous in saying that this marvellous machine deserved a much better fate.

After this very brief overview, let us examine, with the full benefit of hindsight, how lack of in-house D &D capability in the Air Force contributed to faulty decision-making and poor project management which contributed to the premature demise of the Marut.

- Had the IAF maintained an in-house D&D capability, the following facts and complexities/difficulties would have been apparent and taken cognisance of and perhaps a more practical approach adopted to build indigenous D&D capability, instead of issuing such an ambitious ASR.

  (i) In the aeronautical field, the only D&D experience the country had was that of designing a basic piston trainer called the HT-2 and the production experience of manufacturing the Vampire under licence.

(ii) The Chief Designer of HAL, Dr Ghatge, was vehemently opposed to such an ambitious venture. In fact, he resigned from HAL when he was overruled.

(iii) The entire infrastructure at HAL, including its runway, was totally unsuited for this class of aircraft.

(iv) At the time of conceptualising the Marut, the IAF knew well that only the world powers like the USA, UK, USSR and, to a lesser extent, France, were undertaking development of this class of aircraft. Since this aircraft would be in direct competition with theirs, no help could be expected from them in this venture.

- Having pushed the country into a venture of this magnitude, the IAF should have led from the front in managing the programme, by appointing a dedicated Project Management Team (PMT), backed by sound technical advice, instead of leaving it to HAL and the bureaucrats.

- To a dedicated and technically sound user driven programme management, it would have been apparent that without the Orpheus BO-12 engine, the Marut as a supersonic MRCA would remain a pipedream. The IAF should, therefore, have prevailed upon the government to accept the funding of the remaining development of this engine. After all, Pounds Sterling 3 million was not such an astronomical sum even by the standards of those times. (In some places, it is also mentioned as Pounds Sterling 1 million, which is a small fraction of it.).

- While it was a good decision to engage Dr Kurt Tank and his team of engineers for the design and development, the IAF should have insisted that a similar approach was necessary for overseeing the upgrade of the production infrastructure and processes at HAL.

- Even the transonic Marut had to be prematurely phased out because of poor reliability and maintainability. It certainly casts serious aspersions on the manufacturing infrastructure, practices and processes at HAL and the Quality Assurance (QA) oversight provided by the CRIs under the then DTD&P(Air).

Ajeet Development

It is well recognised that the Gnat was one of the most compact designs for its time. So much so, many major functions in it had been combined, e.g. flaps with ailerons, airbrakes with the undercarriage, etc. Taking advantage of its small size and light weight, it could outmanoeuvre and outperform most of its contemporaries. However, it was a very unforgiving aircraft. Perhaps it was for this reason that it was never inducted in the Royal Air Force (RAF), the air force of the country of its origin. In the IAF service, it had the dubious distinction of the poorest flight safety record, that too when only average plus pilots were posted to the Gnat squadrons. The fatal accident rate on it was several times higher than on any other aircraft in the IAF inventory. Despite all this, the decision to allow HAL to develop it into the Ajeet with wet wings and four drop tanks and giving it an air-to-ground role was certainly not based on sound technical appreciation. Developing the Ajeet trainer with ambitions to use it as Advanced Jet Trainer (AJT) was even more inexplicable, as the Gnat trainer already existed and was in use with the RAF. If the IAF had an organic D&D capability, these aspects would have been analysed in depth and such a project not attempted. Possibly, we could have saved one full decade by launching *de novo* D&D of a fighter aircraft or at least an AJT, as a follow-on to the Marut programme.

LCA Development

In the late Seventies, the IAF projected a need for MiG-21 replacement, which was planned to be a simple and rugged aircraft, to be produced in large numbers to replace the MiG-21 variants in the IAF. The requirements were deliberately kept simple and even the high altitude performance, both in terms of altitude and mach number, were significantly lower than the MiG-21. The Air Staff Target (AST) 201 was issued for this project in 1982. The Ministry of Defence (MoD) formed a team under Dr Valluri, with members from the IAF, HAL and DRDO to examine various aspects connected with indigenous D&D and production of such an aircraft, including foreign collaboration and project management. The committee added an innocuous goal to this programme: "all round advancement in indigenous D&D and production capability in the field of aerospace by mastering cutting edge technologies such as Digital Flight Control System (DFCS), Multi-Mode Radar (MMR), flat rated turbofan engine, composites, etc'. It recommended creation of the Aeronautical Development Agency (ADA), a dedicated design coordination and programme management agency for marshalling design capabilities existing in various DRDO and other government labs, academic institutions and PSUs, as well as for seeking design consultancy from abroad on various aspects.

In 1983, the Light Combat Aircraft, (LCA) programme was formally approved by the government and ADA came into being in 1984. Detailed discussions were held between the IAF and various other associated agencies and the formal ASR was issued for the LCA in 1985. Project definition was completed by ADA in 1987. It was decided to simultaneously launch development of the 'Kaveri' engine, MMR, DFCS and a whole host of avionic Line Replaceable Units (LRUs) along with the launch of aircraft development. Physical (weight and volume/dimensions) and performance characteristics were assigned to each one of the systems/LRUs under development and it was hoped that all of them would be ready in the desired timeframes and fit in like a grand 'jig-saw' puzzle. At this stage, the IAF expressed severe reservations with this approach, as recorded in the note of dissent by the IAF members in the Srinivasan Committee report. Consequently, it was decided to split the Full Scale Engineering Development (FSED) in two phases. In the first phase, critical technologies were to be successfully developed and demonstrated to the IAF and then only the was the go-ahead to be given for FSED Phase II, comprising full prototype development. The IAF decided to adopt a 'hands off' approach until demonstration of critical technologies. The IAF was finally demonstrated the core technologies and it recommitted itself to the LCA development programme in 2005 and it was decided that a multi-disciplinary IAF Project Monitoring Team (PMT) would be positioned at ADA for close monitoring of the project and to coordinate various requirements with the IAF. Soon thereafter, a contract was concluded with HAL for the supply of 20

Tejas in Initial Operational Clearance (IOC) configuration, equipped with GE 404 IN-20 engine and ELTA's MMR. However, it took another couple of years for the IAF PMT to be positioned at ADA, over two decades after commencement of the LCA design.

Let us now examine how ignoring the in-house D&D capability has affected the LCA programme.

- In the absence of a dedicated in-house D&D group, there was no organisational appreciation of the complexities involved and it was left to the whims and visions of the individuals occupying seats of power to take vital decisions which had far-reaching consequences. What was worse was that these visions were not necessarily shared by their successors:

  (i) The IAF allowed the Dr Valluri Committee to tamper with the original objectives by agreeing to an additional goal of "all round advancement in indigenous D&D and production capability in the field of aerospace by mastering cutting edge technologies" being added to the programme objectives. This single act, perhaps due to the non-availability of institutional technical advice, caused the burial of a simple and rugged MiG-21 replacement aircraft for induction in the IAF in 1995 and gave birth to an ambitious R&D programme with indefinite time-lines.

  (ii) Once the above 'innocuous' goal was allowed to be added to the programme, there was no stopping the DRDO from building a huge design infrastructure in the form of ADA, parallel to HAL's existing aircraft design bureau.

  (iii) The most important lesson of the Marut debacle, i.e. the need to follow the time-tested approach of designing an aircraft around well proven engine and other critical systems, was forgotten and simultaneous launching of design and development of the 'Kaveri' engine, MMR, DFCS and a whole host of avionic LRUs was permitted.

  (iv) In 1989, within six years of the formal sanction of the LCA development, the IAF had a major change of heart which culminated in a "total hands off approach" during the most crucial phase of D&D where close interaction is required between the designers and the user. It was only due to the continuous hand holding by the IAF test pilots and test engineers on deputation to the NFTC that the LCA design achieved the present level of maturity. While they did yeoman's service, there were serious limitations in their interaction vis-vis a user's empowered PMT.

* Various joint project monitoring meetings for LCA related projects, normally took place in Bangalore and, invariably, ASTE was asked to send a 'suitable' officer to represent the IAF. Because of its own trial commitments, it invariably sent a different person each time as no dedicated LCA team had been created at ASTE for this project. Even at Air HQ level, LCA project monitoring was largely a part-time activity of the officer handling fighter projects, barring very short durations when a dedicated DD was posted for it in the Directorate of ASR. A few examples of the result of this lack of user involvement are:

(i) Since the ASR had defined 2xCCMs as operational clean configuration, no tests had been planned by the designers in absolute clean configuration (without any external loads) until pointed out half way in the programme that during training, aircraft will very frequently be flown without any external load.

(ii) At the time of project launch, the IAF had specified R-60 as the CCM for the LCA. The ADA persisted with it even in 2002-3, long after the IAF had changed over to the R-73.

* In the absence of any in-house D&D set-up, the IAF has no means for training its officers in managing or even monitoring D&D projects. Thus, vacancies at the LCA PMT continue to be manned as per P staff considerations rather than an officer's ability to contribute to a project of this magnitude.

MiG-21 Bis Upgrade Programme

In the mid-1970s, the bulk of the IAF inventory comprised MiG-21 variants, and the MiG-21 Bis licensed production had also been launched at HAL. The Air Staff recognised two major weaknesses of the fleet, i.e. lack of a contemporary weapon suite and an accurate nav-attack system and ordered flight trials for the same. In 1977-80, flight trials of the contemporary Inertial Navigation and Attack System (INAS), Matra Magic I CCM, and various air-to-surface Western origin weapons were carried out on the MiG-21 Bis. I am happy to say that that I was personally associated with these trials and that all these systems could be successfully integrated at ASTE and accuracies achieved during the trials were within the claimed specifications. A limited number of aircraft was indeed modified for the Matra Magic and some other advanced Western weapons but, unfortunately, no decision was taken to integrate all these together with the INAS as a package on the entire fleet to make it one of the most potent MRCA fleets of its time. The irony is that a similar upgrade was undertaken 20 years later, that too with the D&D component being provided by the Russians. The only major difference was the addition of Kopyo to replace the then obsolete Almaz radar and the Russian weapon suite.

The official reasons quoted in the files may be any, but I am firmly of the opinion that the main reason was that the IAF was not confident of undertaking it on its own, as it had no organisational entity to undertake any D&D related activity, least of all in the emerging field of advance electronics and displays. HAL was just as ignorant and the DRDO had never been seriously involved with the MiG 21 fleet. Only if the IAF had not ignored the in-house D&D capability, with such an upgrade, the IAF would have been the torch bearer among the MiG-21 operating air forces and imagine how much of business it could have generated for the indigenous aeronautical industry.

Other In-Service Upgrades/Modifications

DARIN System Development: While finalising the Jaguar deal, it was apparent that the obsolete NavWASS system had to be replaced and the BAe Systems solution was not the most optimum. The selected sub-systems of diverse origins had to be integrated but there was no single agency in the IAF or outside which could do it. Once again, the IAF failed to capitalise on this opportunity to create an in-house D&D capability. Instead, it allowed an INAS Integration Organisation (IIO) to be formed under the MoD as a temporary establishment. I would reiterate, if we had in-house D&D capability, by this time the MiG-21 upgrade package would have been in an advanced stage of integration and we could have readily adopted it for the Jaguar too.

DAWN Pod Integration: Once again, while finalising the procurement of the DAWN pod, the question arose as to who would integrate the pod on the Jaguar and develop PFMs and be responsible for in service support, etc for it. This time too, we allowed DRDO to set up a brand new establishment called Aircraft Systems Integration and Evaluation Organisation (ASIEO), now renamed as DARE, instead of creating an in-house capability in the IAF.

Software Development Institute (SDI): In the late 1980s, at the time of closing down IIO after completing the Maritime Jaguar related tasks, the software source codes, documentation, integration rig and other Information Technology (IT) related assets had to be taken over by some user organisation for in service DARIN software maintenance. The IAF did not have any unit which could take on this type of commitment. At last, it was decided to create a new establishment to take on various software related tasks. With in a short span of its existence, SDI has not only taken on various DARIN related tasks but also performed similar tasks for the upgraded MiG-21 Bis and Su-30. It has played a major role in the indigenous development of DARIN II and MiG-27 avionics upgrade package and is even supporting the LCA software development programme.

DASH and Crystal Maize Integration on Mirage 2000: The Mirage 2000 uses the digibus instead of the 1553 bus. Its protocols and data flow and coding, etc are entirely different and proprietary of the French. M/s Elbit and Rafael, Israeli Original Equipment Manufacturers (OEMs) of DASH and Crystal Maize systems, undertook the responsibility of integrating their systems on the aircraft but we had to give them access to the aircraft for it. They, by extensive trials, were able to decode the bus protocol. etc and integrated their systems on it. Thus, while we could be blamed for the Intellectual Property Rights (IPR) violation, the Israelis were the beneficiaries of gaining an insight into this system architecture.

Miscellaneous Modifications: For various modification tasks which come up from time to time, viz fleetwide modification of VUC or IFF or RWR, Air HQ has been creating ad-hoc teams for evolving schemes for various individual fleets and overseeing their incorporation. Such teams have been dissolved after their task was completed. Thus, expertise gained or lessons learnt were allowed to fritter away in the absence of an organic D&D capability.

Impact of Giving up QA, Certification and Acceptance Functions on Operational Potential

In the absence of any organic D&D set-up in the IAF, the Defence Procurement Procedure (DDP) has made it obligatory to seek the advice of various D&D, certification, inspection and production agencies under DRDO and Department of Defence Production while formulating ASRs. Similarly, their participation in field evaluation has been made mandatory. Often, it is seen that the advice/assessment rendered by them is biased by their organisational considerations. Thus, even in an exclusive user domain, the user's role has been undermined.

Allied to the organic D&D capability are the functions of laying down design standards, certification of compliance with the laid down standards and QA cover during various stages of production and, finally, the acceptance of the end product. All these functions are of crucial importance to the user as they determine the efficacy of the final product, and, consequently, have a direct bearing on his operational efficiency and combat potential. Similarly, low maintainability and reliability on account of non-adherence to laid down design standards or production tolerances and processes can seriously undermine operational availability of combat assets. One could argue whether a fighting force should be involved in these support functions. It is not necessary that all the CRIs and CREs must wear uniforms. They may very well wear civil clothes but what is important is that organisationally, they must be answerable to the user. After all, they are his watch dogs, created to protect his interests. The present arrangement of placing them under development and production agencies undermines the basic tenet of the independence of regulators, which is why we continue to have disagreements between the user and CEMILAC on the concessions granted by it to various design deviations which have adverse downstream effects in terms of handling qualities or performance or any other user requirement. In the production arena, the user does not even get to know about the concessions granted by CRI for various deviations and the equipment gets accepted on his behalf without him even knowing about it. He comes to know of these only during collection when the end product does not meet any performance parameter or if there are deviations from the laid down standard of preparation. Often, he has to wait for months before these shortfalls are rectified.

Conclusion
Organic D&D capability the an air force is essential for being able to critically examine complexities of various technology and design options, absorb design the related know-how and know-why of various imported operational systems in its inventory and to respond to various emerging threats by evolving in-house solutions, using the best available technology option. It also assists in evolving realistic requirements for future acquisitions, whether by indigenous design and development or out right purchase, based on proven concepts rather than wishful thinking. It would also be a permanent repository of design data and generate a pool of experts well versed with complexities of combat aircraft design. The Air Force can gainfully use them for managing various developmental and acquisition projects in a professional manner. By ignoring this vital capability, the IAF's decision-making pertaining to various acquisition and indigenous D&D projects has been inconsistent and based on individual perceptions rather than well researched and technologically sound institutional advice. In the absence of suitably qualified personnel in this field, the IAF was also not able to play its rightful lead role in these projects, with disastrous consequences, as seen above. It is high time the Air Force made amends for it and created a well structured organic D&D capability.

Laying down design standards, design certification, QA cover and acceptance are related activities, which are of critical importance to the operational efficiency and combat potential of the air force. Placing them under DRDO and Department of Defence Production has resulted in dilution of user requirements and production standards and led to avoidable friction between the user and development and production agencies. Therefore, these need to be brought under the control of the Air Force for smooth execution of various development and production projects, as per user requirements. By rectifying these organisational deficiencies, the Air Force can achieve quantum improvement in its operational efficiency and combat potential and further the cause of indigenisation.

Technical and Operational Requirements of Joint Operations: 2025

There is no sense in being precise when you don't even know what you're talking about.

—John von Neumann

To talk of ... the future warfare, and all ... only doubles uncertainty, with claims merely tall!

—The Author

Introduction

Notwithstanding the good Hungarian-American mathematician's dire observation as above, it behoves the extant generation of professionals to cast the net, long and firmly, amidst the troubled waters of the coming years. A modicum of preciseness in 'knowing what one is talking about', or rather, 'the method in the madness', can well accrue by ascertaining whence we have arrived and whither we are intended to. If one were to acquire the perspective of recent history, it would be manifest that, in the midst of the "Third Wave",[1] India continues to bear legacy issues related to territory, ideology and competition. As a matter of fact, since the 1980s, there has occurred a perceptible change in the global economic pattern; with the trans-Pacific trade initially reaching comparable dimensions, and, thereafter overtaking its traditional trans-Atlantic counterpart.[2] Further, in the aftermath of the 2008 economic crisis that has had a deleterious effect on the developed countries within the Organisation for Economic

Cooperation and Development (OECD), the emerging economies of Asia have adorned the mantle of the global economic renaissance. The single most important consequence of such happenstance is the likelihood of strategic manipulations and manoeuvres of the 21st century being played out in Asia.

For India, however, the corollary of economic growth being the handmaiden of conflict takes on portentous dimensions within the context of inimical geopolitical realities. With the country being precariously positioned in a geographical region marked by a contiguous cluster of 'failed or failing' states, and thereby having the potential for conflict spillover, refugee flow, and weapons proliferation[3], the genealogical subcontinental reality of being entrenched within the disruptive (violent) conflict-spectrum, once again, raises its hydra-head. The country, therefore, faces multi-dimensional issues that impinge directly, and, in a sense, adversely, on its continued well-being as a nation-state. In articulating India's strategic conundrum, it must be said that unlike other countries, and especially in relation to the wars of the past few decades, what the country has to contend with are three parallel wars, viz., one at the nuclear level (and the mechanism for defence through deterrence), another at the conventional level (although likely to be limited in scope and extent, the possibility exists for an escalation to the nuclear level), and the third, at the sub-conventional level (through proxy war, terrorism, etc, that could spin out to the other two levels)[4]. As such, the genealogical legacy of violent conflict, potentially as well as in practice, will remain the subcontinent's existential *leitmotif* for the time being.

Further afield, as technology matures across a host of diverse fields, ranging from nano-technology, bio-technology, and robotics, the inevitable military application will greatly influence the design and development of sensors and weapons in the coming years. The jury is still out on the issue of 'technological push' impinging upon the concept of operations, as compared to that of 'operational pull'; although, in a sense, both the aspects appear as being the conjoined sides of a coin. On its part, nonetheless, the Indian Air Force (IAF) will need to continuously address the core, and enduring, quotient of aerospace power towards maintaining the crucial advantage so as to countenance the emergent challenges, adversaries and threats. For, in a metamorphosing world, the complexities will only increase with time.

Aim

The aim of this paper is to underscore the technical and operational imperatives that impinge upon the ongoing IAF transformation, and, by implication, on **joint operations** in the foreseeable future.

Mission Assessment

As part of the overall security necessity of the country, the IAF has launched itself along the trajectory of an enterprise-wide endeavour towards achieving the status of a balanced force; and one that is capable of strategic reach, whilst being modelled on network-centricity and effects-based operations. As one looks out towards the blue yonder of the next 15 years, the force's *raison d'etre* of generation and employment of effective, efficient aerospace capabilities will need to revolve around the triad of dominance, jointness and interoperability.

The charting of a well-thought out programme of modernisation will *inter alia* include the common aspects of integrated planning process and Intelligence, Surveillance and Reconnaissance (ISR), on the one hand, whilst duly addressing the unique characteristics of Command and Control (C2) and 'deliverable effects' on the other. The underlying effort must allow for a systems approach towards 'decisional ergonomics' that relates to intellectual capacity across the technical and operational continuum. In terms of wide-ranging engagement with friendly foreign countries, the mission-set must incorporate the 'code of best practices' during the course of combined exercises and military operations.

Of Matters 'Aerospace'

In a manner of speaking, the value proposition of aerospace power is its direct effect on the speed, velocity, and momentum of military operations. In the same vein, the shift of perspective, from 'power' to that of 'dominance', increases the said value by an order of magnitude through the derived effect on the cognitive domain. It is, after all, the salutary effects on the adversary's mind that is the archetypal arbiter of conflict *per se*. Aerospace dominance, in the sense of transcending the physical domain, embodies the essence of strategic capability by endowing 'favourable asymmetry' across the spectrum of 'disruptive conflict'.

In physical terms, aerospace dominance is a dyadic concept; on the one hand, it is definitely about air-to-air dominance, and, on the other, the technological advancement that increases the value of air-to-surface engagement. The former aspect has evolved into Beyond Visual Range (BVR), all-weather and round-the-clock operations, duly enhanced by Space-Based Assets (SBAs), Airborne Warning and Control System (AWACS), and in-flight refuelling. But, it is in the latter aspect that has been truly transformed on account of long-range, persistent ISR and strike capability; the force enhancement, in this case, accruing on account of long-endurance unmanned platforms in conjunction with SBAs and specialised support platforms such as the Joint-Surveillance Target Acquisition Radar System (J-STARS). The fundamental corollary to achieving the effects of aerospace dominance in the physical domain, both in the air as well as on the surface, is 'actionable information', that is, accurate and timely intelligence[5]. Thus, air dominance is intrinsically related to a robust Command, Control, Communications, Computers, Intelligence, Surveillance and Reconnaissance (C4ISR) programme. Thus, aerospace dominance is the ability to control the aerospace environment, such that all types of air and joint operations are enabled to be executed with peak effectiveness. Consequently, aerospace power becomes the lynchpin of *jointness*.[6] In the words of Gen Eikenberry, the former Commander of the Combined Forces Command in Afghanistan, "Control of the air enables freedom of air and surface manoeuvre, and, therefore, the ability to retain the initiative".[7] And, given the inextricable linkage between the physical and cognitive, or behavioural, effects, dominance is the ability to influence the adversary to the point of impunity. The lack of air dominance will also make it difficult and costly for the military instrument of power to conduct its growing role in deterrence and Operations Other Than War

(OOTW). Aerospace dominance contributes to the safe accomplishment of these missions, thereby achieving the desired end-states at the three levels, namely, strategic, operational and tactical.

Modus Operandi of Aerospace Dominance

Within the ambit of a holistic campaign perspective, aerospace dominance is facilitated through the entire spectrum of capabilities. As a matter of fact, aerospace strategy options towards achieving dominance would dynamically encompass the entire gamut of manned and unmanned, agile and stealth, close combat and BVR, control with Man-In-The-Loop (MITL) and autonomous, land and carrier-based, air and space, network-enabled centralisation and de-centralisation, virtual and real C2, lethal and non-lethal, and finally, explosives and directed energy. Whilst, at all times, the operational solutions would need to be relevant to the soldier and the sailor on the surface.

An assured access to information through an articulated intelligence plan is of the essence. Network-Centric Warfare (NCW) transforms information superiority into combat advantage through highly responsive networking of geographically dispersed forces. In other words, the aim is to leverage shared battle space awareness to allot, apportion and allocate assets; whilst being enabled to modify these assignments and employment as per the dynamics of the situational awareness. Networks collate the partial data of multifarious sensors, and fuse them into a Common Operational Picture (COP). The sensor nodes share information with the decision-maker and the war-fighter alike; the resultant network increases battle space awareness, facilitates greater self-synchronisation and accelerates the decision-cycle, thereby enhancing combat-capability and mission-effectiveness. The ongoing projects of the Indian Air Force (IAF) towards developing NCW capability include the operationalisation of the Integrated Air Command and Control System (IACCS), Modernised Air Defence Ground Environment System (ADGES) Communication (MAC) system and Operational Data Link (ODL).

In the event of overt hostilities in our context, given the developed nature of air power capabilities vis-à-vis the potential adversaries, the primary operational concept would necessarily encompass the attainment of *control of the air environment*. The said 'counter-air' effects are achieved through the application of aerospace combat power *offensively*; that, in the main, would revolve around the ingress into hostile air space by '4+' generation aircraft. The critical element of force employment, at this juncture, would be the force enhancement measures through the combat-support function of anti-radiation Unmanned Aerial Vehicles (UAVs) and sensor-coverage by aerostat and Airborne Warning and Control System (AWACS) platforms. Further, the resultant *dominance* would be 'dynamic' on account of the nature of AWACS control; wherein air-to-air engagements would be simultaneously directed in conjunction with air-to-surface attacks. The aerospace spectrum would shift from *parity* to *dominance* in a sectoral sense.

The individual elements of the modern battle space are integrated through a robust C4I2SR architecture. As a matter of fact, effective command and control of operations is dependent upon secure communication and decision-support systems. In the 'here-and-now', it is pertinent to continuously identify, and update, the adversarial centres of vulnerability, as also that of gravity. The focus must be to achieve decision-superiority towards making, and implementing, sound decisions at a tempo that enables own forces to operate within the contours of a compact Observe-Orient-Decide-Act (OODA) cycle vis-à-vis the adversary. The 'orbital' aerospace assets would be the prime drivers of these endeavours, equally serviced by the cyberspace component of the 'military information infrastructure'. Whilst a structured approach can significantly increase situational awareness at the strategic and operational levels, the factor of uncertainty still endures at the tactical and close-in levels of warfare.[8] The detrimental effects of such a situation would require mitigation by way of innovation in tactics, techniques and procedures. Suppression of surface-to-air engagement and prevention of attacks on own bases are important tasks in ensuring the effectiveness, and thereby dominance, of aerospace power.

To sum up, aerospace dominance would be attained through superior decision-making (C2), based on timely information (sensors) and effective communication (network), the capability for persistent presence, the availability of high-performance by airborne assets (speed, height, range, endurance), the discriminate and proportional delivery of kinetic and non-kinetic effects (weapons); whilst ensuring appropriate measures to maintain invulnerability to enemy effect (counter-measures).

C2 and Planning Process

In a sense, the erstwhile construct of C412SR has been relegated as a mere buzzword; with C2, of military operations, regaining its central criticality. Although the individual aspects relating to computer network, communications, and intelligence continue to hold their respective importance, these could be delegated to the level of Service Headquarters (HQ) and joint staff. The primacy of 'joint planning for operations' has become the *sine qua non* for meaningful and successful operations. At this juncture, it is worthwhile to dwell on the unique aspects vis-à-vis aerospace power.

The defining feature of effective aerospace utilisation is 'centralised control' under professional masters. Nonetheless, the equally critical conceptual requirement towards efficient effects-based operations, and effective jointness, relates to the necessity of 'joint planning'. Subsequently, the joint staff could very well execute the operational orders in conjunction with the operational and tactical level field-operators.

Cascading Effect on Escalation Dominance

The terrorist attack of December 2001 on the Indian Parliament resulted in Operation Parakram, the operational deployment along the entire International Boundary (IB) and the Line of Control (LoC) facing Pakistan. The result was a stalemate at the operational and tactical levels, the *casus belli* presumably being diffused at the strategic level. In the case of a possible confrontation, and armed conflict, with a nuclear-armed adversary, the control of belligerence becomes the primary focus on the strategic agenda. At this juncture, the ability of the operational-level to execute the joint campaign towards credible 'aerospace dominance' will translate into significant deterrence value. The clear enunciation of the intent, by way of rigorous training under realistic scenarios, would convey the existential capability to effectively deliver damage mechanism. The aim must be to render the adversary bereft of any offensive action through the provision of conventional deterrence capability.

Also, there is the further derivative of coercive capability that can possibly address the subcontinental malaise of vacuous rhetoric and posture. At the lower end of the conflict spectrum, towards engaging irregular, cross-border forces, aerospace power would provide the optimum operational solution; through the application of punishment whilst maintaining the conflict below the strategic threshold.

To Rest a Debate: Quantity vs Quality

Given the immense cost of development and deployment of exceptional aerospace capabilities, a continuing conundrum relates to the aspect of balance between preponderance and technology. Whilst it could be said that quantity has its own quality, the modern military system needs an elaboration. Such a war-fighting system is characterised by an inter-related complex of concealment, dispersion, suppression, small-unit independent manoeuvre and combined/joint forces at the tactical level; and, strategic depth, reserves, and differential concentration at the operational level of war.[9]

During the 1991 Persian Gulf War, the Coalition Air Forces had deployed a total of 3,380 aircraft against 600 of the Iraqi Air Force[10], with a resultant advantage of 5:1 that shortly translated into aerospace dominance. To be able to 'turn the flank from the top', the concept of force employment, the very trestle of operational art, will continue to be critical as it has been the single-most dominant factor leading to victory in wars. The principles of force-employment exist essentially in the conceptual domain,[11] and, therefore, they relate directly to intellectual capacity. Consequently, it is imperative to focus, to a great extent, on intellectual power by way of the people manning the systems and the leadership that impacts the operational OODA loop. It is important that the adversary is subjected to continuous, and intense, scrutiny in terms of its strategy and capabilities.[12] Competitive advantages in force employment during a conflict situation commence with planning during the time-period below the threshold of overt hostilities, so as to derive the options to achieve favourable asymmetry.[13]

But having said that, as a matter of the highest priority in India's case, it may be underscored that there is the need to restore the authorised IAF combat force; otherwise, there is the pitfall of accepting any temporary arrangements. It is necessary to plan for, and implement, the decision of the 1963 Emergency Committee of the Cabinet (ECC); whereby, the envisaged force level is based upon a 64 squadron Air Force that includes 50 combat squadrons and 14 transport ones.[14] The force-multipliers would be additional to the basic force-structure. The recently published figure in a periodical of 60 squadrons[15], by 2025-2030, that includes the Su-30 MKI, Light Combat Aircraft (LCA), Multi-Role Combat Aircraft (MRCA), Fifth Generation Fighter Aircraft (FGFA), and upgrade on the MiG-29 and Mirage-2000 would offer the opportunities for competitive advantage, and favourable asymmetry, by allowing for aerospace dominance.

Aerospace Strategy

Comparisions are odious, while 'military-parity' tends to be a chimera in most of the cases; but then again, it is imperative to generate a strategic riposte to any regional aerospace imbalance, initially as a countervailing strategy before, hopefully, achieving a prevailing one in the years to come. Consequently, to derive combat advantage in a conflict-situation, the country's aerospace strategy would emanate from a multi-dimensional national security strategy, whilst being ensconced firmly within the national military strategy. In the coming years, the broad contours could well commence from the standpoint of 'aerospace strategic depth', whilst encompassing capability in terms of robust C2, ISR, (nuclear) deterrence, and a holistic campaign. Further, in keeping with the truism of 'national interests' being the ultimate arbiter of international relations, the continuum of strategy must consider the viable likelihood of technical and operational capability towards coercion and partnership-building. The indigenous implications reside within a robust Research & Development (R&D) programme and resource-allocation vis-a-vis budgetary funding.

Consequently, there arises the need for a comprehensive national aerospace commission. In a manner of speaking, the absence of a succinct, and dynamic, source-code related to an aerospace strategy is akin to placing the 'cart before the horse'; in fact, a distinctive non-starter. The fulcrum of aerospace development would, necessarily, be contingent upon the establishment of a suitable legislative commission that articulates a viable, long-term perspective. In fact, such an empowered body would consider the pursuit of aerospace capabilities, of an exceptional order, across the dyadic segments of the military-civil, the public-private, and the indigenous-foreign enterprises.

Of 'Jointness'

In any sphere of human endeavour, the amalgamation of various discrete elements, in the attainment of a concomitant objective, is driven by the basic need to acquire a competitive advantage vis-à-vis the operating environment and the opposing protagonist. And warfare, being the archetypal arbiter of competition between nation-states, evolved in conjunction with military capabilities. A potential adversary cannot be expected to be oblivious to an ongoing transformation in own military capabilities, or, otherwise, be lacking in strategy to either exploit, bypass, or counter these. In other words, in the face of perceived superiority in military capability and competent fighting personnel, the adversary is likely to change the terms and conditions of conflict *per se*, and, thereby, attempting to render the manifest advantages as irrelevant. A nation-state proceeds at the risk of own peril if such possibilities are either dismissed outright or accorded scant attention. As could be expected, the paradigm of a paradox afflicts the concept, too; in that, a matter today considered to be of utmost import, in belief and doctrine, stands as being elusive, in practice and performance. What is critically important to note is that joint operations are the foundations on which a modern military has to fight and win wars.[16]

The global access and interaction at the societal level superimposes the 'disruptive' conflict matrix upon the security-triad; thereby, in effect, giving rise to a multiplicity of challenges, vulnerabilities and threats to the constituent elements within the triad continuum. The inimical vectors could equally manifest in the physical as well as the virtual domains; at times, being discriminate, but otherwise nebulous, below the eastern horizon, whilst moving towards the inexorable rise. The de-confliction paradigm of the armed forces must be premised on the process of **jointness,** so that the entire 'jungle gym' of the security architecture is proportionate, discriminate, and flexible in nature, whilst being effective across the conflict-spectrum. The conduct of optimum joint operations, to a large measure, depends upon the constituent agencies having gained the professional mastery of the joint environment; and thereby, being able to assure the government machinery of the ability to support the national security initiatives, or responses for that matter, by way of a wide repertoire of joint military capabilities.

One of the barriers, to 'practise-what-is-preached', relates to inter-Service differences in terms of culture and ethos vis-à-vis the conduct of training and operations[17]. On the other hand, the dissonance could be due to honest, professional differences as is the experience in the bulk of the cases; or on account of institutional biases/loyalties, which need to be fostered and guarded zealously[18]. The apparent discord could also be attributed to the lack of mutual confidence and trust amongst individuals and different components of military power (hence, the desire to keep capabilities and forces 'under control'), that often arises from a lack of understanding of the role, limits, and capabilities of each other, as well the problem of institutional and individual egos.[19] Clearly, the remedy to the conundrum, or paradox for that matter, lies within two critical aspects; the first being the formulation of supporting guidelines by way of characteristic principles of *jointness,* that could relate simultaneously to the joint structure as a whole, as also the specific levels of execution (strategic, operational and tactical). The other enabling factor would be to envisage *jointness* as an ongoing, dynamic continuum which is mostly process-driven, and one, that transcends peace-time evolution (including joint exercises), as also, contingency-situations (including war-fighting).

The concept of *jointness* is primarily contextual in nature, rather than an end in itself. It is a truism to state that any rational activity must have a purpose; and in the context of military-force application, the *raison d'etre* of *jointness* is intricately enmeshed with the 'conflict-spectrum' and the 'security-triad'. In fact, an understanding of the said aspects can, well and truly, enable the acquisition of the fundamental sense of what is required to be attempted in order to be achieved. Looking out into the future, the 'next-step' goes beyond the current network-centricity to the interim mode of 'capability-centricism', before eventually realising the optimal goal of 'effects-centric' operations. The joint effort must push and heave along such a trajectory.

Force Employment as Capability

It is necessary at each level of command and staff alike to realise the fundamental aspects of warfare from the standpoint of the operating environment, as a clear understanding will enable 'force employment' to develop as the crucial capability. In two-dimensional operations, such as on land and maritime (both the surface as well as the limited sub-surface element), the responsibilities are allocated by splitting 'space'; whilst in the air, the same is related to the splitting of 'time'.[20] Thereby, essentially, the surface forces can 'hold' space / territory, which then becomes the decisive derivative for these forces in a conflict situation. On its part, aerospace force can 'dominate' time on account of reach and speed; resultantly, the third operational environment achieves 'rapidity of effects' across the strategic, operational and tactical continuum.

The central logic of joint operations rests in complementing the capabilities of a particular Service with those of the other Services. The specific capabilities need to be optimised as per the unique characteristics of the operational environment. For example, air power exploits the inherent factors of ubiquity, translucency and homogeneity of the vertical dimension. It is, thus, in a position of being able to influence and, if appropriately configured and employed, to control the employment of the surface forces in the land and maritime domains.[21] To achieve the central goal of defeating the adversary strategy, jointness enables the attainment of synergy through the orchestrated exploitation of relevant roles and effects of specific capabilities. Thus, the land forces, through overwhelming tactical dominance capabilities, can bring about an operational reaction on the part of the adversary through concentration of forces, or committing the reserves.[22] The joint plan must synchronise the air power effects to engage the resultant manoeuvre, thereby shaping the battle space at the operational and strategic levels. Air power would enable synergy through close support, lift and transparency functions.

Beyond the Conventional Narrative

It was the employment of air power as a military capability that forced the debate and the concept-development process of joint military operations[23]. In a manner of speaking, the value proposition of the said power lies in its direct effect on the speed, velocity, and momentum of military operations. That is to say, the tempo of operations can be dynamically orchestrated, in terms of operational art, through a rapid effect on the operational-triad of space-force-time. In the same vein, the shift of perspective, from 'power' to that of 'dominance', increases the said value by an order of magnitude through the derived effects on the cognitive domain. It is, after all, the inducement, or imposition for that matter, of salutary effects on the adversary's mind that is the archetypal arbiter of conflict. Consequently, air power is the lynchpin of jointness.[24]

With the advent of space power in 1957, and that of cyber-space in the extant century, the perspective of joint military force application has, once again, undergone a metamorphosis. Given the global nature of Space-Based Assets (SBAs), and the all-pervading domain of cyber-enabled information, jointness migrates from an environment-specific, and essentially a platform-centric, approach, to that of a network-centric structure. The resultant synergy allows   for a transformation of roles, missions, force-structures through the impact of ubiquity, access, and speed. It is time to go beyond the conventional sense of jointness, or for that matter, operational art.

Key Emerging Technology

The perpetual saga of the growth of technology, both linear as well as exponential, has been the common denominator in the historical sense. As a matter of fact, the world is in the midst of a global technology revolution, wherein, over the past 30 years, advances in biotechnology, nanotechnology, materials technology, and Information Technology (IT) have been occurring at an accelerating pace[25]. As technology maturation takes place over the next 10 years, the outcome will manifest itself through integrated development across multiple scientific disciplines in a 'converged' manner, such as to transform various aspects of economy and society, thereby resulting in a profound effect on human life[26]. The implication for 'force propagation', through myriad applications, is the natural corollary; in that, newer forms of warfare will hold centre-stage. After all, history bears out that conflict has evolved along as many domains and dimensions as have developed at various points of time.

In terms of emerging aerospace technologies that will then impact on 'future warfare', the repertoire includes extreme stealth, hypersonic vehicles, increased precision weapons (kinetic as well as non-kinetic), persistent ISR through micro-UAVs (Unmanned Aerial Vehicles), and the evolutions related to directed energy weapons. SBAs will perhaps take on the role of 'force application', thereby validating the physical reality of the doctrinal tenet of the 'high ground'; in that, warfare will first be unleashed in the exo-atmospheric vastness of space prior to taking on the air and surface evolutions. It is, indeed, a moot point that the 'victor' could well be established as a *fait accompli* even as the traditional forms of warfare take place as mere 'additionalities'.

Law of Armed Conflict (LOAC)
Inherent in the recourse to sanctioned conflict lie the presumptions of rationality, proportionality and discrimination. Thus, the limits to armed conflict will be the *leitmotif* in the emerging knowledge world. Any perpetrator, or protagonist for that matter, of warfare will need to dwell upon the dichotomy that 'military necessity' brings to the table of expediency. Such an inextricable embrace will be the defining challenge to commanders and staff alike as one looks out to 2025 and beyond.

In fact, 'zapping' is emerging as an operational concept in consort with enabling precision and ISR technologies.

Conclusion

It is but a truism to state that a nation must be determined to make its own choices vis-à-vis its legitimate security concerns; failing which, the adversary could then make these. The fundamental nature of such a 'reactionary' occurrence would be the foreclosure of viable options, thereby limiting the very essence of aerospace power, namely, flexibility. Serendipity is no longer an option for India's military strategy, nor that of the archetypical 'ostrich syndrome'. Or, for that matter, finding ourselves too late, and far out, at a strategic 'cul-de-sac'. In the foreseeable security calculus, the Indian armed forces will continue to stand as symbols of the country's bastion and bulwark, as hitherto since independence.

The inherent dilemma in modern security lies in the difference between preparation and expectation; with the eventual question being, how prepared can one be to face the unexpected? In the final analysis, it behoves us to understand the central philosophy that in true jointness lies our deliverance. As a result of the said understanding, the country can attempt the necessary wherewithal for joint force-employment in order to deliver itself unscathed into the forthcoming Knowledge World, and the Wisdom Era that lies beyond. The spilt blood of countless brethren, military and civilian alike, commands it; as much as the unravelling security environment, both external as well as internal, demands it. Our position in the coming years, either of privilege or predicament, is contingent upon the sagacity and foresight that we bring to bear in the present moments. The central point is that, were the national security-mechanism to be sacrificed at the altar of crisis-management, repeatedly, *ad nauseam,* the expedient options would merely vacillate between the extreme points of the 'pendulum's swing'; namely, a pusillanimous acquiescence along one of the trajectories, and the extremes of indiscriminate force-application on the other. Either one of the two extreme decisions begets opprobrium rather than plaudits. In looking out towards 2025, one would, indeed, do well to remember that any future, envisaged or otherwise, has to have a past; and that, the start-point of the desired trajectory could truly lie ensconced within the present times. We have our tasks cut out, and, therefore, let us reach out to our collective future...starting from the here and now.

Notes

1.   For a detailed treatise on the Third Wave characteristics, see Alvin Toffler, *The Third Wave* (New York: Bantam Books, 1990).

2.   Sanu Kainikara, *Australian Security in the Asian Century* (ACT Australia: Air Power Development Centre, 2008), p 4.

3.   Sonali Huria, "Failed and Failing States and Armed Conflict in South Asia" in D. Suba Chandran and P.R.Chari, eds., *Armed Conflicts in South Asia 2009* (New Delhi: Routledge, 2010), p.211.

4.   Jasjit Singh, "Whither Joint Operations?" in Jasjit Singh, ed., *Air Power and Joint Operations, Second Edition* (New Delhi: Knowledge World, 2008), p.15.

5.   Jasjit Singh "From Air Superiority to Air Dominance" in Jasjit Singh, ed., *Air Dominance : Proceedings of the Seminar* (New Delhi: Knowledge World, 2010), p.xv.

6.   Ibid., p.175.

7.   Ibid., p.77.

8.   Alistair Byford, "Afghanistan Operational Lessons", Guest Lecture delivered at IAF College of Air Warfare, June 3, 2009.

9.   Stephen Biddle, *Military Power* (New Jersey: Princeton University Press, 2004), p.3.

10. Singh, n.5., p.35.

11. Singh, n.4., p.283.

12. Ibid.

13. Ibid.

14. Jasjit Singh, "India's Aerospace Options", Panel Speaker at HQ EAC - CAPS Seminar on "China's Rise: Implications for India", Air Force Station Tezpur, November 7, 2009.

15. Tathagata Bhattacharya, "Russia, France for MRCA", *The Sunday Indian*, May 10- May 16, 2010, p.34.

16. Singh, n.4., p.273.

17   Sanu Kainikara. "Capability Born Joint : Towards a Seamless Force", Working Paper 22, Air Power Development Centre, ACT, Australia, September 2007.

18. Singh, n.4, p.14.

19. Ibid.

20. Regis Chamagne, *The Art of Air War* (Sceaux, France: L'esprit du livre editions, 2007), p.180.
21. Singh, n.4, p.286.
22. Ibid., p. 292.
23. Kainikara, n.17.
24. Singh, n.5, p. 175.
25. RAND National Security Research Division, The Global Technology Revolution 2020, Executive Summary (Santa Monica: USA, 2006).
26. Ibid.

What Ails Indigenisation of Air Launched Weapons?

✿ S. BHANOJI RAO

Introduction

For any combat force, the weapon systems used to achieve the combat objective becomes a prime concern. In the case of the Indian Air Force (IAF), the weapon delivery platform, the weapons and associated sub-systems required for accurate delivery of weapons for both offensive and defensive roles would be the most important. Therefore, air armaments are vital components of the war machinery.

The air armaments can be classified into two categories i.e. the externally mounted stores and the armament stores fitted inside the aircraft. The externally mounted stores are the aircraft gun, ammunition, unguided rockets, bombs, Precision Guided Munitions (PGM), air launched missiles, etc, and the internally installed stores are the release carts, escape aid explosives and various power cartridges. Design and Development (D&D) of air armament stores is a complex activity. It needs close coordination with the user, production agency, airworthiness approval agency and flight testing agency. Indigenisation of low technology weapons like bombs and cartridges, either through reverse engineering or through new development could be achieved by our Research and Development (R&D) agencies to some extent. However, till date, the Defence Research and Development Organisation (DRDO) has not been able to develop high-tech weapons like air launched missiles and PGMs. Even in the case of low-tech weapons like unguided rockets and fuses for aerial bombs, the Indian R&D has failed to develop credible air armaments. Most of the air armaments, including low technology weapons, are being imported.

India is emerging as a major economic power in the world. Also, India is the regional military power. In most sectors of industrial technology, we are surging forward at a brisk pace. We have the largest pool of technical personnel. We are developing our own military aircraft. We have launched lunar missions and various satellites. Despite all these credentials, why does India still depend on import of air armaments? What ails our air armament industry? How come the Ministry of Science and Technology succeeds and the Ministry of Defence (MoD) fails? It is necessary to delve into the reasons for the failure to design, develop and produce air armaments in India. We need to introspect and alleviate the problem areas to achieve self-reliance.

Aim

The aim of this paper is to analyse why India is unable to design, develop and produce air armaments for all the three Services. The aim is not to find fault with the system but to introspect and identify the deficiencies of the major players in the business of armament design and development i.e. the user, R&D, producer and MoD so as to adopt corrective measures in the respective establishments for enabling indigenisation of air armaments.

History

The requirement of air armaments depends on the type of military aircraft in use. Initially, a majority of the air armament stores was imported. During the British rule, the technology to manufacture the bombs was provided to Indian agencies by the Ministry of Supply, Royal Aircraft Establishment, London. Some of the documents like those of the ADEN gun ammunition and 1,000 lb Mk 6/7 were prepared in the late 1940s. In the early 1950s, certain stores, viz. aircraft gun ammunition and bombs were produced by the Ordnance Factory Board (OFB) using these original technology documents. At that time, there were no separate agencies responsible for design, airworthiness certification and quality assurance. The IAF started an establishment called

'Inspectorate of Explosives' at Khamaria, which was under the functional and administrative control of Air HQ (Directorate of Technical Services—Aeronautical Inspection Services). This unit was involved in design as well as inspection/production of air armaments. Subsequently, upon the formation of the Directorate of Technical Development and Production (Air) [DTDP (Air)], a large number of low-tech weapon systems viz. bombs, rockets and escape aid cartridges were developed through reverse engineering, and drawings and specifications were formulated. Even now, **the IAF is using the 1,000 lb bombs and ADEN gun ammunition, whose specifications were issued in the 1950s.**

During the DTD&P (Air) times, the designer, quality assurance agencies and user representatives were working together to design and a develop air armaments. Therefore, the coordination was good and a large number of projects were successfully accomplished through reverse engineering. Subsequently, the task of indigenisation was assigned to individual DRDO labs. Initially, the development activities of the Armament Research and Development Establishment (ARDE) and High Energy Materials Research Laboratory (HEMRL) (then Explosives Research and Development Laboratory—ERDL) were well coordinated and the products were successfully developed in the prescribed timeframes as IAF representatives were coordinating the projects and the Regional Centre for Military Airworthiness (Air Armament) [RCMA(AA)] was headed by an IAF officer. However, the progress of development activities became rather slow in the subsequent years due to various reasons.

The Air Staff Requirements (ASRs) for new generation bombs like 250/450 kg HSLD and the fuses for these bombs were issued in the late 1970s. Though the bombs were developed in 1993, the bulk production could commence only from 2002 onwards. The delay in bulk production was primarily due to delay in the formulation of documentation and initial production problems. **Since the designer was not responsible for bulk production, this time lag from design to bulk production was very high, compared to international standards.** Till the late 1990s, indigenisation of air armaments was tasked to DRDO only. Due to inordinate delays in development and DRDO's reluctance to take up reverse engineering projects, the IAF had tasked OFB to indigenise certain low-tech weapons like Russian origin bombs and rockets. However, except for one bomb i.e. 100-120 kg natural fragmentation bomb, none of the air armament stores could be produced by OFB till date. The success story for designing the 100-120 kg bomb within one year is mainly due to the involvement of the Director General of Air Quality Assurance (DGAQA) and employment of a retired IAF officer, Air Cmde K.V. Rao, as a consultant to OFB for one year.

Development of air launched missiles and PGMs has been going on for the last two decades. The progress is very slow and the IAF continues to depend on imports.

Present Scenario

The design and development of air launched weapons is different from that of ground launched ones. The design safety and airworthiness are of paramount importance. Malfunction of the fuse FBRN-4I on the 1,000 lb bomb released by the Jaguar aircraft is a classic example of the designer, certification agency and producer not being able to ensure fail safe design primarily due to lack of knowledge. Each agency has an important role to play in the indigenisation of air armaments. Once the product is developed, the transfer of technology would take place to the bulk production agency. In the case of original R&D work, the task is still primarily with DRDO whereas OFB is involved in the R&D of certain reverse engineering projects.

At present, there are two sources for production of air armament stores i.e. OFB and ARDE. The bulk production of a majority of the stores is through OFB whereas certain stores viz. power cartridges, release cartridges, etc. are supplied in limited numbers by ARDE. Therefore, depending on the type of weapon system, the indents are placed by the Services. Bharat Dynamics Limited (BDL) is trying to refurbish/ life extension of Russian origin air launched missiles. The air launched missiles under development are also dealt with by BDL. Since DRDO could not successfully develop any air launched missile, BDL has not been included as a supplier of air armaments.

Indigenisation of Air Armaments

The indigenisation projects may be classified broadly into two categories. i.e. new projects or reverse engineering projects. For new projects, the procedure is clearly defined whereas for reverse engineering projects, different directorates at Air HQ follow different procedures.

In the IAF, the externally mounted stores are indigenised by the Operational Branch and the power carts are indigenised by the Maintenance Branch. In both cases, the indigenisation is not the primary duty. It is an additional duty. Therefore, the IAF is not able to devote adequate time for indigenisation activities. Scrutiny of the technical specifications and drawings of the indigenous air armaments designed in the 1970s/1980s revealed that IAF officers (Technical Armament Branch) had worked on these products during the development stage and all specifications were formulated by them. A sizeable number of armaments were designed by the IAF officers during the DTD&P (Air) times. In the case of power carts, considering the expertise in pyro systems in India, ARDE could develop a large number of carts which are in use by the IAF.

Amongst the air armaments, the indigenous production is very limited. Only low technology weapons are being produced in bulk. The list is given below:

- 1,000 lb bombs—production based on British documents.
- 250 kg HSLD bomb—designed in 2000 by ARDE.
- 450 kg HSLD bomb—designed in 2000 by ARDE.
- 100-120 kg bomb—designed 2002 by OFB.
- 68 mm rocket—designed in the late 1980s by ARDE.
- 30 mm ADEN ammunition—through Transfer of Technology (ToT) by OFB.
- 30 mm GSH—through ToT by OFB.
- 23 mm GSH—through ToT by OFB.
- Various power cartridges and escape aid explosive carts.

The fuses for the aviation bombs were developed by ARDE. However, their use has been discontinued as incidents of air burst occurred due to certain design deficiencies. The ARDE was initially reluctant to accept that there were deficiencies in the design. However, by the time ARDE accepted the need to redesign the fuzes in a fail safe mode, the IAF stopped using these fuses and adapted a Russian origin fuse as the common fuse for all bombs. For the live ammunition for aircraft guns, the OFB was unable do so due to difficulties in the quality of the fuses. Therefore, the live ammunition is still being imported and the practice ammunition is being made in India.

In the case of the 68 mm rocket, a large number of amendments are pending for ratification by the ARDE. Since the rocket group of ARDE had been wound up a long time back, there is no response from ARDE despite being the designer. Certain life stipulations were granted provisionally in 1977. The designer and user were to conduct trials to enhance the extension of shelf life. But, till date, no trials have been done. As the life of the igniters and rubber seals is 5 years, of the propellant 9 years and of the rocket hardware 15 years, maintenance of such stores becomes a problem for the user.

In the case of power carts, the indigenisation efforts were successful to a large extent. However, there are minor deficiencies in the existing design of certain carts which need to be rectified. Also, the production documentation is mostly incomplete due to which OFB is unable to produce in bulk.

The stores which are being manufactured by OFB under ToT are of vintage technology of the early 1950s. OFB did not seek any amendments or updates from the Original Equipment Manufacturers (OEMs) to improve these old specifications. **Some of the test parameters are of 1946**. The validity of these specifications in the 21st century is not clear.

At present, the following air armaments are under indigenisation:

OFB
- 57 mm rocket—1st flight trials in 1999 & 2nd in 2007. Still pending.
- 80 mm rocket—development stage.
- 240mm rocket S-24B—development stage.

DRDO

- 100-120 kg pre-fragmented bomb—under pilot lot production.
- 250 kg pre-fragmented bomb—under development.
- 500 kg pre-fragmented bomb—under feasibility study.
- 500 kg M-62 Russian origin bomb—under feasibility study.
- Laser guided kit—under development for 20 years.
- Anti-tank missile—under development.
- Air-to-air active radar guided missile (Astra) —under development.
- IN/GPS guidance kit with range enhancement—under development.

The projects of OFB are going at a snail's pace. In the case of DRDO, indigenisation of unguided bombs and power carts is progressing satisfactorily whereas development of guided bombs and missiles is rather slow.

Dificiencies of Agencies Involved in Indigenisation
The main agencies involved in indigenisation are the user, R&D organisation, quality assurance and production units. Since all these establishments are under the MoD, the policies formulated by the MoD play a major role in the success of indigenisation. It is, therefore, necessary to identify the areas which affect the process of indigenisation. The details are given in the subsequent paragraphs.

Deficiencies at User Level
- Domain knowledge on air armaments plays a major role in expeditious development of indigenous air armaments. Earlier, the IAF had a Technical Armament Branch which had the expertise on air armaments. Now very few experts on armaments are available. Every AE(M) officer would like to work on aircraft instead of armaments as the recognition of the work effort on aircraft is clearly visible and better appreciated by the commanders. Armament activities are least visible. Very few commanders give importance to the armaments in the field units. The flying task gets paramount importance compared to any other activity in the field units. Since the working environment

is not conducive to development of core competence in armaments, the number of officers, who have the capability to lead the armament indigenisation projects, is limited.

- At Air HQ, the policies are driven by the Operation (Ops) Branch. A majority of the armament functions like procurement, WWR/AAT scaling, allotments, utilisation policies, trials and indigenisation of main stores are looked after by the Ops Branch. The highest ranking officer to look after armaments is a Group Captain. In fact, in the chain of command, till the year 2008, there were two officers between the Director Weapons and the Vice Chief of the Air Force. Now, it has been increased to three officers. It indicates the lack of importance given to armaments. Moreover, the total number of officers in the Directorate of Weapons (Ops Branch) is so low that they are barely sufficient for day-to-day fire-fighting. There is no time for policy matters. Compared to the Naval Armament Inspectorate, the total number of officers working in the area of air armaments in the entire Air HQ is very limited despite the fact that the IAF has more variants and numbers of armament stores. Whereas in the Maintenance Branch, the armaments are looked after by an officer of the rank of Air Vice Marshal (AVM). Indigenisation of the power cart was successful mainly due to the attention paid by the dedicated officers of the Maintenance Branch.
- The IAF is not involved in the design of any airborne item, unlike the Indian Navy which is involved in every aspect of design. Its involvement in the design of the missile explosive items (warhead and propellant) is noteworthy. The IAF needs to institute such an agency, responsible for design, so as to expedite the reverse engineered projects.
- Longer tenures could have helped the officers to build up expertise. But due to typical tenure-based posting across the board, the officers working in the armament field are unable to gain core competence. Due to this, the person defining the Services Qualitative Requirements (SQRs) may not have the requisite knowledge of the entire weapon system. Therefore, errors at the project definition stage could occur.

- Indigenisation is not the primary responsibility of the officers in the present system of work. The officers' primary responsibility is the operational utilisation and its maintenance. Dedicated officers, who have a core competence in armaments, need to be posted to both the branches for indigenisation.
- The Services often provide the SQRs of the main weapon system. The associated equipment required to utilise the main system is not defined. It is often presumed that the designer would know the requirement. Due to this, development of associated accessories gets delayed which, in turn, delays the induction of equipment into the Services.
- Project management at the user end needs expertise and continuity. The project manager needs to interact with the R&D teams and testing agency. In case the officers are posted to the R&D team, they could manage the projects efficiently. At present, the IAF is unable to spare officers for all the projects. At the same time, DRDO's insistence to equate the IAF officers as per their grade pay with that of their scientists is another impediment.
- The user feedback is not given to the design agency routinely unless defects occur. The feedback helps in improving the design of the weapon system.
- The IAF had surrendered many vacancies of armament related posts. Earlier the IAF officers were posted at RCMA(AA), ARDE, DGAQA armament units. At present, civilians who have no attachments to the IAF have been given these posts.

Deficiencies at DRDO
- Due to lack of knowledge of the overall requirements of any weapon system on fighter aircraft, parallel R&D of the main system, integration requirements and its associated equipment does not take place. All R&D activities are concentrated on the main item only. Only when the main item is successful, does the R&D team consider indigenisation of the associated items.
- Once the prototype is developed successfully, the project team

declares successful completion of R&D and does not complete the associated documentation on time. At times, after successful flight trials, it takes 10 years for the item to be produced in bulk due to lack of documentation and non-availability of associated equipment.

- Without adequate ground trials, the project team seeks flight trials. The cost of the flight trials is not included in the project cost. One flight trial of air armament stores costs approximately Rs. 1.5 crore. In the case of the proximity fuse development, the project was shelved after the conduct of 11 flight trials, wherein the fuse functioned inadvertently in the last two flight trials.

- The designer is not responsible for bulk production. Therefore, the designer does not spend adequate time in preparing the production technology documents. Preparation of documents for the gauging, manufacture process and Quality Assurance (QA) requirements must be the responsibility of the designer. When any product is produced under ToT from abroad, all production documents are to be properly made by the designer and one representative of the designer needs to ensure production as per the standards. No such methods are followed. The DRDO needs to study the ToT documentation of any air armament product and prepare the documentation accordingly. In fact, two groups from the same DRDO lab prepare different standards of documents for ToT. There is no standard template. When one such template was prepared, the DRDO justified why they could not make efforts to adhere to such comprehensive template.

- During the development phase, the hardware is manufactured under the direct supervision of scientists of DRDO. Since they are the designers, the production process control has to be accomplished under their supervision. When the same product is to be manufactured in bulk by the OFB or trade sources, the educational qualification and understanding of the quality and specification requirements of the product is limited as the technicians are not competent. Therefore, OFB finds it difficult to manufacture certain items due to lack of clarity in the process documentation.

- Once the product is in regular production, the designer closes the project; whereas the production agency faces difficulties in bulk production and certain amendments may be required to the drawings and specifications. Also, there would be a need to introduce additional QA measures based on the feedback from the producer and user. Hence, there is a need for constant upgradation of the product by the designer in terms of quality and performance. At present, once a product is developed successfully, no upgradation is planned.

- After finalisation of the design, the drawings and specifications are issued as 'provisional' documents. Based on the production problems and feedback from the user, the product specifications and drawings are to be changed. However, the latter part does not take place. It is pertinent to note that the **specifications issued in 1952 for the 1,000 lb bomb are still 'provisional'. Till date, almost all the specifications issued for air armament stores are still 'provisional'.** The designer never made efforts to issue final specifications and drawings. A few examples of why 'provisional' drawings are to be converted to final drawings are worth mentioning:

  o The 1,000 lb casing material does not contain alloying elements required for penetration.

  o At the time of the design of the 68 mm rocket, the rubber items (O rings), igniter and propellant could not be designed optimally because of which each item had a different life span. It was clearly mentioned by RCMA(AA) in 1977 that additional tests needed to be conducted for improving the design.

  o The ERU-201 and 204 were designed in 1976 with an improper 'cap' (initiating component), with the resistance value not matching the Jaguar aircraft. It was to be redesigned.

- DRDO is reluctant to accept positive criticism about the performance and quality of the design. The deficiencies in design are never accepted. The user always compares the product with a similar item from abroad. If the performance is not up to the mark, it would be better to classify the item as Mark-I and try to design a better product as the Mark-II version.

Deficiencies at OFB

- OFB is a production organisation. R&D is not their core competency. They are good at production technology. The primary effort of any Ordnance Factory (OF) is to chase targets and increase production turnover. Man-hours spent by the workforce on R&D, which affects production, is not acceptable to the management. Therefore, R&D takes a back seat. Even if OFB is able to produce an item through reverse engineering, it is not able to complete the process of tests and documentation required for the qualification and airworthiness certification of air armament stores.

- A majority of products produced by OFB are meant for the ground forces. The entire staff of OFB i.e. officers and technicians are, therefore, used to the quality norms of the ground forces which are a little relaxed when compared to the air armaments. Since the Quality Assurance/Quality Control (QA/QC) requirements and proof testing of air armaments are much more stringent, OFB finds it difficult to produce items of the correct specification. Since the volume of orders for air armament stores is low compared to the ground forces, OFB is reluctant to take up the air armament tasks.

- The old industrial employees of OFB are not technically competent to read the specifications and devise their process schedules. Most of the old technicians are only 10th class pass. Therefore, adherence to process schedules and process control is very difficult, without which, quality products cannot be made. There is no practice of following a checklist by the technicians/ supervisors. It is based on memory and practice. Therefore, the possibility of non-adherence to the correct process cannot be ruled out. However, OFB is now getting engineers even as chargemen, and must utilise these industrial employees to enforce adherence to process schedules.

- The industrial employees of OFB (below the Group B officers) are entitled for financial incentives based on the number of items produced and overtime work. Since R&D is considered non-productive activity, the work force does not come forward actively for such work. They need to be forced to work on R&D projects. The OFB also puts its best employees into production rather than R&D work. Therefore, the R&D activities remain non-starters.

- The machines, jigs and fixtures are to be periodically calibrated. In practice, it is mostly on paper. Practically, only the gauges are calibrated periodically but the jigs and fixtures are checked only when the quality is affected.

- There is no accountability for rejected items in a semi-finished condition. All higher officials see the cost of the items produced. No one sees the cost of items rejected in each stage of manufacture. Since rejections at this stage are not monitored by the MoD, the OFB adds the cost of the rejected material to the final finished product. In the case of the 450kg HSLD bomb, the rejection at the casting stage was almost 75 percent due to the application of vintage casting technology. If an audit is conducted on the total raw material used and the end product weight, the loss to the state may be assessed.

- Whenever ToT takes place, the OFB does not sign any contract with the ToT firm for regular updates in product specifications as well as proof specification. It may be noted that the ADEN gun ammunition is manufactured under ToT. Test specifications of Fuse 933 of the ADEN gun ammunition, is carried out as per the **proof specification of 1946**. Any designer and manufacturer needs to update the technology and obtain the latest acceptance rejection criteria and testing methodology.

- OFB is not able to produce quality propellants for gun ammunition and rockets. Most of the propellants produced have certain deviations. Whereever required, we must think of importing these components to complete production.

- A majority of the ordnance factories are working on vintage technology in bomb casing manufacture and explosive filling. Quality and numbers cannot be achieved due to this vintage technology. OFB needs to undertake a large scale modernisation plan to meet the current production requirements.

- Middle managers' involvement in development is almost nil. Since the bright officers are involved in production, officers made in-charge of development do not have the will to indigenise armaments.

System Deficiencies at MoD

- The MoD depends heavily on the DRDO. The industry is considered as a 'trader' rather than a 'partner'. The existing process does not permit funding or assigning long-term contracts of defence projects to private industry. Without the participation of major players of the private industry, the new generation weapon systems cannot be indigenised. Design and development of any air armament stores is a complicated process, considering the requirements of flight safety. Only an integrated approach [Joint Venture (JV) of R&D and industry] would be a viable option. Industry would come forward only when there is an assurance that the investment would get proper returns to develop the product. On most occasions, the industry involved in development does not get the contract when it is produced in bulk. Therefore, after a couple of experiences, they do not come forward for development activity. Therefore, the MoD needs to debate this issue and develops suitable policy guidelines.
- The Integrated Defence Staff (IDS) had issued certain convening orders to the IAF for the development of products of air armament stores. These would remain a paper exercise unless a separate expert team is formed to work on the project. When the IDS projects are received by the IAF, the concerned officials consider these as additional tasks. They tend to concentrate on the primary task. Therefore, a separate team needs to look into the IDS projects for indigenisation of air armament stores. We have Project Management Teams for aircraft and helicopters. But till date, no team has been formed for management of air armament projects. Moreover, the projects defined by IDS are very ambitious and some of the project definitions are unrealistic to achieve. Also, the officers issuing the tasks are from the land forces.

- The MoD always seeks the total quantity produced and cleared by the factory and QA agency. While it is necessary for the MoD to monitor the turnover of OFB, the QA agencies must be assessed based on the cost of items rejected or rectified, after QA have identified the lapses in quality. Since the monitoring system is not in place, rejections are not taken seriously and OFB does not spend time to identify the reasons for the occurrence of a defect. This affects development projects.

- At present, the industry is not permitted to do the explosive filling. Therefore, the user has to place the indents on either OFB or ARDE or BDL for any armament products. To make the process more competitive, the government needs to permit the industry to compete with OFB and BDL.

- Every department tries to protect and defend its own system. Departments are trying to expand their domain for the sake of better promotional avenues for their officers. Till date, no credible air armament has been produced by the DRDO. Since the MoD may not get the correct picture of the problems of indigenous development, it would be better to have **an independent body, working directly under the MoD, that would link all the other departments (DRDO, user, OFB, DGAQA and CEMILAC) for expeditious completion of the indigenisation task.** The team needs to assess the feasibility of realisation of projects within the given timeframes. Experts from each department/Service may be pooled to carry out this activity. The tenure of the task force team should be a minimum of five years, considering the gestation period of development projects.

- The educational institutes are not tapped to use their potential in the development of military products. Unless the basic research is established in the educational institutes, the applied research will not be successful. It means that the MoD need to invest in institutes like the Indian Institutes of Technology (IITs) and Indian Institute of Science (IISc) for developing the products. If need be, a separate institute, exclusively meant for feeding the defence research and production units, may be established for effective returns from the investments. Then the question arises: who will assign the task to these educational institutes? If an independent body, as mentioned above, is formed, it would be able to assign the projects to the educational institutes.

Analysis

Military Services are war-fighting machinery. The operation and maintenance of equipment is a primary responsibility. Indigenisation depends on the government's policies and approach. It emerges from the above that the failure of indigenisation of air armaments is primarily due to lack of coordination and focus. Each department/Service has its own agenda in which indigenisation does not figure as a primary task. Since OFB is a production agency, the indigenisation projects should not be assigned to them. They may be involved in producing the hardware by the respective R&D agencies from the beginning of development for expeditious bulk production.

Despite having the largest pool of technical manpower, India is import dependent mainly due to the non-involvement of industry as a partner and lack of thrust in every department. Given authority and accountability to a dedicated team, the low-tech weapons could easily be indigenised. Also, the existing weapons could be improved. For development of high-tech weapons, we need to take industry and foreign companies as partners and make a beginning.

Being one of the largest armed forces, we need to establish a credible weapon industry. The shelf life of a majority of costly armaments is 10 years, extendable to 20 years. It means the entire War Wastage Reserve (WWR) requirements are to be procured repeatedly after every ten years. So far, the focus is only on the weapon delivery platform but not on the weapon itself. We feel happy that we are able to indigenise fighter aircraft but we need to remember that it would carry mostly imported weapons. Therefore, the deficiencies mentioned above need to be examined by an independent body and necessary policy changes are to be initiated in each organisation for self-reliance.

Recommendations

The following are recommended:

IAF

- The IAF is a fighting force. All flying efforts are meant for ensuring the delivery of weapons. But the weapons and people handling the weapons are given least importance. The IAF need to create an environment to enhance core competence in air armament activities. The P-branch needs to deliberate on the system to be incorporated for enhancing the core competence in the field of air armaments. It should plan the training, career profile and promotional avenues. In the case of the Indian Navy, the Naval Armament Inspectorate Branch is actively involved in defect investigation, quality control, design and development of armaments. The IAF needs to think on similar lines to create core competence by training and planning the career profile of AE officers.
- Create certain posts exclusively for indigenisation of air armament stores. The posts could be at Air HQ as well as at DRDO, MoD, CEMILAC, DGAQA and IDS. The primary responsibility of the officers is indigenisation of air armament stores and improvements to the existing products. In fact, the IAF has not been sparing officers for the projects of air armaments.
- The tenures of the project managers must be five years instead of two / three years.
- The Ops Branch may deliberate on the requirement to create a post of ACAS Weapons (Ops), who would come directly under the DG Ops (Air). The ACAS (Ops) could also take the responsibility of operational utilisation of role equipment common to multiple fleets of Air Defence (AD) and Ground Attack (GA) role aircraft. Also, this directorate would be responsible for procurement of associated equipment of the main stores viz training weapons, belting machines, proof equipment, tools, manuals, mandatory spares, etc. At present, the weapon is procured by the Op Branch and role equipment and TTGE are procured by the Maintenance Branch based on the inputs

of the respective fleet's Op Directorate. In case the AVM rank post cannot be created, there could be at least an Air Cmde (PD Wpns), who could directly come under DG Ops (Air). This would ensure expeditious decisions on all aspects related to air armaments for air defence as well as ground attack roles.

• Increase the number of officers posted to DASE and D Weapons in the Maintenance and Ops Branches respectively.

• Create better testing facilities at 28 ED for life extensions and defect investigations of imported and indigenous stores.

• Indigenisation projects must not be given to OFB. All projects are to be given either to DRDO or the industry (if the government permits them to participate). Create a design agency within Air HQ to look after the indigenisation projects.

• When new products are to be developed, formulations of SQRs must be realistic and provide scope for improved versions as Mark-I, Mark-II, so on.

The remedial actions to be taken at DRDO, OFB and MoD have not been specified. Based on the deficiencies mentioned above for each organisation, the respective organisation needs to introspect frankly. If need be, the MoD may form a committee of experts and come to an amicable solution. Firstly, there must be will and resolve to give greater impetus to indigenisation. Then only would some tangible solutions emerge.

Conclusion

Considering the internal and external security scenarios, India needs effective air launched weapons of its own. Except for limited unguided weapons, India is not able to design modern guided weapons. The private industry has the technology to produce modern non-armament related equipment. If this is tapped and translated from generic technology into air armaments, we will be able to produce world class products. However, indigenisation of air armaments is a long drawn process. Unless the government takes certain radical measures, the blame game of DRDO vs. user would continue and we will continue to import for another two to three decades. When we can send a satellite into space, we can also make a missile hit a target. We need to integrate the expertise available with the Ministry of Science and Technology and Ministry of Defence. Involvement of the user is mandatory to coordinate the system. If need be, the IAF may seek additional officers for this task. The WWR and AAT requirement put together would be a very huge amount and even if we produce 20 percent of the items indigenously, we would save thousands of crores of rupees. However, the main thrust must come from the MoD.

Price of Ignoring Organic D&D Capability

✿ A.K. NAGALIA

Introduction

The Indian Air Force (IAF) prides itself in being the fourth largest Air Force in the world. In the last decade, it has been rubbing shoulders with the very best in the world, in various bilateral and multilateral exercises held in India and abroad. The IAF pilots have earned kudos from the various air forces they have exercised with and have been rated among the very best. The IAF has come out with flying colours in the 'Red Flag' exercise held in 2008 in the Nevada desert of the USA, both in the air as well as ground operations. It has fully operational high end force multipliers like the Airborne Warning and Control System (AWACS) and Flight Refuelling Aircraft (FRA) to support its operations in any theatre of war.

One can indeed be proud of the above achievements. However, are these enough for the IAF to rest on its laurels? It has the unenviable task of defending the country against two nuclear armed potential adversaries. Both are in the process of rapidly expanding and modernising their armed forces, especially the air assets. They are also in close alliance with each other and have made no secret of their intentions against India. The IAF, on the other hand, finds itself deficient of nearly 25 percent of its combat assets, both airborne as well as ground based. Also, barring the Su 30MKI fleet and the limited number of recently acquired/contracted weapon systems, all other airborne and ground-based assets in the inventory of the IAF are verging on varying degrees of obsolescence. Despite having produced under licence and operated the MiG 21 variants for over three decades, we had to go back to the Russians for their avionics upgrade. The same is the story for the MiG-29 and Mirage 2000 upgrades. Even six decades after independence, we have to depend on foreign sources to not only make good the deficiencies in the combat assets but for fighting obsolescence as well. How have we allowed such a situation to develop? Is it only the bureaucracy in South Block to blame for it? Has there been any contribution of the IAF itself in it? Let us examine the latter.

Need for Organic D&D Capability in Air Force

It is universally accepted that a user knows best what he wants. However, a wide range of factors is there to influence his choice. The most obvious and desirable factors which need to be taken into consideration are the threat environment and desire to improve self-reliance in sourcing and sustaining the desired capabilities. Not so obvious factors are the numerous agents or lobbyists of various global arms merchants trying to push through their products. Ingenious methods are employed by them to influence the user's choice. The most innocuous ones are sleek glossies and unsolicited presentations, making tall claims about their products, while carefully hiding shortcomings or technological limitations or its impending obsolescence. More enterprising adopt devious methods like employing gullible politicians or bureaucrats or senior Service officers to influence the choice of decision makers in various garbs. Often the systems offered by them or technologies employed in these systems are obsolescent. The state-of-the-art or emerging technologies are zealously guarded or denied by them. Only after an obsolescent system has been bought and later models employing contemporary technologies revealed or offered. Since the imported equipment needs to be well proven, it is normally procured halfway in its life cycle with the parent country or, in same cases, even later. Thus, the parent country support is likely to be available only far a small part of its intended period of utilisation by the buyer. Thus, the buyer needs to safeguard his interest by getting critical design data or 'knowhow' to be able to undertake periodic upgrades and manage obsolescence related hurdles. For gainful utilisation of the design data so obtained, the user needs to have organic Design and Development (D&D) capability.

Organic D&D capability in an Air Force provides a ready set-up, comprising suitably qualified designers and engineers in various disciplines, necessary laboratories and associated infrastructure, for the following functions associated with optimising selection, induction and life time exploitation of various imported systems in the most efficient manner:

- Technical appreciation of various technology options available in the global market and identification of the most optimum.
- Assisting in evolving realistic Air Staff Requirements (ASRs) which will ensure multiple choices and fair competition to achieve optimum balance between operational capability and economy.
- To be repository of design data and 'know-how/know-why' of various operational systems in the inventory of the Air Force.
- Evolve in-house solutions to various emerging threats by using the best available technology options.
- Evolve various periodic upgrade/modernisation packages to maintain operational relevance through the entire life cycle of a weapon system.
- Obsolescence management to avoid disruptions in supply chain.
- Provide pool of experts to manage various outright purchase projects through various phases of acquisition, induction and life time exploitation, i.e. 'cradle to grave' approach.

A major objective of a prudent air force is to promote self reliance in sourcing and life time exploitation of various weapon and support systems in its inventory. For a country like India, which started from a very low industrial base but faced a very grave threat environment, the choices were not easy. While maintaining contemporary war fighting capability, it had to establish *de novo* a military industrial complex and embark on the path of self reliance. Under these circumstances, organic D&D capability plays a crucial role in ensuring that the air force finds an optimum product and technology mix for outright imports, licensed production and indigenous development. To be able to eventually achieve a very high degree of self reliance in a reasonably short time, the organic D&D capability has to perform the following functions:

- Concept development and proving.
- Technical appreciation of various design options.
- Assist in evolving realistic ASRs for progressive compliance during the development cycle.
- Assist design staff of the nominated D&D agency in interpreting the ASR and provide other user related inputs during the detailed designing phase.
- Provide pool of experts to manage complex D&D Projects and allied activities.

Historical Background

At the dawn of independence, the country had a very low industrial base, with practically zero defence industry. By way of aeronautical industry, there was a small factory in Bangalore, set up by Seth Hirachand Walchand in 1940, which was later nationalised and is known as Hindustan Aeronautics Limited (HAL). Out of the three Services, the Air Force has been most technology intensive, followed by the Navy. Know-how about the military aviation in the country existed only in the Air Force. All the technical functions like formulation of technical specifications for futuristic requirements, modifications, inspection/testing, acceptance, etc. were being carried out by the Services themselves.

While the Navy decided to keep the warship design and inspection function with itself, the Air Force decided not to have an organic D&D capability, despite there being no other agency having expertise in this highly specialised field. The giving up of design standard compliance and Quality Assurance (QA) during production and acceptance functions, which are usually the prerogative of the user, was indeed inexplicable. The DRDO and Department of Defence Production gratefully accepted the opportunity and promptly set up Resident Engineers and Resident Inspectors at DPSUs, who were controlled by D Aero and DTD&P (Air), predecessor organisations to the present day Centre for Military Aviation Certificate (CEMILAC) and Director General Air Quality Assurance (DGAQA) respectively. Not only that, the Air Force also supplied them the expertise in these fields in the form of its highly qualified and experienced engineers and other technical staff. The Air Force was now left with General Duty Pilots and Maintenance Engineers and technicians, supported by small complements of admin, logistic and other support staff. It no longer had the expertise to respond to various emerging threats by evolving in-house solutions using the best available technology option, integration of innovative solutions on various fleets, in service upgrades, inspection and certification related activities. Whenever even a simple integration task had to be done, an *ad hoc* team was constituted by Air HQ for the specific task and dissolved after completion of the task without the organisation being wiser of the experience gained. Alternatively, it was given to HAL to manage it.

HF-24 Marut Development
In the mid-1950s, the IAF issued an Air Staff Requirement (ASR) for indigenous development of a supersonic Multi-Role Combat Aircraft (MRCA). Its performance attributes included ceiling of 60,000ft, speed of Mach 2, interception capability at various altitudes, and low level ground attack with a radius of action of 500 miles (805 km). Dr Kurt Tank and his team of 18 engineers were invited to work at HAL to develop such an aircraft in India. The team arrived in India in 1956 and set about converting the ASR into an aircraft, designated HF-24 which was later christened 'Marut'. The aircraft was designed around the Bristol Siddeley's twin Orpheus BO-12 engine configuration. The BO-12 was being designed as 8170 lbf thrust after burning engine, against a British government requirement. Unfortunately, the British requirement for such an engine was dropped and the Government of India (GOI) refused to underwrite the remaining developmental expenditure of Pounds 13 million sterling. As an interim measure, the development and initial production of the Marut was continued with Orpheus 703 engine, which was under licensed production in India for the Gnat programme, while there was

a frantic search to find a suitable engine to realise its full potential. The suitable engine was never found and even in its transonic configuration, the aircraft had to be prematurely phased out in late seventies due to poor reliability and maintainability. Those of us who have flown this aircraft, still swear by its pleasant handling and superb acceleration characteristics and are unanimous in saying that this marvellous machine deserved a much better fate.

After this very brief overview, let us examine, with the full benefit of hind sight, how lack of in-house D &D capability in the Air Force contributed to faulty decision making and poor project management which contributed to premature demise of the Marut.

- Had the IAF maintained an in-house D&D capability, the following facts and complexities/difficulties would have been apparent and taken cognisance of and perhaps a more practical approach adopted to build indigenous D&D capability, instead of issuing such an ambitious ASR.

  o In the aeronautical field, the only D&D experience the country had was that of designing a basic piston trainer called the HT-2 and the production experience of manufacturing the Vampire under licence.

  o The Chief Designer of HAL, Dr Ghatge, was vehemently opposed to such an ambitious venture.

  o The entire infrastructure at HAL, including its runway, was totally unsuited for this class of aircraft.

  o At the time of conceptualising the Marut, the IAF well knew that only the world powers like the USA, UK, USSR and, to a lesser extent, France were undertaking development of this class of aircraft. Since this aircraft will be in direct competition with theirs, no help could be expected from them in this venture.

- Having pushed the country into a venture of this magnitude, the IAF should have led from the front in managing the programme, by appointing a dedicated Project Management Team (PMT), backed by sound technical advice, instead of leaving it to HAL and the bureaucrats.

- To a dedicated and technically sound user driven programme management, it would have been apparent that without Orpheus BO-12 engine, Marut as a supersonic MRCA would remain a pipedream. The IAF should, therefore, have prevailed upon the government to accept the funding of the remaining development of this engine. After all, Pounds 13 million sterling was not such an astronomical sum even by the standards of those times (In some places it is also mentioned as Pound 3 million sterling, which is only a small fraction of it.).
- While it was a good decision to engage Dr Kurt Tank and his team of engineers for the design and development, the IAF should have insisted that a similar approach was necessary for overseeing the upgrade of the production infrastructure and processes at HAL.
- Even the transonic Marut had to be prematurely phased out because of poor reliability and maintainability. It certainly casts serious aspersions on the manufacturing practices and processes at HAL and the QA oversight provided by the CRIs under DTD&P (Air).

Ajeet Development

It is well recognised that the Gnat was one of the most compact designs for its time. So much so, many major functions in it had been combined, eg flaps with ailerons, airbrakes with undercarriage, etc. While it outmanoeuvred and out-performed most of its contemporaries, it was also a very unforgiving aircraft. In the IAF service, it also had the dubious distinction of the poorest flight safety record, that too when only average plus pilots were posted to the Gnat squadrons. The fatal accident rate on it was several times higher than any other aircraft in the IAF inventory. Despite all this, allowing HAL to develop it into Ajeet with wet wings and four drop tanks and giving it the air-to-ground role was certainly not based on sound technical appreciation. Developing the Ajeet trainer with ambitions to use it as the Advanced Jet Trainer (AJT) was even more inexplicable. If the IAF had an organic D&D capability, these aspects would have been analysed in depth and such a project not attempted. Possibly, we could have saved one full decade in launch of *de novo* D&D of a fighter aircraft, as a follow on to the Marut programme.

LCA Development

In the late Seventies, the IAF projected a need for the MiG-21 replacement, which was planned to be a simple and rugged aircraft, to be produced in large numbers to replace the MiG-21 variants in the IAF. The requirements were deliberately kept simple and even the high altitude performance, both in terms of altitude and mach number, were significantly lower than those of the MiG-21. The Air Staff Target (AST) 201 was issued for this project in 1982. The MoD formed a team under Dr Valluri, with members from IAF, HAL and DRDO to examine various aspects connected with indigenous D&D and production of such an aircraft, including foreign collaboration and project management. The committee added an innocuous goal to this programme; 'all round advancement in indigenous D&D and production capability in the field of aerospace by mastering cutting edge technologies such as Digital Flight Control System (DFCS), Multi-Mode Radar (MMR), flat rated turbofan engine, composites, etc'. It recommended creation of Aeronautical Development Agency (ADA), a dedicated design coordination and programme management agency for marshalling design capabilities existing in various DRDO and other government labs, academic institutions and Public Sector Undertakings (PSUs), as well as for seeking design consultancy from abroad on various aspects.

In 1983, the Light Combat Aircraft (LCA) programme was formally approved by the government and ADA came into being in 1984. Detailed discussions were held between the IAF and various other associated agencies, and a formal ASR was issued for the LCA in 1985. Project definition was completed by ADA in 1987. It was decided to simultaneously launch development of the 'Kaveri' engine, MMR, DFCS and a whole host of avionic LRUs along with the launch of aircraft development. Physical (weight and volume/dimensions) and performance characteristics were assigned to each one of the systems/LRUs under development and it was hoped that all of them would be ready in the desired timeframes and fit in like a grand jig saw puzzle. At this stage, the IAF expressed severe reservations with this approach, as recorded in the note of dissent by the IAF members in the Srinivasan Committee report. Consequently, it was decided to split the Full Scale Engineering Development (FSED) into two phases. In the first phase, critical technologies were to be successfully developed and demonstrated to the IAF and then only was the go-ahead to be given for FSED Phase II. The IAF decided to adopt a 'hands-off' approach until demonstration of critical technologies. The IAF was finally demonstrated the core technologies and it recommitted itself to the LCA development programme in 2005. Soon thereafter, a contract was concluded with HAL for the supply of 20 Tejas in IOC configuration, equipped with GE 404 IN-20 engine and ELTA's MMR. However, it took another couple of years for a multi-disciplinary IAF team to be positioned at ADA for coordination purposes, almost two decades after commencement of LCA design.

Let us now examine how ignoring the in-house D&D capability has affected the LCA programme.

* In the absence of a dedicated in-house D&D group, there was no organisational appreciation of the complexities involved and it was left to the whims and visions of the individuals occupying seats of power to take vital decisions which had far reaching consequences. What was worse was that these visions were not necessarily shared by their successors:

  o The IAF allowed the Dr Valluri Committee to tamper with the original objectives by agreeing to an additional goal of 'all round advancement in indigenous D&D and production capability in the field of aerospace by mastering cutting edge technologies' being added to the programme objectives. This single act, perhaps due to the non-availability of institutional technical advice, caused the burial of a simple and rugged MiG-21 replacement aircraft for induction in the IAF in 1995 and gave birth to an ambitious R&D programme with indefinite time lines.

  o Once the above 'innocuous' goal was allowed to be added to the programme, there was no stopping the DRDO from building a huge design infrastructure in the form of ADA, parallel to HAL's existing aircraft design bureau.

o The most important lesson of the Marut debacle, i.e. following the time-tested approach of designing an aircraft around well proven engine and other critical systems, was forgotten and simultaneous the launching of design and development of 'Kaveri' engine, MMR, DFCS and a whole host of avionic LRUs was permitted.

o In 1989, within six years of the formal sanction of the LCA development, the IAF had a major change of heart which culminated in a "total hands-off approach" during the most crucial phase of D&D where close interaction is required between the designers and the user. It was only due to the continuous hand holding by the test pilots and test engineers of the NFTC that the LCA design achieved the present level of maturity. While they provided yeoman service, there were serious limitations in their interaction vis-a-vis a user's empowered Project Management Team.

• Various joint project monitoring meetings for the LCA related projects, normally took place in Bangalore and invariably ASTE was asked to send a 'suitable' officer to represent the IAF. Because of its own trial commitments, it sent a different person each time as no dedicated LCA team had been created at ASTE for this project. Even at Air HQ level, the LCA project monitoring was largely a part of activities of the officer handling the fighter projects, barring very short durations when a dedicated DD was posted for it in the Directorate of ASR. A few examples of the result of this lack of user involvement are:

o Since the ASR had defined 2xCCMs as operational clean configuration, no tests had been planned by the designers in absolute clean configuration (without any external loads) until pointed out half way in the programme that aircraft will very frequently be flown without any external load.

o At the time of project launch, the IAF had specified R-60 as the CCM for the LCA. ADA persisted with it even in 2002-3, long after the IAF had changed over to the R-73.

- In the absence of any in-house D&D set up, the IAF has no means for training its officers in managing or even monitoring D&D projects. Thus, vacancies at LCA PMT continue to be manned as per P staff considerations rather than an officer's ability to contribute to a project of this magnitude.

MiG-21 Bis Upgrade Programme

In the mid-1970s, the bulk of the IAF inventory comprised MiG-21 variants, and the MiG-21 Bis licensed production had also been launched at HAL. The Air Staff recognised two major weaknesses of the fleet, i.e. lack of contemporary weapon suite and an accurate nav-attack system and ordered flight trials for the same. In 1977-1980, flight trials of contemporary inertial nav-attack systems (INAS), Matra Magic I CCM, and various air-to-surface Western origin weapons were carried out on the MiG-21 Bis. I am happy to say that all these trials were successful. A limited number of aircraft was indeed modified for the Matra Magic and some other advanced Western weapons but, unfortunately, no decision was taken to integrate all these together with the INAS as a package on the entire fleet to make it one of the most potent MRCA fleets of its time. The irony is that a similar upgrade was undertaken 20 years later that too with the D&D component being provided by the Russians. The only major difference was the addition of Kopyo to replace the then obsolete Almaz radar and the Russian weapon suite.

The official reasons quoted in the files may be any, but I am firmly of the opinion that the main reason was that the IAF was not confident of taking it on its own, as it had no organisational entity to undertake any D&D related activity, least of all in the emerging field of advance electronics and displays. HAL was just as ignorant and the DRDO had never been seriously involved with the MiG-21 fleet. If the IAF had not ignored the in-house D&D capability, with such an upgrade, the IAF would have been the torch-bearer among the MiG-21 operating Air Forces—and imagine how much business it could have generated for the indigenous aviation industry.

Other In-Service Upgrades/Modifications

NavWASS Upgrade: While finalising the Jaguar deal, it was apparent that the obsolete NavWASS system had to be replaced and the BAe Systems solution was not the most optimum. The selected sub-systems had to be integrated but there was no single agency in the IAF or outside which could do it. Once again, the IAF failed to capitalise on this opportunity to create an in-house D&D capability. Instead, it allowed an INAS Integration Organisation (IIO) to be formed under the MoD as a temporary establishment. I would reiterate, if we had in-house D&D capability, by this time, the MiG-21 upgrade package would have been in an advanced stage of integration and we could have readily adopted it for the Jaguar too.

DAWN Pod Integration: Once again, while finalising the procurement of DAWN pod, the question arose as to who would integrate the pod on the Jaguar and develop PFMs and be responsible for in service support, etc for it. This time too, we allowed DRDO to set up a brand new establishment called Aircraft Systems Integration and Evaluation Organisation (ASIEO), now renamed as DARE, instead of creating an in-house capability in the IAF.

Software Development Institute (SDI): In the late 1980s, at the time of closing down IIO after completing the Maritime Jaguar related tasks, the software source codes, documentation, integration rig and other IT related assets had to be taken over by some user organisation for in service DARIN software maintenance. The IAF did not have any unit which could take on this type of commitment. It was decided to create a new establishment to take on various software related tasks. Within a short span of its existence, SDI has not only taken on various DARIN related tasks but also performed similar tasks for the upgraded MiG-21 Bis and Su-30. It has played a major role in the indigenous development of DARIN II and MiG-27 avionics upgrade package and is even supporting the LCA development programme.

DASH and Crystal Maize Integration on Mirage 2000: The Mirage 2000 uses the digibus instead of 1553 bus. Its protocols and data flow and coding, etc are entirely different and proprietary of the French. M/s Elbit and Rafael, Israeli OEMs of DASH and Crystal Maize systems, undertook the responsibility of integrating their systems on the aircraft but we had to give them access to the aircraft for it. By extensive trials, they were able to decode the bus protocol etc and integrated their systems on it. Thus, while we could be blamed for the Intellectual Property Rights (IPR) violation, the Israelis were the beneficiaries of gaining insight into this system architecture.

General

In the absence of any organic D&D set-up, in the IAF, the Defence Procurement Procedure has made it obligatory to seek advice of various D&D, certification, inspection and production agencies under DRDO and the Department of Defence Production while formulating ASRs. Often, it is seen that the advice received is biased by their organisational considerations. Thus, even in an exclusive user domain, the user's role has been minimised.

Allied to the organic D&D capability are the functions of laying down design standards, certification of compliance with the laid down standards and QA cover during various stages of production and, finally, the acceptance of the end product. All these functions are of crucial importance to the user as these determine the efficacy of the final product, and, consequently, these have a direct bearing on his operational efficiency and combat potential. Similarly, low maintainability and reliability on account of non-adherence to laid down design standards or production tolerances and processes can seriously undermine operational efficiency. One could argue about whether a fighting force should be involved in these support functions. It is not necessary that all the CRIs and CREs must wear uniform. They may very well wear civil clothes but what is important is that organisationally they must be answerable to the user. After all, they are his watch dogs, created to protect his interests. The present arrangement of placing them under development and production agencies undermines the basic tenet of the independence of regulators, that is why we continue to have disagreements between the user and

CEMILAC on the concessions granted by it to various design deviations which have adverse down stream effects in terms of handling qualities or performance or any other user requirement. In the production arena, the user does not even get to know about the concessions granted by CRI for various deviations and the item has already been accepted on his behalf. He comes to know of these only during collection when the end product does not meet any performance parameter or if there are deviations from the laid down standard of preparation. Often he has to wait for months before these shortfalls are rectified.

Conclusion

Organic D&D capability in an air force is essential for being able to critically examine complexities of various technology and design options, absorb design related know-how and know-why of various imported operational systems in its inventory and to respond to various emerging threats by evolving in-house solutions using the best available technology option. It also assists in evolving realistic requirements for future acquisitions, whether by indigenous design and development or out right purchase, based on proven concepts rather than wishful thinking. It would also be a permanent repository of design data and generate a pool of experts well versed with complexities of combat aircraft design. The air force can gain fully use them for managing various developmental and acquisition projects in a professional manner. By ignoring this vital capability, the IAF's decision-making pertaining to various acquisition and indigenous D&D projects has been inconsistent and based on individual perceptions rather than well researched and technologically sound institutional advice. In the absence of suitably qualified personnel in this field, the IAF was also not able to play its rightful lead role in these projects with disastrous consequences, as seen above. It is high time the Air Force made amends for it and created a well structured organic D&D capability.

Laying down design standards, design certification, QA cover and acceptance are related activities, which are of critical importance to the operational efficiency and combat potential of an air force. Placing them under DRDO and Department of Defence Production has resulted in dilution of user requirements and production standards and led to avoidable friction between user and development and production agencies. Therefore, these need to be brought under the control of the Air Force for smooth execution of various development and production projects as per user requirements. By rectifying these organisational deficiencies, the Air Force can achieve quantum improvement in its operational efficiency and combat potential.

Strategic Directions: Indian Air Force— Research to Operationalisation

✿ T.M. ASTHANA

Introduction

In December 1903, the first powered and 'heavier than air' manned flight flew 20 feet above the ground, to a distance of 120 feet, for a duration of 12 seconds. A little over a century since, the air forces of the world have emerged as a technologically intensive arm of the nation's military forces. Such intense development in technology could never have been be predicted in December 1903. Each successive decade, and even each progressive year (at times) has witnessed aviation technology progress by leaps and bounds. We have witnessed how the Revolution in Military Affairs (RMA) has introduced concepts like Information Warfare (IW), sophisticated smart bombs and Precision Guided Munitions (PGMs), and a marked change from platform-centric warfare to network-centric warfare thereby reducing the Observe, Orient, Decide, Act (OODA) loop to near real-time execution. The virtual adaptation of the 'system of systems approach' to all aspects of warfare has led to greater synergy and interoperability.

Gradually but surely, air power has been asserting itself as an increasingly potent factor in conventional warfare. The single most important variable that has altered the calculus of conventional capability mix and elevated air power to a dominant status is technology. Compared to the land and maritime forces, air power is unique in its reliance on technology. Because an air force is a technology-intensive outfit, technological progress, or lack of it, will ultimately determine the potential and limits of air power. Technological advances have traditionally yielded military advantages from the earliest times and in so doing, changed the relative balance between offensive and defensive capabilities. In this, emerging and existing technologies presently favour air power at the cutting edge which has provided a fillip to air power to the extent that air power can today claim to be offensive by definition. This is because air power is now relatively invulnerable and exponentially more capable, thanks to stealth, electronic warfare and precision munitions technologies. A yet more significant force-multiplier lies in Information Warfare (IW) capabilities with the exploitation of space-based and airborne sensors coupled with real-time data transmissions. Such capabilities of aerospace power will enhance not only 'dominant battle space awareness' and 'operational synchronisation' but also the tempo of war as decision cycles have been shortened.

The generation gap in military technology between informationalisation, on the one hand, and mechanisation-cum-semi-mechanisation, on the other, is widening, and the military imbalance worldwide has increased. The role played by military power in safeguarding national security is assuming greater prominence. The vital aerospace capabilities are translating into an RMA by leading to a fundamental change in the nature of war primarily due to three significant developments:

- Information dominance in time and space contributing to real-time situational awareness and precision engagement.
- Breakdown of the classical division of the levels of war—strategic, operational and tactical into a seamless operation.
- Transformation from linear to non-linear prosecution of war.

Any fundamental change requires to be nurtured to maturity delicately, deliberately, precisely and with clarity of thought as well as execution. The elements of aerospace power are virtually limitless, where each existing and new element has to be so conceived, designed and produced that it meshes into the architecture of the system to fine tune and/or enhance the overall capability and efficiency of the system.

Changes in the world order, coupled with rapid developments in technology have encouraged many governments to examine the relationship between defence research and civil applications. A traditional view is that defence research creates advanced technology, which may subsequently spin-off for civil use. This only represents a one-sided view of the current scene. Many technologies relevant to defence now have major roles in civil use. Many countries are now encouraging increased collaboration between civil and defence research and dual use technologies centres are being established by defence research agencies all over the world. Increased alignment and collaboration between the civil and defence sectors leads to improved economic benefits, with defence having at least as much to gain from civil spin-in and access to mature civil technology. This aspect is significant to defence Research and Development (R&D) since adoption of dual use technology in military applications is increasingly becoming the norm.

It is considered imperative, therefore, to create an integral organisation in the Indian Air Force (IAF), which will contribute to research in two distinct fields. Firstly, to forecast future requirements in the design, capabilities and avionics in aircraft, munitions, equipment, infrastructure and communications leading to network agility. Secondly, to provide a catalytic edge, by suggesting upgradations and modifications to the existing inventory. In other words, planning and executing basic research to ensure continued technological superiority; developing and transitioning new technologies for Air Force weapon systems and their supporting infrastructure; and ensuring responsive technical support for emerging problems whenever and wherever they occur.

Aim

The aim of this paper is to suggest a self-sufficient and effective integrated organisation of the IAF to support the IAF's strategic vision with a mission to discover, integrate and deliver affordable technologies for war-fighting by harnessing and steering a partnership of the IAF, industry, and academia.

Defence R&D

The ambit of defence R&D is far too expansive to cover in one paper or presentation. I shall, hence, restrict myself to a few aspects that merit consideration. There was a time when everything to do with production of material, goods and acquisitions for the military that were indigenous was done only by the public sector/government agencies. This did create employment but the technological growth of the nation and, consequently, defence R&D was very slow indeed. Supporters of yesteryears' policy may lay the blame entirely on the adverse international regime of sanctions, export controls and technology denial, but that is only half the truth. Today, there is an overwhelming demand for the private sector, to participate at every level to provide a catalyst to the overall military production, and that too, of standards that are comparable or better than the available contemporary standards. Logically, the cycle of defence R&D should include its involvement right up to the stage when the finished product is evaluated, tested and produced to the satisfaction of the user; in this case, the armed forces.

A raging debate takes place when "value for money" is weighed in realistic and practical terms, primarily because it was argued that the quantities or numbers of the products for defence would be restricted, and hence, amortisation benefits could not be relied upon. On the other hand, the armed forces would naturally like to insist on delinking "financial value" from "military value". Today, much has changed with the acceptance of dual use technology and involvement of the private sector from R&D to the production stage. In addition, the defence sector all over the world does not hesitate to seek contributions from the academia, technology training institutions, autonomous research organisations, and private companies that are keen to participate. After all, the armed forces comprise the most lucrative market.

Technological Push Vs Operational Pull

A major issue that practitioners, strategists as well as scientists grapple with is: what should be the link between policy and guidance? Who should be responsible for achieving this synergy? When the net outcomes do not generate major issues, everyone would like to take credit for it, but when it is otherwise, the less said the better. Experience tells us that even where precise technical parameters and performance capabilities were quoted as a requirement, the IAF had to remain content well short of the requirements because either indigenous capabilities fell short, or the internationally available equipment was not affordable economically. This is particularly true in relation to munitions. The reasons are manifold but the end result was not satisfactory. It is also a fact that advanced and futuristic technologies that are available in the international market had no possibility of achieving indigenous capability. **The IAF had to acquire what came its way by the available "technological push".**

The same situation prevails in all air forces where integrated operational research is absent. Though indeed desirable, the projected operational requirements of accretions, modifications and upgrades were pushed into the background and "technological push" has ruled the roost. It is the dream of all airmen that the accretions, modifications, upgrades and munitions of the IAF's inventory be primarily responsive to "operational pull", be it for the present or the future. **In other words, we would like to see the days when "operational pull" scores well over "technological push".**

I have mentioned accretions, modifications, upgrades and munitions virtually in the same breath. In case one desires to ensure excellence in all departments, all these stages need to be catered for. More importantly, all these stages need to be pursued vigorously with "operational pull" as the basic denominator. Let us look at the programmes planned for development of a new entrant in the international market, viz, the Eurofighter Typhoon. Barely a couple of years have passed since its induction in service and the Eurofighter is already working on the first batch of enhancements for the Typhoon—Phase I Enhancement (PIE). The company also refers to this as the "First Batch of Enhancement for the Eurofighter". This modification will be available to customer nations from 2011 with the final release available in late 2012. This phase includes a new software architecture, enhanced multi-role Man-Machine Interface (MMI), full LDP integration, enhancements of the Multi-Function Information and Distribution, Global Positioning System (GPS), defensive aids sub-system, including decoys, communications and network-centricity, as well as the integration of additional weaponry such as the Paveway IV and EGBU-16. The Phase 2 Enhancement (P2E) is currently being negotiated with customer nations and is scheduled to be available from late 2014. P2E includes the integration of the MBDA Storm Shadow and Taurus standoff cruise missiles as well as the supersonic Paveway IV. Additionally, Phase 2 includes the addition of an enhanced communications suite and improved network-centric capability. Further enhancements planned for the Typhoon include the MBDA Meteor beyond visual range air-to-air missile integration, which is required to be operational by 2012. The Meteor flew on the Typhoon in the UK in 2005, in Italy in May 2007, and Spain in October/November 2007. The Meteor has not flown in Germany as yet. Thus, we see that **the time has come for us now not to be satisfied only by accretions: we need to plan modifications and upgrades well in time to remain on top of prevalent technologies, which has been an ongoing process for the developed nations for a long time.**

With the introduction of Commercially Off the Shelf (COTS) equipment and components in the aviation industry, several aspects of traditional military weapon system design are either modified or eliminated. By opening the architecture, future upgrades and new mission capabilities may be integrated with minimal integration and testing requirements. In order to take full advantage of COTS, the design team needs to determine if certain components can be used. For example, the temperature range specified in the original AWACS system specification required that all electronics operate within the operating range of -55°C to +85°C. After flying the E-3 more than 20 years, the Air Combat Command determined that such a wide operating temperature range was not necessary in most cases. The requirement was modified to specify use in the +50°C range that is typical for most COTS electronics. This modification to environmental requirements provided the opportunity for use of an increasing number of hardware components from various vendors. Coupled with the COTS components, some custom hardware and software will also be required to interface the architecture to the remaining system. **This involvement of the Air Combat Command provides the proof of modifications suggested and accepted by "operational pull".**

Defence R&D and the Air Force

I shall now onwards restrict myself to the air force, which is the foundation as well as the edifice of aerospace. At this stage, suffice to say that air forces would prefer to be in control of all the relevant defence R&D meant to be for them. For numerous reasons, it has not been possible for all air forces to achieve this, including the IAF. However, a few of the so-called advanced countries have achieved this but in various categories. The top of the line, of course, is the United States Air Force (USAF). It would not be out of place therefore, to briefly analyse the *modus operandi* of defence R&D in the USAF.

USAF: Air Force Research Laboratory (AFRL)

The Department of Defence (DoD) itself has a long history of successfully supporting innovative research and development efforts for the future advancement of war-fighting and battle systems capabilities. Since the 1980s, DoD, including the Defence Advanced Research Projects Agency (DARPA), Office of Naval Research (ONR), Army Research Office (ARO) and the Air Force Office of Scientific Research (AFOSR), has initiated numerous development programmes.

The AFRL in its present state was formed in 1997 from an organisational consolidation of four former air force laboratories. AFRL's goal is to create a more efficient, effective organisation to support the air force's global engagement vision. The laboratory is responsible for the air force's annual $1.2 billion science and technology programme, including the full spectrum of air force basic research, exploratory development, and advanced development. The laboratory is the air force's manager for technology transfer to, and exchange with, civilian enterprises. It is also the manager for the Small Business Innovation Research; Dual Use Science and Technology; the Air Force Science Fair Programme, which encourages high school students to pursue a technical education; and for monitoring the aerospace industries' independent R&D programmes.

AFRL employs more than 6,300 military and civilian personnel (1,600 military and 4,700 civilian). The lab and its predecessors have overseen more than 80 years of critical research efforts for the air force and Department of Defence (DoD). AFRL has contributed to significant advancements in modern communications, electronics, manufacturing, and medical research and products. The lab is organised along nine technology disciplines. As the coordinating office, the AFOSR manages the entire air force's basic research programme, its technical experts sponsor and direct basic research conducted in the nation's universities, industry and government agencies. In effect, in my terminology, the AFOSR exercises "operational pull" from research to the evaluation, testing and production of the final product. Its technological breakthroughs can be found in all of today's modern aircraft, spacecraft, and weapon systems, including the F-117 stealth fighter, B-2 bomber, C-17 airlifter, and F-22 fighter.

AFRL has contributed to significant advancements in modern communications, electronics, manufacturing, and medical research and products. The lab is organised along nine technology disciplines as under:

- **Air Vehicles Directorate:** This directorate is organised into four technology divisions (Structures, Aeronautical Sciences, Control Sciences and Integration and Operations), which collectively cover or interface with all research and development areas associated with the conception, analysis, experiment, simulation, design, and test of aerospace flight vehicles over the entire flight spectrum.

- **Human Effectiveness Directorate:** This directorate is organised into six technology divisions (War fighter Training Research, Crew Systems Interface, Directed Energy Bioeffects, Integration and Operations, Biodynamics and Protection, and Development and Sustainment). It is responsible for improving human interfaces with weapon systems to assure the preeminence of US air and space forces.

- **Information Directorate:** This directorate develops systems, concepts and technologies to enhance the air force's capability to successfully meet the aerospace information technology needs for the 21st century.

- **Materials and Manufacturing Directorate:** This directorate develops materials, processes, and advanced manufacturing technologies for use in aircraft, spacecraft, missiles, rockets and ground-based systems.
- **Munitions Directorate:** This directorate's emphasis is on the weapon's capability to operate with complete autonomy and with high accuracy.
- **Propulsion Directorate:** This directorate provides "one-stop shopping" for all forms of propulsion science and technology of interest to the air and space forces. The directorate is also responsible for most forms of power technology (other than those required for spacecraft), making it one of the nation's leaders in the field of energetics.
- **Sensors Directorate:** This directorate conceives, demonstrates, and transitions advanced sensors and sensor technologies for air and space reconnaissance, surveillance, precision engagement, and electronic warfare.
- **Space Vehicles Directorate:** This directorate is organised to develop space technologies that support the evolving war-fighting requirements.
- **Directed Energy Directorate:** This directorate develops, integrates, and transitions science and technology for directed energy to include high power microwaves, lasers, adaptive optics, imaging and effects to assure the preeminence of the US in the air and space.

In addition, the Air Force Office of Scientific Research manages the entire air force's basic research programme, and its technical experts sponsor and direct basic research conducted in the nation's universities, industry and government agencies.

Defence R&D in India
In India, the core activities in defence R&D are primarily handled by the Defence Research and Development Organisation (DRDO), which

celebrated its Golden Jubilee in 2007. The vision and mission statement of the DRDO stipulates the following:

- To develop state-of-the-art defence technologies.
- To achieve self-reliance in defence technologies and systems and provide indigenous systems to the defence Services.
- To create synergy in the efforts of R&D organisations, ordnance factories, public sector units, academia and industries of the country to achieve self-reliance in defence systems.

The Department of Defence R&D of the DRDO is working for indigenous development of weapons, sensors and platforms required by the three Services. To fulfill this mandate, the Department of Defence R&D, is working closely with academic institutions, R&D centres and production agencies of Science and Technology Ministries/Departments in the public and civil sectors, including the defence public sector undertakings and ordnance factories. From the user Services (Army, Navy and Air Force) the DRDO expects participation in the development process from raising Qualitative Requirements (QRs) to product development and productionisation. It includes participation in the periodical reviews and financial commitment in the staff projects.

Procedures have been streamlined over the years but experience tells us that the IAF has had to acquire what came its way by "technological push". Perhaps the Indian Navy (IN) is better off since, firstly, it has its own Cadre of Naval Constructors comprising officers trained overseas for a considerable length of time (between 5 to 7 years), and secondly, for every DRDO project, a fair number of career officers are sent to DRDO to oversee the proceedings as per the quality and schedule. Presently, this is not the practice in the IAF and time delays are common for DRDO projects. Above all, the indigenous products lack the involvement of "operational pull". It is an undisputed fact that the indigenous route is the best and only route to follow in the long run. However, it must be ensured that that the reequipping/upgrades as also acquisitions must operationally cater for the near and distant future in most cases, and probably, for the present and contemporary standards in the case of some selected items. It is also true that no country is fully capable of providing indigenous articles for its air force since the number of sub-units involved in production are many and each one of them demands specialised research. Hence, you have an American aircraft with a British engine, a Spanish undercarriage, etc. How does one put all these pieces together in the puzzle?

The answer lies in creating an organisation whose main contribution is to ensure that the IAF inventory is "operational pull" orientated and that the same organisation is held responsible to discover, integrate and deliver affordable operational technologies.

Operationalisation Recommendations

Achieving an IAF inventory that smarts with the state-of-the-art "operational pull" is easier said than done. The organisation so established must be able to accomplish five distinct spheres of research as its objectives:

- It must be in a position to peep into the future in terms of appreciated emerging trends in all departments and prioritise them in time to remain well ahead of the contemporary standards. This applies to accretions, modifications, upgrades and integration with new munitions as well as avionics suites.
- Analytically assess indigenous capability as well as the will and economic capacity of indigenous participants who will execute the planned task after the basic inputs are provided by the IAF, and they must be able to convert thoughts and plans to products in time, including additional research, if any.
- As and when required, work out the trade-offs in terms of theoretical and optimistic capabilities versus practical ability of the participants and crew capability with the finished product.
- Suggest procedures for harnessing and steering partnerships in the processes of development, trials, and production towards a win-win situation for all the participants.
- In the absence of an all aspect indigenous capability, identify affordable COTS technologies of today, or even the near future.

It must be borne in mind that this list of objectives may be expanded in an incremental fashion as and when deemed fit and expedient. It is, hence, considered inescapable that the IAF establishes an organisation and effectively exercises "operational pull" to equip its present and future inventories. This organisation will also work in conjunction with DRDO but the responsibility and accountability should be the domain of the IAF organisation.

The Time Factor

A major question that comes to mind at this stage is: "When should such an organisation commence functioning?" The answer is "It should have commenced functioning years ago". There is reason to believe that it is time now also for the Indian economy to apply itself in the role of contributing towards building an enviable inventory for the military for the nation. Towards this effort, the essence will lie in building and steering indigenous production. It is emphasised that the strategic direction for defence R&D must be provided by an organisation integral to the IAF, which will be accountable to the IAF and the nation to ensure that every accretion, modification and upgrades to the IAF's inventory is the direct result of "operational pull".

Recommended Action Plan

I visualise five basic steps. These are:

The First Step: The IAF already has a technological sensitive unit called "Software Development Institute" (SDI) manned totally by IAF personnel. This unit took over from the IIO and was initially involved in developing follow-up marks of the DARIN system. Today, it is involved in design, development, testing and production of avionics components for the Su-30, Bison and an Air Traffic Control (ATC) simulator. There may be more tasks allotted (I am sure), which the author is not aware of. The seminal point is that the IAF already has a readymade platform to take-off from. The SDI is a self-accounting unit and its members accompanied the IAF team for the Red Flag exercise to cater for on the spot changes in the software programmes for interoperability. This unit could commence as the hub of activities for the entire operational pull programme. Along with this move, it is proposed that an institution called the Aeronautical Development Agency (ADA) be handed over to the IAF by DRDO. There should no apprehensions in the minds of the present civilian staff in respect of their jobs, since this IAF organisation will also have civilian staff at all levels. It is observed that the expertise built up during the manufacture of HF-24 aircraft just disappeared when the project was foreclosed. The ADA is presently involved in the design of the Light Combat Aircraft (LCA). Such a developed expertise pool must be put to good use by the IAF and the nation. It is hoped that the combination of the IAF and civilian personnel will provide the sought after operational pull inputs for the IAF with a scientific backing.

The Second Step: Assuming that it is accepted that the time is right now, we need to be clear about how to proceed in a planned manner to achieve the operational pull. We have already established the facts that the indigenous route is the best available option, and that involving the private sector is an inescapable necessity. The organisation created must, therefore, in the first place, ensure that the organisation builds the minimum credibility (to start with) to guide and propel the indigenous capabilities of both the public and private sector units towards perfection in the state-of-the-art in design and production of the components (big and small) to be used in aerospace power. It must be emphasised that these products or their variants will also, to a large extent, be capable of adoption in dual/triple use articles. Secondly, where possible, place such demands on multiple agencies to generate a competitive spirit that they will ultimately get used to in the future; like the USAF tasks companies like Boeing and Lockheed to do additional research for an aircraft and then chooses one out of the competitors' proven products for mass production. Thirdly, suggest the employment of selected ex-Service personnel in the private/public sector units who will assuredly contribute to the operational pull of the IAF. And, fourthly, suggest methods and procedures that ensure that the logistics footprint of the finished product is minimal. It is recommended that the first two steps be restricted and practical to ensure satisfactory achievement of objectives. When such restricted objectives are achieved, then and then only, should action be taken to enlarge the scope of the organisation.

The Third Step: "Tomorrow's war will be digitised and communications sensitive" is a statement we hear over and over again. Also, the qualities of precision weapons today permit an aircraft to fire and forget, and yet be assured that the cruise missile released will self-navigate through streets in urban areas and hit targets through windows with NO collateral damage. The question that I pose is this: "Will anybody willingly give you this technology even if you purchase it? The answer is NO. A very structured plan must be evolved to acquire this technology. My suggestion is to follow the philosophy of "beg/borrow/steal". I need not enumerate the various success stories where nations have achieved their objectives through this route.

The Fourth Step: Identify the public/private sector agencies, the academia and educational institutions for research that should be given contracts for the specified research. The research contracts could and should be given to more than one agency for the same subject, thus, creating the desired sense of competition in an advanced economy nation. In the ultimate analysis, such a move will ensure the highest standards of perfection and capability. In the event that no such research agency can be identified, identify the COTS equipment that will ensure uninterrupted supply of the equipment and its spares.

The Fifth Step: I have purposely not called it the last step since this will ALWAYS remain an incremental organisation. Here, I would like to suggest that a separate branch of officers and trade of airmen be created to man the organisation. It must also be ensured that there is a mix of civilian and uniformed personnel but the head of each organisation must be an officer in uniform who is professionally seasoned. This proposal will ensure continuity, which is so essential in the fields of analysis, research, design and production. Above all, the secret contents that every military arm needs to preserve and cherish should be well looked after when the core knowledge is restricted to the minimum personnel.

Research to Operationalisation

Finally

To meet this requirement, the IAF requires an independent 3-star officer to head this organisation. He could be called "DG Concepts and Design". Instead of a staff orientated function, this 3-star officer's function should be designated as a command and executive function and should be detached from Air Headquarters. He could be located at a place which is close to most of the units that will be under his command. As stated earlier, the SDI and Aeronautical Development Agency (ADA) should functionally be placed under his executive command. The testing facilities of ASTE should also be directly under his command. A suitable Electronic Warfare Development Department under his direction could form part of a modified 5 BRD whose charter of duties should also cater for a practical laboratory responsible for concept proving capabilities. This modified 5 BRD should be staffed with 60 percent civilian and 40 percent service personnel to ensure continuity and desired development of expertise levels. And, finally, this modified 5 BRD should be relocated in and around Bangaluru.

It is hoped that as and when the DG Concepts and Design is appointed and commences to function, he will ensure future design and development of platforms, systems and armament, will find true guidance and accurate and critical analysis, providing the IAF with independent and in-house capabilities in design, development and operationalisation across the entire spectrum.

Building Resource Efficiency: Case Study Armaments

✿ MANOJ KUMAR

Environment and Material Parsimony

The application of human intellect has led to many innovations. Knowingly or unknowingly, these innovations have had a tremendous impact on life on this planet. From the advent of wheels to the journeys in space, human quest for "development" has been exciting and equally frightening. It is frightening, because of the innovations that have brought the human race to a point of no return. The invention of dynamite and atomic devices fall in this category. Does this mean that innovations are an anathema for mankind? Far from it, innovations are an integral part of the evolutionary process. It is the methodology involved in development that demands introspection.

Nature has been accommodating and innovating to keep abreast of the rapid deterioration brought about by unsustainable consumption of natural resources. The beauty of innovation on the part of nature is that it is doing so by using and reusing mostly the same set of elements that it began with—namely carbon, hydrogen and oxygen. It does not allow these elements to be wasted and reuses them in some form or another for various applications. In contrast, human beings have been using and discarding nature's resources, unmindful of the burden that it causes on the ecosystem. Consider the invention of Ozone Depleting Substances (ODS) like halons and Chlorofluorocarbons (CFCs) for fire-fighting, refrigerants and solvent applications. These chemicals were hailed as wonder chemicals as they met all the 'human' criteria of development on the industrial and economic scales. As is their wont, humans do not study the impact of such innovations on the environment as that does not fall in the 'development measuring' criteria. However, when the ozone layer depleting potential of these chemicals was realised, the 'innovative' race began all over again to find their replacements as the earlier innovations had to be discarded. Quite a few replacements of ODS are Green House Gases (GHGs) and have the potential to cause further harm to the environment. Such a methodology of development is fraught with danger.

Human beings waste most of the resources that they start to work with while creating products. Consider the following two examples:[1]

- In the pharmaceutical industry, a ton of saleable pills requires well over 150 tons of raw materials.
- Coal-fired electric power stations waste two-thirds of their input energy before the current starts flowing.

In that context, this paper would study the armament use in the Indian Air Force (IAF) in order to understand whether their use for training can be optimised to extract greater value from the same resource i.e to increase the resource efficiency. More than efficiency, can the IAF adopt good practices for process improvement in order to reduce the costs of armament usage i.e to reduce consumption even while not denting its operational preparedness? In other words, the endeavour would be to suggest ways by which environmentally safe practices of increasing resource efficiency and reducing consumption can be incorporated in the IAF in particular and the Indian military in general.

Why Focus on Armaments?
The three pillars of the IAF are operations, maintenance and administration. The activities under these pillars go on in the IAF as in any large industrial conglomerate. In the context of consumption of resources, the IAF can take a leaf out of any industrial organisation's working processes, learn from them and optimise the utilisation for reducing environmental impacts. However, there are a few differences too between the two set-ups. Being a military organisation, one of the input resources in the IAF is the armament

inventory that is procured, held in reserve and trained with, for building operational readiness. This use is very different from any other resource that an industrial hub, akin to the IAF, would use. Additionally, the life threatening element, all-time preparedness and ruggedness of work also differentiate the work of the IAF from that of others. Hence, it would be challenging to concentrate on these issues here, while focussing on resource optimisation, rather than on the largely industrial processes for which many examples and studies are available to be emulated.

Armament usage also causes a direct and large impact on the environment. This is due to the particular nature of resource consumption that leads to the release of pollutants like lead, other metal shrapnel/ chemicals and harmful gases. This impact is unavoidable in wars and, thus, their usage during hostilities is not under the purview of this study. The armaments used by the IAF are costly because they are not a normal industrial commodity governed by the market forces. On many occasions, these are customised and, in other instances, they are manufactured against specific orders. Herein lies the leverage that the IAF holds if it wants to work towards optimising the usage and inventory management of armaments and also to lower the cost of training.

It is important to appreciate the business sense of the optimisation process being outlined here. There may be cynical responses to working for environmental safety for the human race, on the one hand, while dealing with life endangering armament stores, on the other. However, it is a harsh reality of human existence that militaries cannot be wished away. For militaries to function, armaments are a necessity. Since every day, the militaries are not fighting wars but only training for being prepared to face them, the focus should be on reduction of the adverse impact of their peace-time operations on the environment. In the process, if the cost of training also reduces, it may be called the proverbial icing on the cake.

Armaments are specific to the particular arm of the military that is going to utilise them. In the IAF, armaments are more esoteric and are commonly termed as air armaments. Since most of them are air dropped/ fired, the shape, charge-by-weight ratio, type of warhead, ballistics and method of precision guidance are some of the attributes that differentiate them from the stores used by other arms of the military. The variety of armament stores utilised by the IAF is very large and complex and, therefore, the scope for increasing their usage efficiency is equally large. Owing to the sensitive nature of the information related to the subject, this statement can only be explained in simplistic and general terms. Only those stores where the principles of resource efficiency can be applied directly, would be used for suggesting process improvements. However, some of the armaments are meant for only war-time usage and they are obviously beyond the purview of this work.

Armament Training in the IAF

The primary aim of any air force is to guard own air space and take the firepower beyond the enemy's borders in the shortest possible reaction time. Thus, air defence and air strikes are the two power projection options available with the air force and for this, it requires different types of weaponry. Obviously, for air defence, air-to-air missiles are used and for strike missions, rockets, air-dropped bombs (precision or simple ballistic) and air-to-ground missiles, etc. are utilised.

'Practice makes perfect'. The oft repeated adage is accurate for the professionals in the IAF too. To hone their skills, the concerned air and ground crew constantly practise firing of air armaments. The training consists of different types of air armaments that are dropped or fired over field/air-to-ground firing ranges. For the purposes of training, either the aircraft detachments are moved to a particular location so as to undertake armament training from there or the armaments are provided at their parent base. There are many operational and training issues that are factored before deciding on the location of planned usage of the armament stores. Each aircrew has a set of armaments to be fired in a year. This is based on a set formula that works out the numbers of specific training stores (light bombs, etc) and normal armaments (that is, the same as war-time stores) that would be used by each aircrew. It is obvious that the bottom line in this training is gainful use of experience similar to a war-like situation for all the personnel involved with this usage.

In line with the need of the military organisation, each combatant member of the IAF also has a set quota of Small Arms Ammunition (SAA) that he/ she has to fire in a year to remain adept in the use of small arms like revolvers, rifles and light machine guns. This quota has been fixed keeping in mind the stage of training of the combatant member and normally plateaus out after initial training is completed. The quantity of ammunition also varies for different branches of the Service. This firing training is carried out in each major formation of the IAF, at the ground firing ranges (called small arms ranges). The lead that accumulates due to firing of ammunition in the butt of the ground firing ranges, needs to be collected (to the extent possible) and disposed of periodically through logistics procedures. If this exercise is not carried out periodically, it is likely to cause ricochet when more and more firing is undertaken at the same spot with embedded lead. The lead then also poses a danger of seeping down over time to the ground water below and contaminating the same. This phenomenon has already taken serious proportions in the US. Consider the following statistics and the set of information:[2]

- According to the US Environment Protection Agency's (EPA's) Best Management Practices:
  - It is estimated that approximately four percent (80,000 tons/year) of all the lead produced in the United States in the late 1990s (about 2 million tons/year), is made into small arms ammuntion. Taking into account rounds used off-range, and rounds used at indoor ranges, it is clear that much of this 160,000,000 pounds of lead shot/bullets finds its way into the environment at the ranges.
- EPA—Best Management Practices states the following site characteristics that may lead to increased potential for lead pollution:
  - Lead reacts more readily and may become more mobile under acidic (pH < 6) conditions. In general, soils in the eastern US tend to be acidic.
  - During and after periods of rain, storm water runoff may wash lead particles or lead compounds off the range. If there are

surface water bodies such as lakes, rivers, or wetlands in the down-gradient, the potential for lead to adversely affect the surrounding environment is even greater.

o   On-site or contiguous surface water bodies: Very high potential for contamination when shot fall zone is located over, or adjacent to, water; increased wildlife exposure; increased lead dissolution.

The methodology of waste disposal in the IAF has much scope for improvement but is beyond the scope of this paper. This issue has been mentioned here to highlight one more way in which armament usage can adversely affect the environment. It is reiterated that the way forward on the subject is not banning usage of armaments as that would be totally counter-productive to the central theme of the military. However, the right way would be to manage these assets by increasing their usage efficiency while appreciating their environmental impact potential.

Inventory Procurement and Classification

The armament stores procured by the IAF can be classified based on their origin – indigenous or imported. Mostly, the specialist stores received with a particular aircraft as part of a package or otherwise, are bought out. In addition, there are armament stores that are role-specific owing to certain features of precision and other complex capabilities that are required to be procured from a few manufacturers of such stores, abroad. Normally, while procuring these stores, their actual and extendable life is an important feature that determines the quantitative requirements over a period of time. Obviously, the complexity of the stores, their contemporary technology and life plays an important part in determining the cost of these stores.

The Indian ordnance factories also produce many types of air armament stores. These are the older generation of air-dropped bombs and training stores. They have also started manufacturing propellants for a few air applications. The manufacturing standards are fairly dated although attempts have been/ are being made to raise the quality and manufacturing standards. India also has an armament Research and

Development (R&D) establishment, the Armament Research and Development Establishment (ARDE) at Pune[3], which has undertaken many indigenisation and new development projects. The IAF buys a lot of its munitions from the ordnance factories.

Considering the above scenario, it would be natural to assume that a synergy should exist between the two processes of procurement. Hence, the latest technology in the armament field that is available internationally, should find its way to the R&D establishment and, finally, the shop floors of the ordnance factories. Only if this was to take place, would India develop its own ways to increase the efficiency of material use and reuse, which would optimise armament inventory. More of this would be described later when the ways and means of optimising the armament inventory are considered.

As with most military procurements, armament stores are procured for reserves to be used in war and training during peace. While some of the stores are physically different depending upon the intended purposes (war or training), the IAF normally does not differentiate between the types of armament stores required for different end use. This is a standard practice with many militaries of the world. This methodology is fairly well-thought out considering that training has to be carried out as close to the real-time scenario as possible and, thus, the same stores would provide the 'right feel'. The older stores that are nearing life expiry are, thus, used for carrying out the training and the principal of 'First In, First Out' (FIFO) is employed for using up these stores for training. Thus, training and inventory management (to avoid life expiry) are very closely interlinked for armament stores. They acquire a different hue when it is considered that armament training is a very elaborate exercise, with deadly adverse consequence of a wrongly planned move, whether in the air or the ground.

Optimising Inventory
After understanding various facets of armament procurement and training, it can be appreciated that the FIFO principle is of utmost importance to derive the maximum value out of these costly stores. In its absence, the

costly armament stores would life expire and then need to be disposed of without extracting any real value out of procurement. **Since the disposal methodology of armaments is still mostly through demolition of stores, the adverse environmental impacts of disposal and usage are the same.** Judicious utilisation of resources would necessitate that the stores are not allowed to life expire but are fully utilised for training before that takes place.

Application of FIFO in the context of armament training and inventory management presents a challenge to most of the militaries. This is due to the fact that these are stored in diverse locations and required in still varied places. Their usage is dependent on the operational training requirement and availability of air-to-ground ranges[4]. Thus, practically the oldest stores in the IAF inventory may not be available at the location they are required to be fired from. Actual usage would require careful planning to reconcile many variables of aircraft and range availability, flying/ operational environment, movement of stores at the right time and right mode of transport. The principle has to be applied at the organisation level and the training programme has to be designed by the Service Headquarters (HQ) keeping this in mind. Thus, the oldest stores *in the entire organisation* should be allotted and moved for training purposes in the first instance even if they are available at a far off location. For operational reasons, if it becomes imperative to utilise some of the stores from the same or nearby location (where the aircraft are operating from), then it would be prudent to apply the principle at least at the regional HQ level. In this case, the oldest stores *in that region* should be allotted and moved for training when the aircraft operation is taking place in that particular region. It is to be understood that this regional issue programme should not be treated as a standard practice or used as a precedent. It must be clear that to follow the FIFO principle on the stores already available at the location of aircraft operations would obviously be the easier operation but totally incorrect.

There is another way of ensuring reduction in the cost of armament training and its environmental impact. It has been mentioned earlier that armament training requires using actual combat stores to generate a realistic training environment. During the time of procurement, it is well known that some part of these stores would be required for training purposes. Therefore, if some proportion of these stores can be so customised as to be filled with lesser explosives, having the same shape, weight and ballistics characteristics, then their usage during training would not adversely impact the environment. The impact of using high explosive bombs on the environment can be gauged by comparing the figures of explosives filled in the low explosive bombs with those filled in a normal combat high explosive bomb. Both would be dropped by air and would show the same aerodynamic properties owing to similar design and weight. A high explosive, air-dropped bomb anywhere in the world, weighing about 500 kg, would have 40-45 percent (by weight) explosives. In comparison, a low explosive bomb would have only 10-15 percent or even less explosives. If a training mission requires only validating the homing/ navigation of an armament store, it would be prudent to utilise a low explosive or even inert store.

There are various options available for dealing with combat stores as they approach their shelf life. These are listed below in the desired order of priority of their implementation.

- If the life of the combat stores can be extended after periodic change of explosives and other life limited components, then this may be the best course of action. Not only would this save cost on future procurements but also help the environment by reducing consumption of resources.

- Another change that can be brought about in the combat stores is to modify a few of them for training at the time of their life expiry. Changes like the instrumentation of combat missiles for using them for training missions at the time of their life expiry is possible and may be resorted to in consultation with the Original Equipment Manufacturers (OEMs). However, deciding on the actual proportion of stores to be modified for training at the time of life expiry, would require adoption of a long-term perspective on training with regards to that particular armament store.

- There would be some combat stores that would still approach their life expiry period. These would be available for training in an as-it-is condition and should be used for training in order to achieve the full value from their procurement.

Fig 1: Optimising Bought-out Armament Inventory

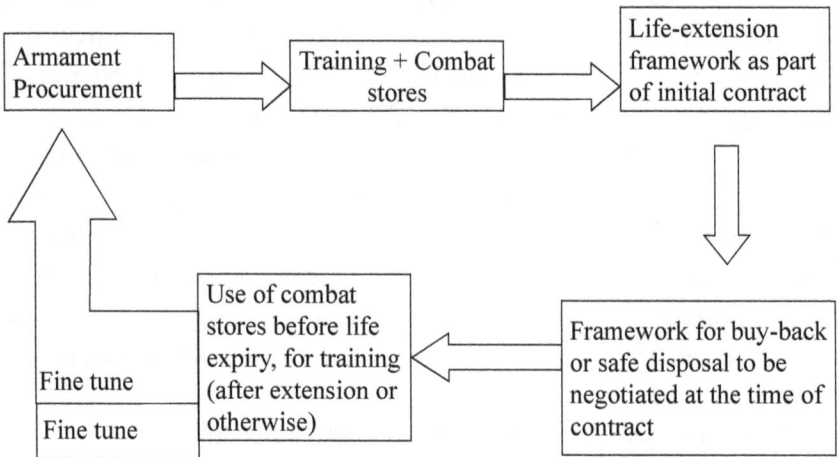

Customisation of stores for specific training needs and extending the life of combat stores can be easily undertaken if their manufacturing has been indigenised as the changes can be easily incorporated when the technology is available in-house. This raises two pertinent questions: (i) what drivers can be used to ensure that the bought out stores can also be life extended or gainfully utilised as a routine? And (ii) how can the technology for indigenisation of armament manufacturing be easily made available?

The answer to the first question is complex. This process has to be thought out at the time of procurement itself and made incumbent on the supplier. This would involve engagement with the OEM over the life span of the stores. As a business practice, it is considered desirable by both the supplier and the customer to remain engaged over the life span of the product. When the armament store is decided to be purchased from abroad, the initial contract for procurement needs to encompass a framework for the following:

- Explicitly seek the framework of life extension after the initial life expiry, duly recording the changes that would be required along with the cost enhancement.
- If combat life extension is not possible any further or has been fully utilised, then seek the framework of methodology to extend life with a view to use the stores for training purposes.
- If incorporation of training life is not possible or achieved, then the user should seek a safe disposal methodology of life expired stores, from the OEM, either by removing the explosives and safe burning (instead of demolition) or any other environmentally friendly means. Including a framework for buy-back of the store after life expiry may also be one option that can be exercised at the time of procurement itself.

The Indian Defence Procurement Procedure (DPP 2006 and later)[5] makes it necessary to execute offset projects by the suppliers for projects of a certain value, in additions to a few other conditions. Amongst the list of defence products that are covered under the offset policy, armament stores are covered prominently. So with regards to the second question posed above, one of the best sources for infusion of the latest armament technology into the country could be the offset route. This would require minor changes to the DPP but would benefit the Indian Ordnance Public Sector Undertakings (PSUs) a great deal. This technology can then be gainfully utilised for the tasks that have been envisaged above (life extension, converting combat to training stores, etc.), for the bought out stores.

To some extent, recycling by increasing life with replacement of explosives, is already being done for some of the older generation stores by the ordnance factories in India. The need of the hour is to make this a standard practice for as many stores—bombs, rockets and missiles—as possible, without depending on outside support. This would be possible if the technology for the same is imbibed at the earliest. This technology would not only include the chemical process, quality and testing techniques but also the latest methodology involved in manufacturing of explosive structures. The era of mixing explosives in buckets in factories should finally be a thing of the past. As an example, the latest explosive technologies are even breaking the chemical boundary by creating lead free detonators so that they have less impact on the environment.

Futuristic Armament Training

We are witnessing rapid technological changes taking places in air power projection. The weapon delivery platforms are witnessing a generational change and the modern aerospace powers of the world can be said to be at the doorstep of 'four plus' generation hardware. Stealth, network-centric warfare, data overload and computer algorithms deciding weapon release timings, are some of the changes that are transforming the air power projection. In such a scenario, the armament training has also got to transform to keep pace with the technological changes taking place. It would be a costly proposition to fire scarce weaponry to gain hands-on experience for each aircrew. This brings us to the concept of quality over quantity. While the need for proving the weaponry and some amount of hands-on experience cannot be denied, the IAF has to seriously consider the use of advanced armament training simulators that can create a virtual battlefield of the 5ᵗʰ generation. Such simulators are already available globally and need to be customised for the IAF's operating scenarios and can integrate Virtual Training Simulators (VTS) with the option to choose different terrains for practising different armament usage. This would, in the normal course, reduce the use of armaments for training missions and would be very cost-effective in the long run. Even maintenance simulators that allow for training of ground crew on armament handling and fusing activities should be procured and extensively utilised. The need of the hour is to show confidence in such methodologies and convert a percentage of flying effort towards such environmentally friendly, but effective, practices.

Another paradigm shift that can prove very effective is applying the principle of 'need-based training' while dealing with armaments. This is already being implemented in the IAF to a large extent wherein a graded syllabus is executed for the aircrew. The concept can be appreciated when considering the efficacy of training with older armaments whilst using the latest military hardware. This may require an overhaul of training patterns. Consider another example wherein all types of small arms training is imparted to each combatant member of the military. It is true that every member of the military is required to be conversant with all types of small arms and ammunition. Therefore, they are authorised to fire a fixed quantity of ammunition of all types each year. If this quantity is the same for each combatant member, irrespective of the domain of operation, then there is a need for introspection. If the military officers are required to use revolvers predominantly during combat and rarely use other types of small arms, then training them at the same level as others who would mostly use other firearms may not be warranted. This is not to say that personnel should not be conversant with all types of firearms but the degree of expertise should depend upon the envisaged need. It may even be argued that for developing expertise on all types of small arms, increased need-based use of small arms simulators may be considered. These simulators are now readily available off the shelf. Actual firing training may be done on the types of arms where combat experience is a must and, for all others, only minimal actual training, carried out with the desired expertise built through the use of small arms firing simulators.

Disposal of Life Expired Munitions
With the aforementioned recommendations, it is envisaged that there would be a limited need for disposal of armament stores whose life expires before they are gainfully utilised. Holding of life expired munitions is not safe due to deterioration of the chemical properties of the explosives filled in them. Thus, these stores would have to be disposed of. At present, such stores are disposed of by Open Demolition/Open Burning (OD/OB), thus, adversely impacting the environment. Disposal of unwanted munitions, rocket motors, and other explosives by OD/OB releases a huge quantity of toxic chemicals into the environment and shakes buildings far away from the blasts. Safer disposal methodologies like, for instance, removing and gainfully utilising the nitrogenous explosives by converting them into fertilisers can be perfected in consultation with either the OEM or experts

in the field. This approach may reduce many man-hours and armament associated risk, and highlight the military's environmental leadership.

Environmentally safe disposal techniques of armaments may be worked out only in consultation with OEMs. If it is made incumbent on the supplier to take care of disposal of life expired stores, it would be a win-win situation for both. This could be done as a buy-back option and a framework negotiated at the time of procurement of the stores. The supplier may then be able to utilise some part of the stores before actually disposing of the remaining portion and, thus, recover the cost involved in buy-back. Also, the users would have been spared the onerous task of disposal on their own accord.

As an alternative to the process suggested above and as an interim measure for legacy stores, the concerned military organisation may approach the OEM to suggest ways to safely dispose of them. The OEM may be in a better position to guide the users on safe disposal, having designed the stores themselves. They may even be interested to retrieve certain portions of the stores and pay for the same even while working towards the environmentally desirable activity of waste reuse. This process does not find favour with the users as it involves discussion on life expired (and, thus, inconsequential) stores. Correct environmental orientation of the organisation should make this a priority.

Recycling of armament stores, by the use of the old shells or casings of the stores and changing the explosives, has already been mentioned earlier under the section on "Optimising Inventory". This practice is effective wherever the life of the casing so permits. In case the life of the casing cannot be increased, it would still be better to recycle the metal case after removing the explosive safely.[6] Open demolition should be considered the last alternative for disposal of armament stores. It is unfortunate that presently this method remains the first way of disposal of armament stores even in modern military organisations.

Management of air-to-ground firing ranges where the armament training is carried out is another area where environmental concerns can improve the working conditions of communities in the vicinity. First and the foremost, it should be appreciated that these ranges are used for heavy aircraft fired/ dropped munitions. The safety distances that are mandatory for ensuring the safety of communities in the region have to be strictly enforced. With more and more pressure on real estate due to the rising population in India, this is fast degenerating into a dangerous situation. The encroachment near these ranges needs to be curbed by effective governance. The local government has to be alive to the situation to ensure the safety of the population.

The recovery of shrapnel from these ranges is also of paramount importance to ensure that it does not cause ground contamination. The IAF has well drafted procedures that allow for outsourcing the waste collection from these ranges. Since higher waste retrieval implies higher cost advantage to the contractor, it is normally ensured that much of the shrapnel is retrieved. The military has a responsibility to ensure that the outsourced waste retrieval job is performed with due safety and under authorised labour laws on their ranges even though the labour is employed by the contractor. These details should be built into the outsourcing contract so that it becomes legally binding on the contractor.

Armament Safety and Storage
While talking of armaments and their environmental impact, it is important to consider their storage and transportation conditions as these directly affect the life of the stores. Most of the precision stores require special conditions of storage (like controlled temperature and humidity) and restricted modes of transportation. When stored in a non-controlled environment, the life of the stores decreases drastically and their performance also becomes suspect. Transportation by road or train and by air, affects their life differently as the filled explosives are likely to deteriorate when transported over an uneven surface. There are specific guidelines on safety of armaments during storage and transportation. These are issued in India by a department under the Defence Research and Development Organisation (DRDO). While safety is the paramount concern, the military also has to ensure that the life of armament stores is not wasted on avoidable transportation and storage in non-controlled atmospheric conditions. The development of infrastructure to store the

armaments should be given as much importance as the military hardware itself. After all, the military hardware would be rendered inconsequential if the armaments for delivery are not available or serviceable. Thus, it is essential that a precious resource like armament is so treated as to avoid unnecessary life expiry that would directly impact the operational and training capabilities of the military and also affect natural resources.

Lean and Mean Military
Financial pressures are being faced by almost all countries. One of the expenditures that any nation is reluctant to reduce, even marginally, is the expenditure on defence, due to the sensitivities involved with national security. In such a scenario, it is essential that the military establishment appreciates its responsibility and uses the resources put at its disposal, judiciously. Since armaments comprise a critical resource for any military organisation, their optimum utilisation would not only make economical but also operational sense. Management of the armament inventory is a complex process because it does not follow all the essential parameters of a traditional industrial resource but is still the most essential element of the military's existence. Its environmental impacting potential is also one of the largest. To study armaments as a part of a resource efficiency drive, for furthering the cause of the environment is a difficult but essential connect to make.

Optimising the armament inventory has to start at the time of the initial procurement contract itself. Distinguishing between, and amalgamating, the combat and training armament stores at different stages of their life is a complex process that has to be performed by the operators with a high amount of accurate planning. While some part of the inventory should be procured as training stores at the time of the initial contract, there might be a requirement to convert the combat stores to training at the time of their life expiry. Some combat stores would still get life expired in storage due to the peculiar nature of the inventory and the need to store them as war reserves till the end. These stores would need to be disposed of in the most environmentally friendly manner in consultation with the OEMs. Militaries normally resort to open demolition of the stores. This causes the same adverse effect on the environment as actual firing of the store, with no value derived from it. Thus, this state is to be minimised to the least possible and to do so, the practice of following an organisation specific FIFO principle for training stores, needs to be adopted. The option of safe disposal of armaments like buy-back after life expiry needs to be explored, to derive maximum value from the product. The flexibility available in managing the inventory increases manifold if the production line is indigenised. The need of the hour is to invest in transfer of armament technologies, mostly under the offset clause of DPP. This would lead to long term-gains and is strongly advocated in the Indian context.

Training on armament delivery is an integral part of the military's operational readiness. There are ways by which armament training can be modernised without actually firing of these stores. Realistic simulators are available, allowing for an actual feel of the armament stores, whether on the ground or in the air. The provisions of new defence procurement policies should be suitably modified to facilitate procurement of this training hardware. In the long run, this would prove cost-effective even while building the operational capability of the military.

Preserving the life of the armament stores by correct storage and transportation practices is of utmost importance. This is not only essential for the safety of the stores, and, thus, the personnel working with them, but also for ensuring that they are available for their full intended life. Non-utilisation, early life expiry, armament accidents, and inadequate training on the armament are all causes for concern and cry out for optimising the resource, in line with what has been suggested above.

Notes

1. Gregory Unruh, *Earth, Inc. Using Nature's Rules to Build Sustainable Profit* (USA: Harvard Business Press, 2010), pp.xii-xiii.
2. This information has been taken from http://noflac.org/ accessed on April 13, 2011.
3. For more information, readers may visit http://www.drdo.gov.in/drdo/labs/ARDE/ English/index.jsp?pg=homebody.jsp
4. For more on non- availability of firing ranges, readers may refer to the news article at this site. http://economictimes.indiatimes.com/news/politics/nation/army-faces-

dearth-of-firing-ranges/articleshow/7759709.cms, accessed on May 3, 2011.

5. For details on the subject, readers may visit http://mod.nic.in/dpm/welcome.html, the official website of the Indian Ministry of Defence.

6. For more on safe recycling of armament store casing, please visit http://www. aria.developpement-durable.gouv.fr/ressources/34585_vierzon_ih___anglais.pdf, accessed on May 6, 2011.

Air Intelligence in Future Wars

✿ SHIV RAM KRISHNA PANDE

Nature of Future Wars

World War I was labelled as the "War to end all Wars". At that time, nobody could possibly imagine that humankind could plan and carry out a horror even worse than World War I, hence, it was christened The Great War.

Even after World War II, while the concepts of War, Victory and 'Victory in War' have undergone a number of changes, human nature is such that conflict there always was, is, and will occur. As this paper is being written, there are no less than eight major wars raging, with about two dozen 'lesser' conflicts ongoing with varying levels of intensity.[1]

May be Thomas Hobbes was right way back in 1651 when, in his epic work, *The Leviathan,* he articulated that human beings are selfish, brute and rash creatures. They will always have a tendency to fight and cause chaos, even if they are living within the same realm.

The Democratic Peace Theory says that two democracies will have a lesser tendency to go war with each other as the respective governments are directly answerable to the people who attach great importance of living in an atmosphere of peace and tranquillity.

Thomas L. Freidman, on the other hand, in his much celebrated work, *The Golden Arches Theory,* says that two countries that have McDonalds, will not go to war as the cost to the various multinational corporate giants is simply too high and they will ensure that their interests are protected.[2] This is also in line with the neo-liberals who say that economic interdependence in a globalised world will ensure that peace prevails between states.

Combine these two theories and it is not hard to see why it has been observed that wars post World War II have been largely limited in nature. By the same logic, it is not hard to see why it has been emphatically articulated that wars of the future are also going to be limited in nature.[3]

War has now come to be seen as something evil that has the power to wipe out civilisations with one single strike (especially with the presence of nuclear weapons). Hence, no government is willing to take that chance and be dislodged from power (especially in a democracy). This, however, has not stopped armed conflict in the world. War/armed conflict is now seen as a way to leverage the view and direction of international affairs towards a particular side. A war is not waged with the aim of annexing territory in order to expand one's horizons, but to attain politico-military objectives in the short and long terms. These politico-military objectives can have a social component to them as well. Hence, in the future, wars will be fought as a last resort to resolve issues, after ensuring that legitimacy has been gained (first, domestically, and then, in the international system), to attain certain pre-defined politico-military objectives while keeping the scope of the conflict limited and close to the borders, especially if the war is being fought against a nuclear backdrop.

In such a war, the question of the legitimacy of the war gains supreme importance. The country going to war has to impress upon its people and the international system that there is no option left but to fight.

We have seen, time and again, that a government can be toppled if its decision to undertake military action is seen as illegitimate by its own people. If the action is also seen as illegitimate by the international community, then it can invite economic sanctions or worse, negative publicity by all forms of the media for a very long time.

The definition of victory in war has also changed. If the war is asymmetric, the weaker side could hail its defences against the stronger side and if it manages to use the media effectively, it could easily make the stronger side appear defeatist, as happened in the case of the 1965 Indo-Pak War.[4]

Hence, the effective use of the media has become a crucial component in the concept of a limited war. We saw live pictures of Tomahawks bombarding Iraq in 2003 and the message of those images being broadcast at prime time on international television was loud and clear. Not only did it convey how seriously the USA had gone into Iraq but it also fully publicised the quality and quantity of armaments at the disposal of the world's lone superpower. Magazines and newspapers from around the globe carried out detailed pieces of writings on the weaponry, tactics and strategy of the US forces fighting in Iraq to rid the Middle East of the supposed presence of Weapons of Mass Destruction (WMDs). When no such WMDs were found, the same media created havoc for the Pentagon and the White House combined. Not only were images of parents mourning over the loss of their sons in a highly disputed combat operation telecast but the term 'body bags' was introduced and gained widespread acceptance. Movies like Green Zone were made which showed the state of a soldier's mind when he realises that the presence of WMDs in Iraq could be just an empty theory which has been sold to the American people and other parts of the world. The power of the media has both sides of the coin: it can push a person to the pinnacle and it can overthrow governments from power.[5] Even a global power like the USA could not escape from that.

The Iraq War, however, was not the first time that America went to war against Iraq. The first time America went into Iraq was to defend the sovereignty of Kuwait against an Iraqi invasion in 1991 which came to be known as the First Gulf War and the military action that was undertaken was codenamed Operation Desert Storm. Operation Desert Storm changed the way the world thought about, and saw, war-fighting. It took the US forces not more than 42 days to wipe out the Iraqi forces from Kuwait. This was achieved as a direct offshoot of the Revolution in Military Affairs (RMA) which called upon war machines to be heavily technology intensive, with cooperation and integration a must, with help from eyes in the sky (and space) in order for all the Services to fight like one single undivided force.

RMA was not undertaken with the sole purpose of reducing the duration of the fight, it was undertaken to reduce the size of the force required to defeat an enemy, to reduce the collateral damage, and to avoid direct contact with the enemy during war.

One can safely say that with the defence industry now firmly focussing on technology intensive weaponry, future wars are going to be limited in nature, with decisive firepower. It could be a non-contact war, with an adequate number of boots on the ground.[6] These wars could be fought against a nuclear backdrop even if there is no clear nuclear threshold defined by the adversary.

In all circumstances, care must be taken to ensure that even if a conflict escalates, it should remain within the contours of a conventional war. It must be noted that when we say the concept of a future war being a limited one, it is limited only in its objectives. It is not limited in the number of fronts it may open up; it is also not limited in the quality or the quantity of the conventional weapons that can be deployed.

The human psyche is such that the possibility of escalation of a conflict into a nuclear conflict is greater with the deployment of land forces. The presence of boots on the ground in captured territory is seen not only as an infringement of sovereignty, but also as a threat to the very existence of the country, which can lead to a catastrophic mistake by the military/political leadership under attack to use the nuclear option.[7]

Here comes the frontal and decisive role of air power in future wars. Air power, which has barely turned a century old this year, has quickly become the preferred means of choice to inflict maximum damage upon the adversary while minimising collateral damage.

Post World War II, air power was not very reliable or accurate. Technological limitations often came in the way. But due to the development of the Military Industrial Complex (MIC) and the RMA, competition in the international private defence sector shot up to such an immense level and technological barriers were overcome sooner or later. The accuracy of an Intercontinental Ballistic Missile (ICBM) which was eventually reduced to a couple of metres is one such shining example.

The intrinsic nature of air power is such that it can reach locations that the other Services possibly cannot. This gained another shot in the arm when the Sputnik was launched on October 4, 1957, and opened up the skies to endless exploration and application. Thus, the term air power transformed into aerospace power which, as mentioned before, was on display for the very first time during the First Gulf War in 1991.[8]

Aerospace forces can conduct deterrence, denial, coercion and decapitation of the adversary. As technology has improved, aerospace power has moved towards near perfection due to its speed, reach, precision engagement, freedom from constraints of ground friction, firepower, and minimum loss of human lives.[9]

Air power can not only create the 'shock and awe' effect that was so evident during the Iraq War in 2003, it can effectively **'strike the fear of God'**, even behind enemy lines.

As mentioned, air power earlier was not very accurate or reliable. But as RMA gained a foothold, we saw the advent of Precision Guided Munitions (PGMs) and the conversion of dumb bombs to smart bombs.[10] Now precision needs precise information. Information given to the pilot must be quick, accurate, reliable and as close to real-time as possible. So, PGMs might be the 'in fashion' method of bombing targets of high value in any conflict, but they are nothing without accurate intelligence. This now brings us to the second part of the paper: air intelligence.

Air Intelligence
An air intelligence system normally has very simple and basic aims. It must meet three criteria: global coverage, instantaneous discovery and absolute accuracy. This will not only help neutralise enemy targets with great precision but also avoid collateral damage.

Thus, when there is talk about the Indian armed forces acquiring more and more PGMs as the choice of ammunition for future conflicts, we first need to acquire the basic infrastructure to use a 'PGM like a PGM'.

This infrastructure starts off with acquiring basic spectral bandwidth exclusively for military purposes. Unless and until the country possesses the required electromagnetic spectrum and the corresponding bandwidth, it does not matter how expensive or state-of-the-art the intelligence system is. It is like buying the best cellular handset available in the market enabled with the best service provider, but without any signal coverage! In India, which is the among the world's fastest growing cellular markets, the government is often caught between releasing a section of the spectrum either for civilian use in order to discharge its duties towards the public or reserving the same spectrum for defence in the name of national security. The Antrix-Devas scam was an eye-opener on the issue of how precious the spectrum is in the current global scenario.

Secondly, the human team sitting in the command and control centre of such infrastructure should be technically capable of operating such a system. Such training even if imparted to those who already have some technical qualification/background, tends to take months together. Air Cmde Jasjit Singh (Director, CAPS) has time and again pointed out that it is not gaining new technology that takes time; it is the maturity of the technology from procurement to operational status that needs to be given supreme importance.[11]

Thirdly, once we have a trained and competent set of personnel working behind a state-of-the-art command and control centre, they have to be trained in making the right call at the right time. They must have enough independence and confidence to call 'X marks the spot'.

Fourthly, the factor of integration is the key. Once a state-of-the-art intelligence centre is manned by a competent team, integration of various sensors onto a common platform is required. This ensures that information has the least delay in being relayed from one system to another. This was seen in battlefields like Kosovo where pilots were given coordinates after they were airborne. Thus, not only is the time of the military operation reduced, the element of surprise is also automatically added, and taken care of.

Following the collapse of the Soviet Union, the USA became the world's lone superpower. It was during the Cold War that air intelligence started breaking every single technological barrier. But during the Cold War, the impetus was on perfecting the early warning systems required to detect the launch of an ICBM in order to give the defending country enough time to position and activate its missiles defences. Since the end of the Cold War, the threat of nuclear risk has reduced but certainly not disappeared.[12] The fact to remember is that detection of the launch of an ICBM was not done in the air—it was done in space. So right from the days of the launch of the Sputnik, the boundaries between air and space have blurred. Both these dimensions have now been fused into one. So one cannot talk about air intelligence without considering space as the first and final frontier.

Air intelligence in some ways is not a complete term. Intelligence gathering is done hand-in-hand with surveillance and reconnaissance and this fact was picked up by the US Air Force (USAF) which realigned its Air Intelligence Agency (AIA) to Air Force Intelligence, Surveillance, and Reconnaissance (AF/A2) on June 8, 2007. Make no mistake, the AF/A2 might be a new term but the USAF constituted an air force unit to handle special information way back in 1948 under the name Air Force Security Group. All USAF airborne and orbital intelligence collection, reconnaissance and surveillance now falls under the control of AF/A2.

Lt Gen David A. Deptula, Deputy Chief of Staff for Intelligence, Surveillance, Reconnaissance (ISR), USAF, in an interview with the magazine *Defence Today* has given the main facets of the future of air power and intelligence.

According to him, first and foremost, ISR is indivisible. Essentially meaning that intelligence, surveillance and reconnaissance are not different things but are deeply interconnected and overlapping. ISR is spread over multiple domains and can achieve total success only when it attains mastery over all the domains—maritime, air, space and cyberspace.[13]

Intelligence is nothing but good and useful information, something that has been mentioned way back in the 6th century B.C. in Sun Tzu's *Art of War*. The only thing that has changed is the way we gather, assimilate and distribute information since all these processes have become highly technology intensive and their unwanted proliferation can be extremely counter-productive.

If crucial information about the enemy's strategy is intercepted, it will always lead to the handing over of a huge advantage to the other side in warfare. This does, in fact, fall in line with what Air Cmde Jasjit Singh articulates as the perennial truth that in order to defeat an enemy, defeat its strategy.[14]

Information will be of no use if it is not available to the right person on the front in time. Hence, integration is the name of the game in this regard. Updated information has to be made available to the battlefield commander in time and this can be achieved by integrating all the platforms effectively using Network-Centric Warfare (NCW), which has come into being due to an Information Technology (IT) revolution in the 21st century as we move towards the formation of a global village. Metcalfe's Law states that the power of a network increases with the square of the number of nodes connected to the network. The power of the network, therefore, increases significantly with every node that is added.[15]

The need of the hour is to achieve a flying NCW. Hence, we could gain ISR even in the locations and air space where ISR is denied. This is where a platform like the 5th generation fighter such as the F-22 Raptor defies its price tag. A 5th generation fighter aircraft is not only proof of air dominance but it can act as a flying piece of NCW using the enormous sensor and communication packages that it has onboard. Hence, it can be used for a very large variety of missions. It can even be used to negate adversary anti-access capabilities.[16]

NCW can actually be seen as a major force multiplier. The core objective of NCW is to provide situational awareness by networking. A good, effective and robust NCW system that is resistant to enemy attack is a sure shot way to reduce the conflict time, help cancel out errors in a military operation and minimise collateral damage. But, most importantly, it guarantees the commander a certain peace of mind and improves his confidence and ability to take difficult decisions easily. We might talk about state-of-the-art intelligence systems, RMA, so on and so forth. But, there was, is, and will be, no substitute for a human being. Human Intelligence (HUMINT) is still used as a sure shot way of gathering ISR in a battlefield. Soldiers on the field have demonstrated 'laser tagging' of the target to help the incoming friendly aircraft knock out the stipulated target using laser guided munitions.

Although NCW forms the basis of a robust intelligence system, it is hardware like the space-based assets—Airborne Warning and Control System (AWACS)—that carry out the operation of gathering intelligence as close to real-time as possible in the aerospace domain.

Space-based assets in the polar orbit are usually used for ISR missions. Such space-based assets have panchromatic cameras so powerful that they can read the licence plate of your car from a height of 700 km above sea level. Some of these also are equipped with a Synthetic Aperture Radar (SAR) that uses Electromagnetic Pulse (EMP) to form an image of the area being surveyed. Such a system can be used for ISR missions irrespective of the weather conditions. Be it day, night, cloudy or even stormy on the ground, one single satellite can photograph and transmit your whereabouts with near perfect accuracy. The only drawback is that it depends purely on the time interval in which the satellite goes over an area of interest for the second time in case the subject's information has changed from the last time it was visited. Hence, we require a pre-defined constellation of satellites to maintain vigil on a 24x7 basis. This is a luxury that not every country can afford, especially if a conflict is raging.

Here comes the role of AWACS. AWACS is essentially nothing but a flying radar. It is normally mounted on top of an aircraft that is of the dimensions of a transport aircraft. It has an all weather capability to provide command, control, communications and surveillance and can cover up to 400 km in all directions within a time span of 10 seconds. Thus, it can carry out effective ISR missions staying well within its own borders. The Indian Air Force uses its AWACS procured from Israel aboard the Il-76 aircraft. But, an AWACS is susceptible to enemy air defence systems or even Surface-to-Air-Missiles (SAMs) that may be launched from across the border, and needs to be escorted by fighter aircraft.

Another means to conduct ISR missions over a designated area (much smaller than the coverage of an AWACS) is through employing an

Unmanned Aerial Vehicle (UAV). UAVs are far smaller than any other hardware used to gather information in military operations. They have the ability to fly near the horizon, evade radars and loiter in the atmosphere for long durations. UAVs, as the name suggests, are controlled remotely and, thus, there is a limitation on their range and they are extremely vulnerable to enemy air defence systems. They can even be knocked out by a tank mounted machine gun. But the major selling point of the UAV is its ease of deployment, no loss of human life and access to real-time information. UAVs come in various shapes and sizes—from a UAV that has a coverage area of about 10x10 sq km but can be susceptible to enemy fire to the micro (and even nano) UAVs that can cover only a certain spot but are extremely hard to detect by the enemy. Such a system can gather intelligence information in an environment that could be difficult or even impossible for a human to go into. UAVs can also be hand-held and launched as gliders for very close-in and time-sensitive surveillance. Such systems are used as the final piece of the jigsaw puzzle to confirm the presence and location of the target before it been acted upon. It is indeed the UAVs that have caused havoc along the Af-Pak border. The Predator UAV was modified to carry the Hellfire missiles that have 'fire and forget' capability. Thus, the time lapse between gathering information and conducting an air strike has now been reduced to seconds. We are now seeing the emergence of an UCAV (Unmanned Combat Aerial Vehicle) model, especially in the United States.

Communications are generally provided by the presence of geo-synchronous satellites. In today's age when Lower Earth Orbit (LEO) and Medium Earth Orbit (MEO) seem to be the order of the day in space operations, one tends to neglect the importance of a geo-synchronous satellite sitting up at 36,000 feet above sea level, stationary with respect to a particular point on Earth, providing seamless communications. It is the combination of such a High Earth Orbit (HEO) satellite LEO and MEO satellites and an AWACS that can provide accurate, real-time and updated ISR, if integrated.

The challenge of the future is to not to see fighters, sensors and communication packages as different equipment but something that can be interoperable. Lt. Gen. Deptula stresses on the fact again and again that the need for the future is, "Every sensor must be a shooter and every shooter must be a sensor". [17]

Lt. Gen. Deptula emphasises that in the 21st century, warfare has changed from industrial age warfare to information warfare. Now in order to find-fix-track-target-engage-assess any adversary, we need more sensors and fewer weapons since the adversaries also have become highly flexible. ISR has now gone to such an advanced level that ISR is no longer meant to support operations. ISR is operations.[18]

Kosovo War

The Kosovo War in many ways is a must study case to learn about gathering air intelligence and employing effective air power in limited wars to attain certain politico-military objectives.

In 1997, Tony Blair was elected as Prime Minister of Her Majesty's Kingdom of Great Britain and Northern Ireland after a landslide victory for the Labour Party after almost two decades of Conservative government. Around the same time, Bill Clinton became the first democrat to be reelected for a second term as President of the United States of America since F.D.R. Both the Foreign Offices at London and Washington D.C. saw this as a perfect platform to propagate the building of a special relationship due to the presence of two men who regarded each other highly as both of them had progressive left of centre political ideologies.

Bill Clinton, being the senior partner in this 'special relationship', advised Tony Blair time and again on the need to 'build a legacy' from day one. Something that in his opinion took him four years to build. Tony Blair initially saw the peace process in Northern Ireland as the perfect place where he could do so, but faced daunting problems: 1999 was the year when Yugoslavia under the rule of Milosevic started to burn bright enough for the world to stand up and take notice.

Tony Blair was of the firm opinion that something must be done. An intervention in the name of humanity was called for and the North Atlantic Treaty Organisation (NATO) had to act. Ironically, NATO, formed to counter the Soviet Union (and later the Warsaw Pact nations), was never called into action throughout the Cold War which lasted nearly five decades post World War II.

Now, let us be clear here. Article V of the NATO Charter states that "an attack against one is an attack against all" thereby sanctioning collective military action against the aggressor. Collective self-defence is also enshrined in Article 42 of Chapter VII of the UN Charter. But nowhere does it mention "humanitarian intervention". Even the term "Responsibility to Protect" (RTP) came only in the early 21st century and has not been accepted by the vast majority of the world that sees it as an excuse of the powerful nations to impose their imperialist tendencies.

Yugoslavia did not launch an attack on any neighbouring state. What it engaged in was 'ethnic cleansing' of the Serbs which was nothing but genocide. Outraged by no intervention in Rwanda, Tony Blair made a strong case during the meetings of the European Union that the fellow Europeans in Kosovo facing genocide at the hands of a tyrant needed help and that a Rwanda should not be allowed to happen again.

Thus, legitimacy for the conflict was gained in the European Union, but not the United Nations as it was seen as an internal matter of the Serbs in Yugoslavia. Bill Clinton, in the meanwhile, also agreed to send in NATO forces. But, those troops would be 15,000 feet from the sea level. Here began, possibly one of the most crucial case studies for any air power enthusiast, Operation Allied Force, an attempt to bring a dictator to his knees purely on the basis of air power.

Initially, the defending forces of Milosevic held on. This was not due to superior air defence or counter-air operations. It was due to the fact that NATO's actions were being seen as half-hearted. The number of targets, the PGMs dropped and the fixed-wing and rotary aircraft deployed were nowhere as close to the capability of the forces of the USA and UK combined (among other NATO countries). Milosevic used the media to showcase his resolve in front of the world almost as if he had called NATO's bluff. Certainly more needed to be done to win the first limited war using solely air power.

Tony Blair's top advisers (Jonathan Powell and Alistair Campbell) pushed him to convince Bill Clinton to step up the operation in Kosovo. Having stuck his neck out politically on the matter of Kosovo, Tony Blair made a hurried visit to the Oval Office where he proposed plans for a ground invasion. The first plan consisted of 80,000 troops for a limited invasion and the second consisted of a full scale invasion of Serbia with 2,00,000 troops.

This drew a very sharp response from Clinton's advisers since a majority of the troops had to come from the western side of the Atlantic to fight a battle in Eastern Europe. Clinton remained firm and did not sanction a troop invasion in a country whose 'ground conditions' were not known to a force having a defence budget more than that of the next fifteen nations combined. Instead, a more coordinated attack was ordered with an extended list of targets, including high value civilian infrastructure, more aircraft (fighters and bombers), more satellites and AWACS for accurate and updated ISR. It was from this point that Operation Allied Force truly became an Allied operation.

The campaign that started with a mere 300 sorties a day initially in the last week of March 1999 reached up to 900 sorties a day in the last week of May. Some 45,935 sorties were planned and 38,004 were flown by about a 1,000 aircraft; 10,484 strike sorties were launched against some 7,600 designated presumed mobile targets of opportunity. To support the 10,000 odd strike sorties, an additional 13,000 sorties were required for combat air patrol and defence suppression. The total number of ISR sorties totalled 1,038 with 25 aircraft, and UAVs were flown 496 times. It is also interesting to note that it was after the conclusion of the Kosovo War that the need to arm UAVs was brought into the picture, since the delay between gathering information and launching of an air strike sometimes was enough to ensure the escape of the target.[19]

About 28,018 munitions were exploded—one-third of these were carried by the B-52 and B-1 aircraft during the last two weeks of the conflict alone. About 30 percent of these munitions were PGMs. More than 50 satellites were used to provide round the clock intelligence data.[20]

Two aircraft, one F-117 Nighthawk and one F-16 were lost but the pilots were recovered after an effective combat search and rescue operation (again not possible without effective air intelligence).[21]

After 78 days of conflict, with dwindling power supply affecting commercial, industrial, economic and military capability, Milosevic had little option but to settle for peace. The classic air power theory that air power alone can, given the right circumstances, meet clearly stipulated military and political objectives, was validated.[22]

The Kosovo conflict was also important in many other ways. The gradual increase in operations, command and control tasks, extensive use of bombers, the massive use of UAVs and satellites for ISR operations was seen as a blueprint for future military operations. The other point that is noticed is that NATO has been active and preparing for joint military operations since its formation in 1948 and yet there were massive flaws in the preparation and execution of the air campaign. Arrangements were found wanting and disagreements became a routine among military commanders. This underlines the fact that when we talk about the Services' integration, it is clearly, easier said than done.

Post conflict, Tony Blair outsmarted Bill Clinton when it came to hogging the limelight in the print and electronic media. As a result, in terms of public approval ratings, the Prime Minister from a tiny little island in Europe became the *numero uno* leader of the world for a while.[23]

Notes

1. GlobalSecurity.org (2011), "The World at War", [Online: web], accessed on November 30, 2011. URL: http://www.globalsecurity.org/military/world/war/index. html.

2. The Golden Arches Theory presented by Thomas L. Friedman in his book called *The Lexus and the Olive Tree,* however, fails in the current domain of international relations. It failed when NATO took action against Serbia, the 2006 Israel-Lebanon War and the 2008 South Ossetia War between Georgia and Russia.

3. Jasjit Singh, "Some Aspects of Our Wars in Future", *AIR POWER Journal of Air Power and Space Studies,* Vol. 6, No. 3, 2011, pp.1-24.

4. Ibid.

5. During the Watergate scandal, two reporters from *The Washington Post*, Bob Woodward and Carl Bernstein, uncovered information suggesting that knowledge of the break-in, and attempts to cover it up, led deep into the Justice Department, the FBI, the CIA, and the White House. Such was the magnitude that US President Richard Nixon had to resign as he was facing near impeachment.

6. Jasjit Singh, "Our Wars of the Future", Lecture delivered on November 31, 2011, at the Centre for Air Power Studies, Subroto Park, New Delhi.

7. Singh, n.3, pp.1-24.

8. T.M. Asthana, "Aerospace Power in National Defence", *Defence and Diplomacy in Pursuit of National Security*, Vol. 1, No.1, 2011, pp.15-24.

9. Ibid.

10. JDAMS are dumb bombs that can are converted into smart bombs by attaching them with a GPS guidance kit.

11. Singh, n.3, pp.1-24.

12. The *Bulletin of the Atomic Scientists* at the University of Chicago maintains a Doomsday Clock which is a calculated estimate how near/far is the world is from a nuclear holocaust. Hitting midnight means nuclear war. The clock so far has come as close to two minutes to midnight. It is currently positioned at six minutes to midnight.

13. David A. Deptula, "Air Combat Platforms and ISR", *Defence Today*, 2009, Avalon International Air Show, [Online: Web], accessed Novemeber 25, 2011, URL: http://www.ausairpower.net/DT-Deptula-March-2009.pdf

14. Singh, n.3, pp. 1-24.

15. Vinod Patney, *Essays on Aerospace Power* (New Delhi: KW Publishers, 2009).

16. Deptula, n.13

17. Ibid.

18. David Deptula, "Air Force ISR in a Changing World", [Online: web], accessed November 25, 2011, URL: www.aiaa.org/documents/conferences/presentations/Deptula.ppt.

19. Patney, n.15.

20. Ibid.

21. Ibid.

22. Ibid.

23. All the political aspects pertaining to the Kosovo War have been documented in the movie "A Special Relationship," released on May 29, 2010.

Emerging Missile Threat

✿ DEBALINA CHATTERJEE

The end of the Cold War has made such a strategy [MAD] largely irrelevant. Barely plausible when there was only one strategic opponent, the theory makes no sense in a multipolar world of proliferating nuclear powers. Mutual destruction is not likely to work against religious fanatics; desperate leaders may blackmail with nuclear weapons; blackmail or accidents could run out of control. And when these dangers materialize, the refusal to have made timely provisions will shake confidence in all institutions of government. At a minimum, the rudiments of a defense system capable of rapid expansion should be put into place.

— Henry Kissinger, March 9, 1995.[1]

Weapon procurement has formed one of the integral parts of military modelling. It involves the selection of one weapon system from other competing weapon systems. The concepts of defence, deterrence, disarmament, arms race, arms control directly emanate from the concept of technology. Once a country has acquired nuclear weapons or sophisticated conventional weapons, it is only a matter of time before it develops credible delivery mechanisms. Missiles are viewed by many countries as "cost-effective weapons" and "symbols of national power"[2] and are one of the most dynamic innovations of firepower. In fact, delivery systems like intercontinental missiles have enhanced raw firepower and become a threat to aircrafts, tanks, and many more. From the long range intercontinental ballistic missiles to the smaller unguided anti-tank guided weapons and unguided light anti-tank weapons, countries portray their might in myriad types of missiles. Missiles have several components like the airframe, a propulsion system, guidance system, control surfaces, and a warhead which could be either a conventional or nuclear. Increasing the thrust of the missile could improve the range of the missile which would reduce the cost and also enable the missile to carry more weapons.

World War II had seen the use of missiles like the V-1 and the V-2 (Vergelungswaffe which means a weapon which can be used for retaliation) though the real use of missiles could be dated back to the Vedic times when there was use of missiles like the Brahmastra and the Pasupatastra and even anti-missiles like the Upasamhara.. Post World War II, the world got exposed to a new kind of lethal weapon called the nuclear weapon. The dropping of the atomic bombs, Fat Man and Little Boy in Japan in 1945, revealed the cataclysmic effects that could be caused by these nuclear weapons. By 1959, the USA had developed intercontinental ballistic missiles like the Titan and Atlas which were liquid fuelled.

The era of the Cold War had witnessed the development of missiles with increased range like the Intermediate Range Ballistic Missiles (IRBMs) and the Intercontinental Ballistic Missiles (IBMs), and cruise missiles capable of causing grievous catastrophic effects. The Cuban Missile Crisis or the Jupiter Missile Crisis in 1962 when both the superpowers were on the verge of nuclear brinkmanship with each other have still not been forgotten. Stationing of the US Jupiter missile in Turkey, pointing directly towards Moscow, posed a threat to the security of the erstwhile Soviet Union. The Soviets in return stationed missiles like the Frog missiles in Cuba which were pointed towards important American cities. It was a step taken by the Soviets to make the US aware of what it feels to have a missile pointed at one. By the 1980s, countries were able to station the nuclear weapon systems aimed at the enemy's command centres, thereby making command and control of the country vulnerable to an attack. For instance, the US' Pershing II missiles were stationed in Europe while Soviet Yankee class submarines were near the Atlantic coast, thereby enabling attacks to take only a few minutes from launch to impact. Guided weapons like long range strategic rockets, the dogfight missiles which were carried by aircraft, the short range anti-tank missiles, and the surface-to-air anti-aircraft defence systems had become decisive factors in wars. With both the superpowers possessing around 70,000 nuclear weapons, with some fitted on these ballistic missiles, like Short Range Ballistic Missiles (SRBMs), Medium Range Ballistic Missiles (MRBMs), Intermediate Range Ballistic Missiles (IRBMs), missiles became more cataclysmic.

With the Revolution in Military Affairs the age of missiles has become more dangerous and poses greater threats to mankind as warfare has expanded in both qualitative and quantitative terms. Weapons of mass destruction bring about increase in a country's power "vastly exceeding what could be achieved by any considerable territorial acquisition".[3] High-tech systems are usually made to flirt with these missiles, thereby enhancing their ability to produce cataclysmic effects. Technological advancements have coerced states to shift from atomic weapons to thermonuclear weapons and from single warhead to Multiple Independently Targeted Reentry Vehicle (MITRV).

Today, several countries have developed missiles for security and deterrence. Countries might develop indigenous missile technology, acquire missiles from other country, build them in collaboration with another country or simply be under the missile umbrella of another country. National Defence under Article 51 of the United Nations Charter has given the opportunity to states to develop weapons of mass destruction and their delivery vehicles under this excuse. For example, India has indigenously developed its missile technology under the Integrated Guided Missile Development Programme (IGMDP) like the Prithvi, Agni, Aakash and many more. China, for instance, had proliferated the M-11, M-9 and North Korea, the Taepo Dong categories of ballistic missiles to Pakistan. Argentina's **Condor** missile was developed with contributions from German technology. Russia and India jointly developed the BrahMos supersonic cruise missile, while Brazil and South Africa jointly developed the A-Darter fifth generation short range infrared homing air-to-air missile. Germany's HOT is a Franco-German anti-tank missile.

Missile threats come from both ballistic and cruise missiles.

A ballistic missile could be an SRBM with targets less than 1,000 km, or an MRBM with 1,000 to 3,000 km range and an IRMB with targets ranging from 3,000 to 5,500 km while for the above 5,500 km range ICBMs are used. Every ballistic missile has three flight phases: boost phase, mid-course phase and terminal phase. In the mid-course and terminal phases, a ballistic missile could possess greater destructive capabilities. The Department of Defence in the coming years would invest over \$100 billion in nuclear delivery systems which could "sustain existing capabilities and modernise some strategic systems".[4] The United States possesses SRBMs like the MGM-52 (Lance), M39, M39A; ICBMs like the MIRV-ed Minuteman III, Trident D-5 with 8MIRVs. Russia possesses SRBMs like the Frog-7B, SS-1B, SS-1C, SS-26; ICBMs like the RS-24 with 6 MIRVs, SS-18s with 10 MIRVs, SS-19s with 6 MIRVs, SS-25; Submarine Launched Ballistic Missiles (SLBMs) like the SS-N-18 with 3 MIRVs, 10 MIRV-ed SS-N-20, and 4 MIRV-ed SS-N-23. Israel has also made considerable progress in ballistic missiles like the Jericho 2 MRBMs. Libya possesses Scud-B missiles and Frog-7 rockets. Ballistic missiles are one of the best mediums to carry conventional and nuclear weapons. They may or may not pose a threat; however, the existential threat cannot be neglected. Due to their higher circular error probability and longer ranges, they have the ability to cause severe destruction, especially while delivering nuclear weapons and, hence, could comprise the best deterrent. In fact, it is not just the possession of nuclear weapons which provides the best deterrence but also the possession of effective delivery systems which provides deterrence as nuclear weapons would truly not pose much of a threat without effective delivery systems. However, missiles have now been developed with precision guided weapons which would reduce collateral damage and would only pinpoint the desired target, thereby reducing casualties. Surface-to-air ballistic missiles are smaller in size and easier to transport and, hence, can be an option for guerrilla warfare and terrorist activities. For instance, the Stinger surface-to-air missiles were provided to the Mujahideen by the USA during the Soviet invasion of Russia in 1979. The Sri Lankan Liberation Tigers of Tamil Eelam (LTTE) were alleged to have tried to buy surface-to-air missiles from

Federal Bureau of Investigation (FBI) agents.[5]Russian missiles are always feared to fall into the hands of terrorist organisations or rebel groups like the Chechens.

While F-16s are an option for Pakistan to carry nuclear weapons, the M-11 ballistic missiles seem to be the best option for Pakistan. Iraq had used the Scud missiles in 1991 during the Gulf War. In 1998, former Secretary of Defence, Donald Rumsfeld had said, "Ballistic missiles are attractive, and they're attractive for several reasons. There are no defences against them. They tend to arrive at their targets."[6]Theatre missiles like SRBMs and MRBMs with 'state of art guidance technologies' give countries a unique credibility as they enhance the ability of countries to attack multinational forces, Lines of Control, logistic sites, and populations and cities till the hostility lasts.

Missile development could not only scare neighbouring and enemy countries, but could provoke them too. For instance, acquisition of missiles could be a result of threat perceptions and also be a reason for it. Saudi Arabia faces threats from Iraq, Yemen and Syria. Yemen possesses surface-to-surface missiles like Frog-7s, Scud-Bs and SS-21s for delivering conventional warheads. Even though their operational level is not clear, the existential threat cannot be eschewed. Missile threats from Iran cannot be neglected as Iran could use the surface-to-surface missiles not only to deliver conventional weapons but also nuclear weapons. Iran possesses Scud-B missiles, longer range Scud-C missiles and the Shahab missiles based on the No Dongs. Due to lack of efficient air power and modernised surface vessels, anti-ship missiles were an option. The Seesucker, CS-801, CS-802, CS-801K are anti-ship missiles of Iran. Turkey's quest for nuclear weapons, and its growing friendship with Iran and China, could result in Turkey trying to establish defence ties with China and Iran. In case that happens, Turkey could acquire missiles from China, which could completely alter the geostrategic and geopolitical equations in the Eurasian zone.

Even North Korea has developed ballistic missiles and according to BBC reports, the state possesses more than 800 ballistic missiles. In 2002, North Korea had stated that it had the right to "counter the US nuclear threat" with a credible deterrent. [7] North Korea possesses short range ballistic missiles like the KN-02s. North Korea acquired the Scud-B ballistic missile from Egypt in return for its support provided to Egypt against Israel during the Yom Kippur War. However, by 1984, North Korea started to develop its own Scud-B missiles and also developed Scud-C missile also known as the No Dong. Later, North Korea also developed the Taepo Dong missiles. Today, cruise missiles have also become a favourite of the military due to their versatility like stealth accuracy and ability to be guided even after the missile has been launched. The evolution of the cruise missile could be traced back to World War II with V-1 missiles in Germany. However, the second generation cruise missile lost its importance against ballistic missiles and bombers. The cruise missiles were no match for the intercontinental ballistic missiles. The ballistic missiles were proving to be more accurate and reliable than cruise missiles and could evade missile defences while bombers were also far more destructible than ballistic missiles. Those were the times when cruise missiles would follow a steady path and would not carry any active or passive defences along with them. Moreover, ICBMs could reach their targets in a few minutes, thereby enhancing their accuracy, while it would take cruise missiles hours to reach the target. However, with time, cruise missiles became more sophisticated. The Tomahawk cruise missiles found greater use during Operation Desert Storm in 1991, Deliberate Force in 1995, Allied Force in 1999 and many other wars. India's BrahMos supersonic cruise missiles could evade any defence system in the world, thereby posing a great threat to Pakistan and China. In case Pakistan develops a Ballistic Missile Defence (BMD), the BrahMos could be used to destroy Pakistan's command and control systems and nullify the BMD. [8]

The new missile threat emerging from China is not just the threat from ballistic or cruise missiles, but the threat of these ballistic or cruise missiles being developed with counter-measures against ballistic missile defences. With China's new "three attacks three defends" strategy, it has become important to develop stealth aircraft, long range cruise missiles and attack helicopters which would enhance its attacking capability.

It also needs to defend from precision strike, electronic warfare, and reconnaissance and surveillance. [9]Chinese missiles pose a threat not only to India, but also to countries in the Asia-Pacific region, especially Taiwan. The Pentagon has been worried about the garrisoning of Chinese missiles like the DF-15 and the DF-11 opposite Taiwan in the Nanjing Military Region which includes Jiangsu, Zhejiang, Anhui, Fujian, and Jiangxi provinces.[10] Solid propelled ballistic missiles like the DF-21s, the DF-15 could help China evade any ballistic missile defence at the boost phase as they would have shorter boost phases than liquid propelled missiles. Chinese ICBMs are less likely to be a threat in the South Asian periphery but a big threat to the US.

Fig 1: Missile Threat Modelling[11]

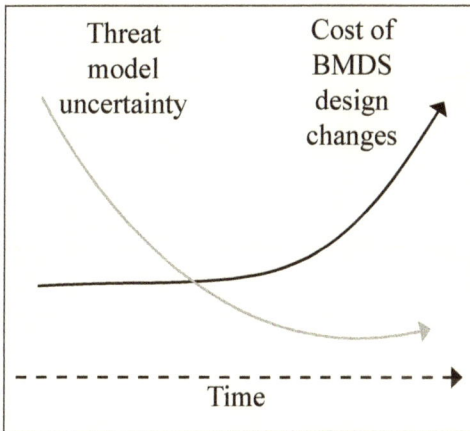

Both missile threats and missile defence system should sychronise well with the time line and this remains the biggest threat for missile threat modelling. Sometimes, a Ballistic Missile Defence System (BMDS) is developed to counter a threat which has not been developed or tested or deployed. Certain characteristics of missiles could easily be changed and, hence, missile defences have to be built in such a way that they may accommodate a range of alternatives.

Fig 2

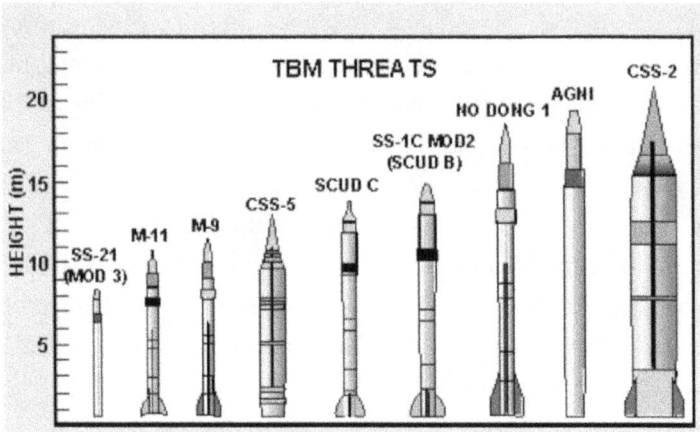

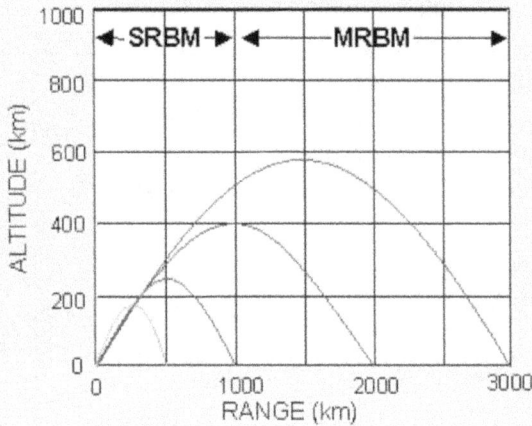

Fig 3: Theatre Ballistic Missiles Threat[12]

Theatre Ballistic Missile		
Targets	**Capabilities**	**Warheads**
• Geopolitical population Centres	• Range = 3000+km	• Ideal for WMD
• Air and sea ports	• Accuracy = within 100m	• Nuclear
• Command and control centres	• Pre launch detection extremely difficult	• Biological
• Logistical areas	• Low Radar signature	• Chemical
• Troop concentrations		• Conventional high explosives
		• Submunitions

Features which make theatre ballistic missiles threatening[13]

Counter-measures on missiles make them more dangerous.

Today, there is growing concern about missile defences. These missile defences could be both ballistic missile defences and cruise missile defences. Gen Ronald Kadish, Director of the Ballistic Missile Defence Organisation (BMDO) had warned in the year 2000 that ballistic missile threats emerging from states which pose a threat to international security would increase with the ability to acquire and launch longer range missiles with just simple counter-measures.

While deterrence by denial appears to be a good option, this process can face severe challenges against counter-measures. Counter-measures are designed by ballistic missiles to overwhelm the missile defence and reach its assigned targets. In other words, while there are defensive measures against offence, there are further defensive measures against these defences. Hence, defensive defence has actually become more expensive than offensive defence or rather 'deterrence by denial' bears a more exorbitant burden on the defence budget than 'deterrence by punishment'. Deterrence by punishment means to inflict punishment on a country in response to an attack. The development of missiles like the IRBMs and ICBMs to deliver conventional and nuclear weapons is a clear example of deterrence by punishment. Deterrence by denial means to provide resistance against any attack. States in their attempt to provide better defence against missile threats, have enabled these missiles, both ballistic and cruise missiles, to pose a greater threat to a territory. Any country which is capable of developing long range ballistic missiles would surely develop counter-measures to make these ballistic missiles more credible.

Biological and chemical warheads could be made into sub-munitions which could be released after the boost phase and make the missile defence more effective. China, for instance, uses biological and chemical warhead sub-munitions. In case nuclear weapons are used, they could be deployed into balloons and then several empty balloons could be released simultaneously. These are called 'anti-simulation balloon decoys'. Liquid fuelled ballistic missiles are now being replaced by solid propelled ballistic missiles in order to overwhelm a ballistic missile defence effectively.

Ballistic missiles are now being fitted with decoys to confuse between a missile and decoy. The Agni I could be fitted with decoys. Missiles could be fitted with electromagnetic pulse bombs to cause severe destruction. Cruise missiles could be fitted with these kinds of bombs and since cruise missiles have the ability to stay unintercepted, these bombs could be used to damage the command and control systems of a country. [14]

Ballistic missiles like ICBMs have now become more destructive than they were earlier. With time, the delivery accuracy was improvised for these missiles with increase in the values of the ballistic coefficient[15] by using "slightly blunted slender sphere cone geometrics, thus, increasing the impact velocity so that the final descent was less affected by winds."[16]

Multiple Independent Reentry Vehicles (MIRVs) and Manoeuvrable Advanced Reentry Vehicles (MARVs) on ballistic missiles further make them cataclysmic due to their increased warheads. For instance, the Chinese DF-21s are equipped with MIRVs. The Indian AgniV is expected to be fitted with MIRVs. Stealth technologies on missiles could help them evade a ballistic missile defence as is the case with the Indian Agni I. Sometimes, a ballistic missile's trajectory could be made depressed in order to enable it to evade a ballistic missile defence as could be the case with Chinese DF-31s. MARVs, with global positioning systems, could make the ballistic missiles more devastating. The Chinese short range ballistic missiles CSS-5 and the US intermediate range ballistic missiles like the Pershing II are some examples.

Pakistan's Missile Arsenal: A Case Study
The development of missiles is viewed from a **realist** paradigm in any country, and Pakistan is no exception. In realism, the state is the most important actor and securing the state becomes the most important task, and, hence, hard power prowess is necessary for this. Pakistan had always been a realist state, and its foreign policy against India is based on **real politik:** it would not compromise on military modernisation even at the cost of keeping its people hungry.

Robert Jervis had described the **security dilemma** as a situation in which "the means by which a state tries to increase its security decrease the security of others".[17]In Pakistan's case, India's growing missile technology programme was a direct threat to Pakistan's security. The region of South Asia is anarchic and Jervis states that the "heart of the security dilemma" emanates from the "anarchic contexts of international relations". The security dilemma has another aspect linked with it—the **action-reaction** model. This means that if India acts by enhancing its missile technology capability, Pakistan would react by enhancing its missile capability too. This would lead to an arms race.

However, maintenance of the stability-instability equation in the region requires Pakistan to also have the same missile capability as India. This has called for **missile proliferation** as the state does not have adequate technological know-how to build up its indigenous missile arsenal. Pakistan was provided the M-11 category surface-to-surface missiles by China. Pakistan is not only acquiring missiles but is exporting versions of missiles like the Hong Qing to countries like Sri Lanka and Bangladesh so as to deter India from all sides of the South Asian periphery. Pakistan's strategists have adopted the doctrine of **'offensive defence'** and their missile technology is being developed according to this strategy. It is not very likely that Pakistan would be able to build a Ballistic Missile Defence (BMD). It is also less likely that it would want to be under the BMD umbrella of any other country. With an offensive defence strategy, Pakistan would want to enhance its offensive capabilities rather than adopt a defensive defence strategy. This could be done by developing counter-measures on its missiles which could negate the credibility of the Indian ballistic missile defence.

Pakistan conducted its **nuclear tests** immediately after India's nuclear tests in 1998. Its nuclear capability was aimed to deter aggression and also for the 'defence of sovereignty'. It announced that its force would follow the principle of 'minimum deterrence'. However, nuclear weapons need delivery systems and missiles are often the best mode for delivering nuclear weapons. Delivery of nuclear weapons and conventional high explosive munitions with the help of ballistic missiles is a cost-effective option. The need for missiles to deliver the nuclear weapons was important for Pakistan, as aircraft had certain limitations. They could not deliver nuclear weapons to a greater range and also could not easily penetrate India's air defence. Hence, it was important for Pakistan to hasten up in its missile build-up process. The M-11 missile can carry both nuclear and conventional high explosive munitions. Pakistan had also bought the No Dong missiles from North Korea which was confirmed by the DCI Nonproliferation Centre in 2000. Pakistan also received the Harpoon missiles from the USA. Imported missiles would be in semi-knocked down or completely knocked down state. The imported missile which would be in semi or completely knocked down state would enable the Pakistanis to enhance their indigenous missile production expertise as it would help them analyse the technical aspects of the missile. It would also help them act rationally in times of conflict.

Pakistan is a state comparatively smaller and weaker than India and suffers from the **small state syndrome**. Therefore, it has always had apprehensions of being dominated by India. Pakistan has developed ballistic and cruise missiles. It developed three categories of missiles— the short range ballistic missiles, the medium range ballistic missiles, and intermediate range missiles. Short and intermediate range ballistic missiles were termed "tactical" and "battlefield" by the Cold War superpowers. Pakistan wants to match India's level at any cost. This might be reflected as the **power transition effect** whereby, smaller states want to become powerful like the bigger state around them. Pakistan is a **revisionist state** and, hence, had been dissatisfied with its small state status and thereby wanted to compete with India in its hard power potency. Pakistan's missile technology would enable it to improve its **Composite Index of National Power** against that of India, though it would adversely affect its **Comprehensive National Power (CNO) equation** against India.

Pakistan's quest for missile technology reveals a **domino effect** in the South Asian region. Many might conclude that Pakistan is developing missiles as deterrence against India, which is, on the other hand, developing missiles as **deterrence** against China and Pakistan. However, it could also be concluded that Pakistan now sees Iran as a potential threat as Iran is nuclearising with assistance from China. This has made Pakistan go in for a sophisticated missile programme to deter Iran and the Central Asian countries. The missiles could be also developed to prevent Afghanistan from influencing the Pashtuns in the region of Pakistan to make demands for a new Pashtunistan. Thus, there seems to be a **reversed domino effect** in the region, which would mean that India is developing its missile technology as it has no other option but to keep up with Pakistan's missile technology pace, thereby revealing an arms race in the region.

Both India and Pakistan could choose to limit the arms race by not increasing their missile arsenals. This could have stopped the arms race and thereby made the region of South Asia less volatile to threats. However, since because both countries are suspicious of each other, they preferred to arm themselves rather than disarm in order to bring stability in the region. This reveals a situation of **prisoner's dilemma** in the region. One aspect that might be taken into consideration is that since India and Pakistan are both developing countries the **Pareto efficiency** of building missiles in one country does not make the other worse off to a greater extent.

Third World countries often consider missiles to be the **best option** against conventional weapons. This is because due to lack of adequate resources to modernise and the opportunity cost of modernisation, the conventional weapons, especially for India and Pakistan are of very poor quality. As a result,. Pakistan has to use missiles for defence. 'Missile posturing' in Pakistan is the 'best' way to deter Indian conventional attacks.

Pakistan sees nuclear weapons delivered by missiles as a "vital deterrent to India's much larger conventional forces, and as a necessary counter to India's nuclear program".[18]Pakistan's battlefield short range ballistic missiles include the Hatf-1, the Hatf-2, Hatf-2A, Hatf-3 and Hatf-4 missiles. The Hatf-2 or Abdali poses threats to Indian military's airfields. The Hatf-1 could be used as an unguided artillery rocket. This could be catastrophic as the Hatf-1 could be nuclear tipped. The Hatf-3 or the Ghaznavi is a threat to airfields, military bases and cities. The warhead could be high explosive, nuclear or sub-munition. Sub-munitions could act as counter-measures against ballistic missile defences and could also be effective against a military column. The Hatf series could be used for both offensive and defensive purposes. The Hatf-4 or Shaheen-I can carry both conventional and nuclear warheads and Pakistan is also developing MIRVs, thereby nullifying an Indian BMD at the terminal phase. its Ghauri-1, Ghauri-2 and Shaheen-2 are capable of providing effective deterrent credibility to Pakistan against India. The Ghauri could be a threat to India's armoured tanks as it has the capability to carry anti-tank warheads. In 1999, in a flight test of the Ghauri-II, the missile indicated that it had "reached the target distance of 1,165 km in 12 minutes".[19] However, Pakistan's ballistic missiles are in semi-knocked down or completely knocked down state, thereby reducing the chances of an accidental attack on India in times of peace. Pakistan's missile proliferation, for example, the proliferation of the Bakhtar Shikan or the Hong Ying missile defence systems to Sri Lanka and Bangaldesh further escalates concerns for India.

Multi-Launch Rocket Systems: The Threat Overlooked?
Today, even artillery has undergone a complete revamp with missiles replacing guns, sometimes for combat. The Multi-Launch Rocket System (MLRS) fires surface-to-surface rockets and the Army Tactical Missile System (ATMS).[20] These MLRS could be used as ballistic missiles with extended range. These systems can deliver high volumes of fire and a variety of warheads and the high mobile launchers can effectively support forward artillery missions. Due to the mobility and the short burn time of the rocket, it results in "little warning for manoeuvre forces" and the short range "precludes engagement" by the present missile defence systems.[21]MLRS have multiple warhead capabilities, thereby making even limited warfare catastrophic. MLRS are equipped with dual purpose improved conventional munitions bomblets which further enhance their efficiency. The original MLRS launcher is the M-270 or the self-propelled loader. There are also the M142 HIMARS (High Mobility Artillery Rocket Systems). These could fire either six rockets or one ATACMS. The unguided M-26 was the first MLRS rocket and

is armed with dual purpose improved conventional munitions and was used during Operation Desert Storm in 1991. The Chinese AR3 MLRS is able to fire guided and unguided 300mm rockets. Low cost autonomous attack sub-munitions have been pursued by the US Army as payloads for the MLRS.[22]

Fig 4

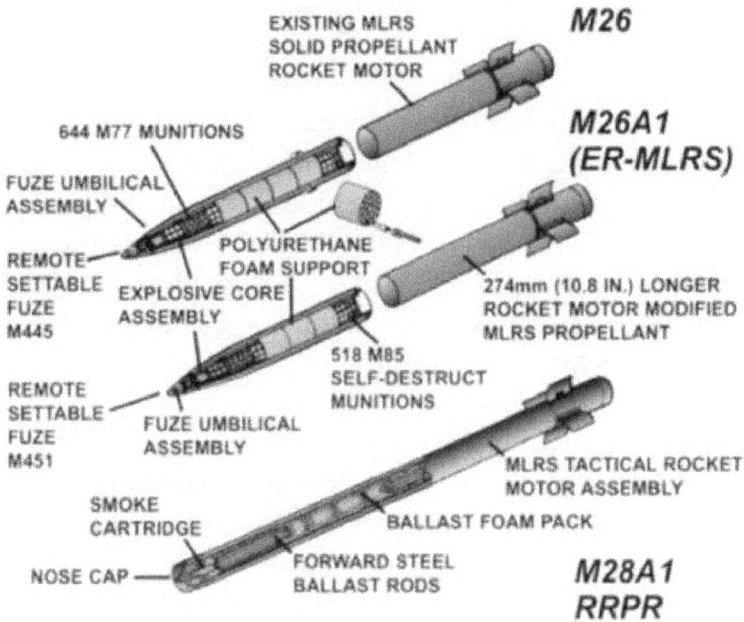

Image: Lockheed Martin

MULTIPLE LAUNCH ROCKETS		
Targets	**Capabilites**	**Warheads**
• Assembly areas	• High rates of fire	• Ideal for massive
• Missile defence/artillery	• Highly mobile ("shoot	ordnance delivery
locations	and scoot")	• Chemical
• Defensive positions	• Rapid reload	• High explosives
• Troops in the offence	• Area denial	• Bomblests
• Chokepoints/routes of	• Low signature/fligh	• Mines
advance	ttrajectory	

Do the Indian Missile Systems Pose a Threat to the World?

India's Prithvi missiles are nuclear tipped short range ballistic missiles. Hence, limited conflicts against Pakistan, for instance, could result in severe destruction. If the Agni V is inducted and proves to be credible, it would be a serious threat to Pakistan and also China to some extent. With MIRVs fitted on the Agni V, the devastation caused would be much higher than that caused by a single warhead. India is also making progress in cruise missiles. The BrahMos supersonic cruise missile is the fastest cruise missile in the world. India is also planning to develop the BrahMos hypersonic cruise missiles. In case the Surya ICBM project becomes a success, it would have serious implications. Any range within 8,000 km would not pose much of a threat to the West, but a range more than that could make the West suspicious of India's motives. India's PINAKA Multi-Barrel Rocket Launcher (MBRL) enabled India to win the Kargil War. India has also concentrated on the Prahar missile which has enabled India to bridge the gap between MLRS and SRBMs.

Conclusion

With emerging security threats to states from non-state asymmetric powers, the big question is whether the Westphalian system formed in 1648 after the Thirty Years of War (1618-48) still exists or is now a 'Westfailure system'. Today, states have crossed the boundaries of their territories to develop relations with other states in order to acquire sophisticated weapon systems. Today, the security dilemma plays such a vital factor that sometimes states prefer to befriend even enemy countries in order to be able to acquire credible weapon systems. For example, during the Cold War, the world witnessed a Sino-Soviet split. However, post Cold War, the Sino-Russian relations started to develop again and China acquired technologies and equipment for missiles, nuclear weapons and anti-missiles from Russia. This was one of the factors which had enabled Russia to sustain economically after the Soviet collapse. Even though Russia kept denying it, the fact was that it had sold S-300 surface-to-air missiles to China.

Often states have to depend on other states for missile and nuclear technology due to the comparative cost advantages. This happens mostly in developing countries where the cost of acquiring these technologies is expensive. For instance, Pakistan developed strong ties with China and acquired some of the sophisticated missile systems like the M-9s and the M-11s.

It has been a strange factor that in spite of terrorist organisations having easy access to missiles due to their ties with some countries, they had never posed a missile threat to any country. It leads us to believe that terrorist organisations do not want to cause collateral damage but rather create mayhem in the area they choose to attack in order to jeopardise the stability and tranquillity of the area for some time. However, with surface-to-air missiles disappearing from military depots in Libya, the threat that these missile could fall into the hands of terrorists cannot be negated.

Missiles, whether ballistic or cruise, would pose a threat and any country could be a threat for that matter. At the same time, every country has the sovereign right to protect itself and enhance its security. If a state is a referent object, its security is the utmost priority for every state.

If analysed carefully, both ballistic and cruise missiles tipped with nuclear weapons could form a credible deterrent and prevent states from entering into a war. South Asia could be the best example for this. Both India and Pakistan have not been involved in any war, not even a limited conflict, since the Kargil episode. This is because both countries had acquired nuclear weapons and were enhancing their missile arsenal with sophisticated missile technologies.

The best way to deal with the threat is to keep enhancing arsenals in order to enhance deterrence. This is because it is a known fact that disarmament would not be an option. Arms control could be an option to reduce missile threats, but not many countries would be willing to go for it. Today, possessing missile and nuclear capabilities enhances a state's hard power prowess and helps it earn honour in the fora of world politics. However, parity has to be maintained in the missile arms race in order to maintain the stability-instability paradox. In case India acquires ICBMs,

Pakistan too will need acquire them or else, due to the security dilemma, Pakistan could indulge in a 'first strike'.

Notes

1. Cited in "The Threat", *MISSILETHREAT.com.*
2. "Ballistic and Cruise Missile Threat", http://www.fas.org/irp/threat/missile/naic/ NASIC2009.pdf
3. Henry A. Kissinger mentioned it in an article, "The Rules on Preventive Force: Nuclear Weapons, Terrorism Require Rethinking a Time-Honoured Approach", *The Washington Post,* April 19, 2006.
4. US Senate, Committee on Foreign Relations, The New START Treaty, Treaty doc. III-5 (Washington DC: US Government Printing Office, December 2010), p.87.
5. Amy   Zalman,   "Surface-to-Air-Missiles",   http://terrorism.about.com/od/ tacticsandweapons/g/SAMs.htm
6. "Unveiling the Ballistic Missile Threat: The Ramification of the Rumsfeld Report", *National Security Report,* Vol 2, Issue 4, August 1998.
7. "North Korea's Nuclear and Missile Programs", *International Crisis Group,* Asia Report N 168, June 18, 2009.
8. I had given similar suggestions in "Counter-Measures", *Force,* November, 2011.
9. Dean Cheng, "China's Active Defense Strategy and Its Regional Impact", *The Heritage Foundation,* February 1, 2011.
10. "The Threat from China", *MISSILETHREAT.com*
11. Figure taken from John S. McLaughlin, "Ballistic Missile Threat Modelling", http:// www.aero.org/publications/crosslink/spring2008/06.html
12. "FM 100-12 Army Theatre Missile Defense Operations", http://www.fas.org/spp/ starwars/docops/fm100-12/chap2.htm
13. Ibid
14. n. 8.
15. Ballistic Coefficient= Vehicle Weight/ Drag Coefficient^Reference Area Used.
16. John C. Adams, Jr, "Atmospheric Re- entry", 2003. http://exoaviation.webs.com/ pdf_files/Atmospheric%20Re-Entry.pdf
17. Robert Jervis, "Cooperation Under the Security Dilemma", *World Politics 30,* January 4, 1978, pp.167-214.
18. "Foreign Missile Developments and Ballistic Missile Threats Through 2015", *Unclassified Summary of National Intelligence Estimate",* December 2001. http:// www.dni.gov/nic/PDF_GIF_otherprod/missilethreat2001.pdf
19. "Pakistan Test-Fires Ghauri II", *The News (Pakistan),* 1999.
20. "MLRS", http://www.army-technology.com/projects/mlrs/

21. "FM 100-12 Army Theatre Missile Defense Operations", http://www.fas.org/spp/starwars/docops/fm100-12/chap2.htm

22. William C.Corkle, Jr., "Future Missile System Trends (U.S.) and Their Impact on Aerodynamic Technology", Paper presented at the RTO AVT Symposium on "Missile Aerodynamics", held in Sorrento, Italy, May, 11-14 1998.

23. "Lockheed Martin (Vought) MLRS Rockets (M26/ M30/ M31)", *Directory of U.S. Military Rockets and Missiles"*, http://www.designation-systems.net/dusrm/app4/mlrs.html

24. Ibid.

Future Trend of MRO and the Indian Air Force

✿ A. AGARAWAL

Definition

Every flying machine is granted a certificate of airworthiness on completion of its Design and Development (D&D) phase. Aircraft Maintenance, Repair and Overhaul (MRO) refers to the steps necessary to be taken to ensure continued airworthiness of these flying machines.

Introduction

The Indian Air Force (IAF) has the responsibility of guarding the skies in the territorial expanse of our country and being capable of projecting our strength anywhere in the world if so required. To successfully discharge these responsibilities, the IAF requires weapon platforms with different capabilities. In times of need, the Air Force needs to ensure availability of these weapons platforms in the required numbers, with ensured mission reliabilities when launched.

The Indian Air Force started with a few Wapiti war planes and a small group of dedicated professionals. Over the last 78 years, it has grown to be the fourth largest air force in the world, with a large number of state-of-the-art weapon platforms. In the next decade, the Air Force has plans to induct Medium Multi-Role Combat Aircraft (MMRCA), Fifth Generation Flight Aircraft (FGFA) and Advance Medium Combat Aircraft (AMCA), making it even more formidable. The IAF's inventory of transport aircraft and helicopters is equally impressive and would become even better after induction of the C-130J, C-17 and new helicopters.

The rapid expansion of the Indian Air Force necessitated procurement of aircraft from diverse sources, initially mainly from Europe (France and the UK) and subsequently from Russia. The indigenous aviation industry was limited to Hindustan Aeronautics Limited (HAL), which mainly produced aircraft under licence with a few of exceptions like the HF-24. To successfully operate this fleet of aircraft, it became incumbent on the Indian Air force to set up extensive MRO facilities due to the following reasons:

- Original Equipment Manufacturers (OEMs) located far away.
- Transportation facilities not very good and time consuming (specially in the middle of the last century).
- Very large turnaround time for the equipment sent to OEMs for repair.
- National policy on non-involvement of private industry in defence.
- Need for self-reliance (specially after the wars of 1962 and 1965).

The Present Status

MRO Philosophy
The present MRO system in the IAF follows the OEM's guidelines in the form of manuals issued by the OEM. (Or CSDO schedules prepared based on the basis of OEMs' manuals.) In addition, there are supporting maintenance directives issued by Air Headquarters (HQ)/Command HQ and even local Chief Executive Officers (CEOs). Upgrades and modifications are carried out to overcome operational and technical inadequacies of the system. All this work is carried out at different echelons, based on the complexity involved. These echelons are:

I Line	'O' Level	Operating squadron/unit.
II Line	'I' Level	Operating bases.
III Line		Started with R&SUs and now expanded to include the concept of service support centres.
IV Line	'D' Level	Base Repair Depots/Public Sector Undertakings (BRDs/PSUs).

Effectiveness of Present System

We are the fourth largest air force in the world. We are today recognised as a potent force with global reach. Our squadrons have flown across the globe to participate in international exercises and won praise for their professionalism. In addition, we are operating permanent detachments in Congo, Sudan and other countries.

Now, let us look at the other side of the story. We all know that the average serviceability of our various fleets hovers between 50-60 percent. Sometimes, commitments have to be revisited in the absence of adequate resources to meet the challenges. We need to ask ourselves: has the present system delivered what a fighting force like ours deserves, and if not, why?

We have created a huge MRO infrastructure in the form of BRDs, PSUs, Service Support Centres and facilities at operating bases. In spite of this infrastructure, our fleet availability is less than desired. We have been forced to send systems and Line Replacement Units (LRUs) abroad for repair even after establishing repair facilities in the country. Problems with the TV2/TV3/R-13 engines, main gear boxes for helicopters and LRUs of the Kopyo radar are but a few recent examples. A recent Comptroller and Auditor General (CAG) report indicated that in seven years between 1998 and 2005, the IAF had to send 11,280 LRUs of the MiG-29 abroad for repair in spite of having established repair facilities for the same. The same report blamed IRAL (Indo-Russian Aviation Ltd—a HAL venture) of failing to supply 2,233 LRUs to 11BRD against orders placed by the IAF. This shortfall in spares supply led to 11BRD utilising between 26 to 47 percent extra manhours to complete servicing of aircraft.

Clearly, something is amiss somewhere. Some of the factors that contribute to the above situation are:

- Spare parts supply not commensurate with the requirements.
- Too many bureaucratic hurdles in the procurement process.
- Frequent movement of skilled manpower resulting in too much time taken to absorb newer technology.
- Inordinate delays in creation of required infrastructure. Aircraft and systems are inducted in service before maintenance support facilities

are established. Some recent examples are the induction of the Mi-17 1V helicopter in 2000 for which full IV line facility is not ready even today. To some extent, the same applies to the Su-30/MiG-27 and Bison.

- Even where the facilities are established, the systems/aggregates continue to be sent abroad due to certain constraints.

In a nutshell, the present MRO infrastructure in our country has failed to deliver the expected results except in cases of extreme emergencies. In my view, our approach to the future of military MRO in our country should be derived from the following analysis.

- Analyse operations uncovering ineffectiveness and bottlenecks.
- Identify and address common mistakes resulting from misaligned strategies.
- Simple processes (with advanced technologies?).
- Indepth analysis of future opportunities, and devise appropriate strategies.

Present Trends in Military MRO

Before we start an analysis of our options, let's have a look at the military MRO the world over. The present global holding of military aircraft is around 38,800. We, in the Indian Air Force, always talk about reducing aircraft in our inventory. This, however, seems to be the trend world over. The global holding of military aircraft is expected to reduce by over 800 between now and 2020. Fighter and trainer aircraft constitute a little over 40 percent of the global fleet.

Fig 1: Through 2020, the Military Fleet Drops by Over 900 Aircraft

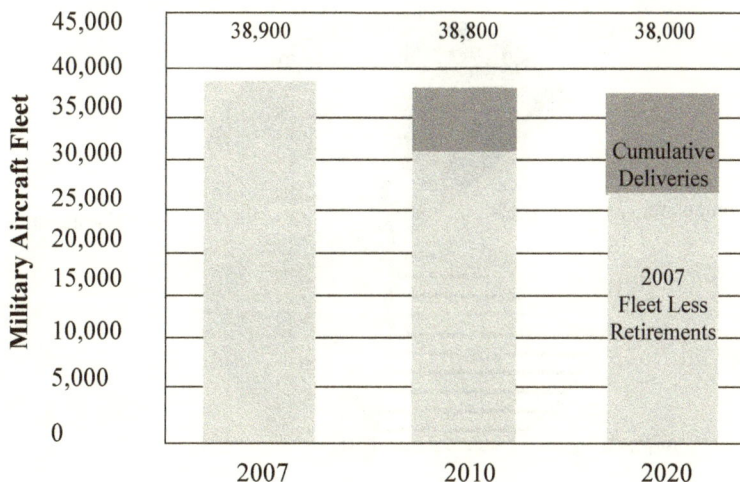

Fig 2: Present Active Military Aircraft Fleet Total—38,800

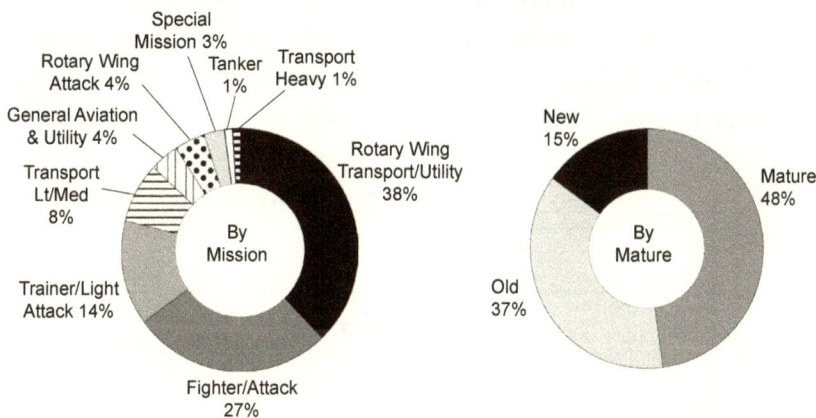

MRO Costs: As per a recent study carried out in the USA, a typical cost breakdown of defence systems as a percentage of life-cycle cost is given below:

- Concept, design and development: 15 percent.
- Production costs: 35 percent.
- Operation and maintenance costs: 50 percent.

Similar analyses by various European agencies have shown almost consistent results. The maintenance costs can be further divided as:

Fig 3: Breakdown MRO Costs

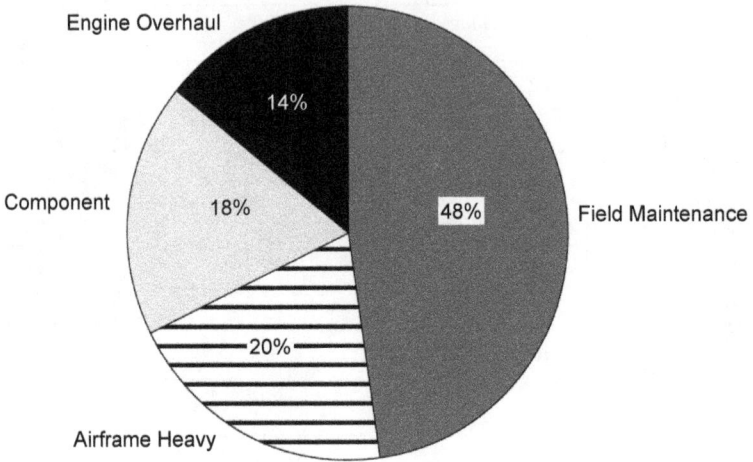

The above expenditure trend is corroborated by a comparison of costs in 2006. While the production costs of all types of aircraft globally was $103 billion, MRO expenditure was $114 billion. This also gave rise to a demand for in-service parts of $ 25 billion.

Fig 4: Why MRO Matters to Aircraft Owners

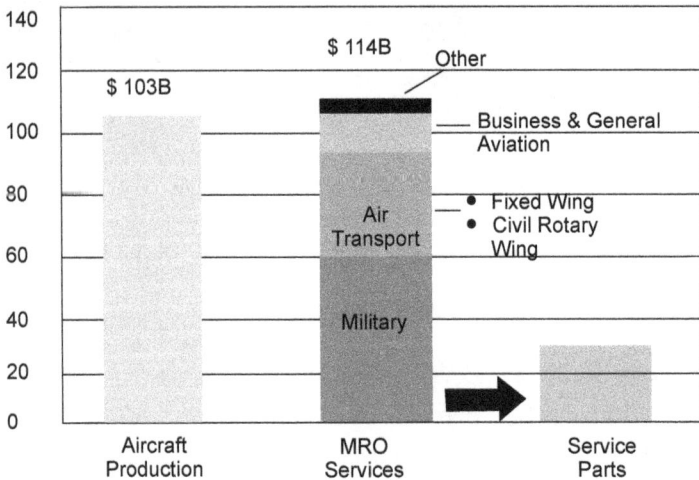

The military aircraft sustainment expenditure alone stands at around $85 billion today and is likely to be around $100 billion by 2020.

Fig 5: Worldwide Military Aircraft Sustainment Spend by Activity

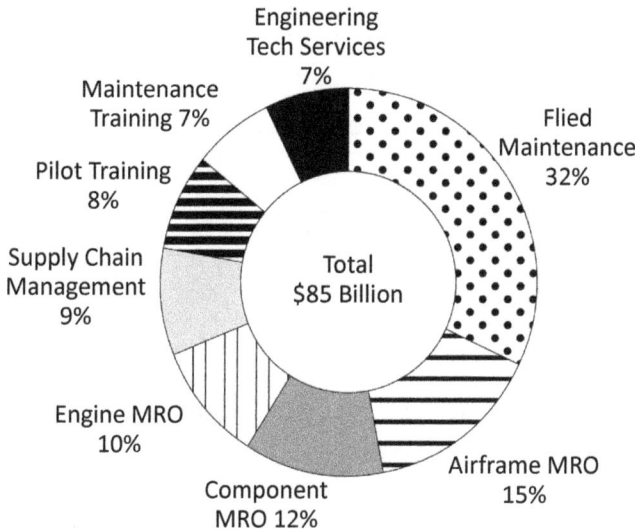

- **Overall market growth of 1 percent per annum is anticipated, despite fleet shrinkage.**
- **A key assumption is the impact of ageing, which increases MRO demand by 2 percent per year.**

While the field maintenance expenditure is driven mainly by fighter aircraft, flight deck avionics comprise the single largest category in the component MRO.

Fig 6: Field Maintenance Spending is Driven by Fighters

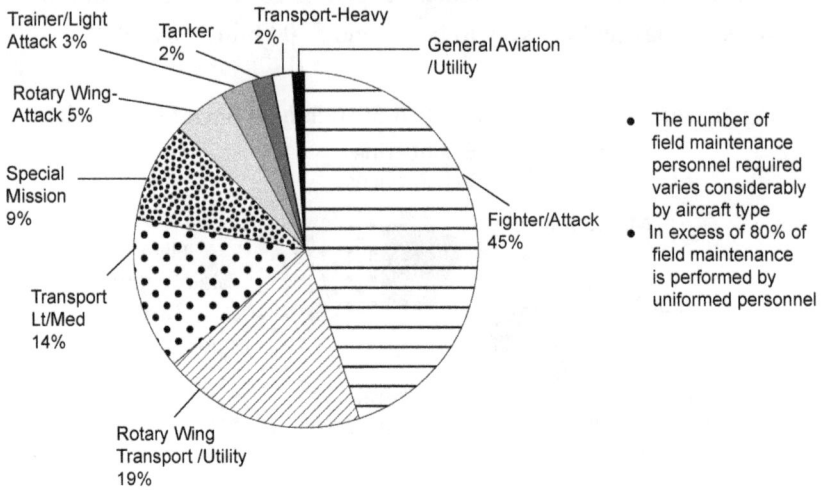

Trainer/Light Attack 3%
Tanker 2%
Transport-Heavy 2%
General Aviation /Utility
Rotary Wing-Attack 5%
Special Mission 9%
Transport Lt/Med 14%
Fighter/Attack 45%
Rotary Wing Transport /Utility 19%

- The number of field maintenance personnel required varies considerably by aircraft type
- In excess of 80% of field maintenance is performed by uniformed personnel

Fig 7: Flight Desk Avionics Are The Single Largest Component of MRO Category

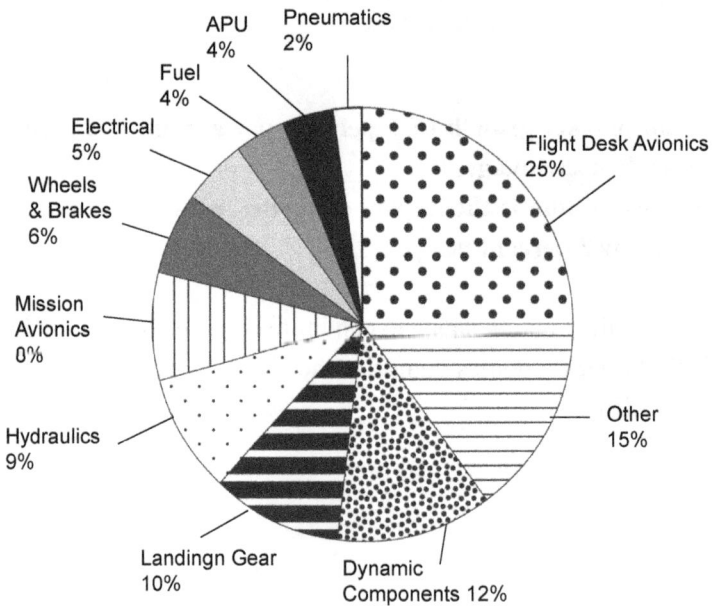

APU 4%
Pneumatics 2%
Fuel 4%
Electrical 5%
Wheels & Brakes 6%
Mission Avionics 0%
Hydraulics 9%
Flight Desk Avionics 25%
Other 15%
Landingn Gear 10%
Dynamic Components 12%

The global trend in military MRO is now driven by market dynamics. Various studies are underway to achieve operational breakthrough demands through innovative solutions. These studies not only suggest structural changes but also focus greatly on optimisation of maintenance procedures. Let us look at a typical model.

Market Dynamics

Operational breakthrough demands innovative solutions

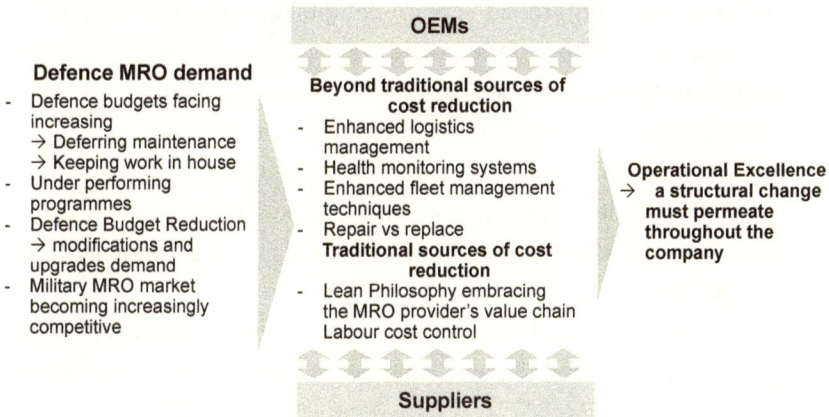

OEMs

Defence MRO demand
- Defence budgets facing increasing
  → Deferring maintenance
  → Keeping work in house
- Under performing programmes
- Defence Budget Reduction
  → modifications and upgrades demand
- Military MRO market becoming increasingly competitive

Beyond traditional sources of cost reduction
- Enhanced logistics management
- Health monitoring systems
- Enhanced fleet management techniques
- Repair vs replace

Traditional sources of cost reduction
- Lean Philosophy embracing the MRO provider's value chain Labour cost control

Operational Excellence
→ a structural change must permeate throughout the company

Suppliers

C-130 APPROACH

Changing paradigms

Approach → create an effective and innovative maintenance process
Lean Philosophy
Remove waste from the maintenance process
 → unnecessary tasks & unnecessary efforts
Standards procedures
Creating flow within the processes
Visual management
Continuous improvement Methodology (Kaizen)

Some achievement
TAT reduction of 40% (on process)
Optimisation of the maintenance procedures
Hangar optimisation around 80%
Safety improvement of 43%

Some of the tools used

- Value Stream Mapping
- Time Observation
- Point-of-Use Tooling
- Visual Marking Standards

Integrate Military and Commercial Maintenance

We shall differentiate within the military environment, the support units (transport, refuelling and surveillance) from the combat units.

- The OEMs are intensively using commercial platforms for developments to produce military applications, pushed by budget restrictions and cost saving policies.
- The maintenance and technical documentation is also quite similar, thus, not being a problem to understand and to execute standard maintenance procedures.
- Infrastructure and ground support equipment are similar enough to obtain a better return of the investment.
- Regarding tooling and test equipment, commonality is quite extensive, although two different groups should be considered:
  o Commercial derivatives (i.e. B707, A310/330, KC-10): almost 100 percent tooling commonality can be found.
  o "Only military use" products: just the standard aviation tools can be used.
- Head of state/official VIP airplanes are normally operated by air forces, but they tend to have "commercial airworthiness regulations and interior standards".

Advantages

The advantages of such a venture will be:

- To take advantage of "core business skills" (productivity, costs, utilisation rates)
- There are common platforms in both areas.
- To maximise utilisation of maintenance infrastructures
- It helps to develop geographical strategies.
- There is technological commonality for systems and equipment.
- To dampen the effect of the economical cycles.

Fig 8: Crossovers Between Commercial and Military MRO

Antithesis

There are also aspects in the military environment that significantly differ from the commercial aviation models, with an impact on maintenance activities. These are, amongst others, the following:

- Low airplane utilisation.
- Unusual/extreme operational conditions.
- Extended ground times.
- Interior equipment and finishing.
- Operation adjustment.
- Low number of fleet units.

Difficulties

Obviously, not all are advantages for the MRO in the duality commercial/military maintenance. The following are some of the issues that can come up, while executing maintenance on military products in an MRO where commercial aeroplanes are maintained.

Fig 9

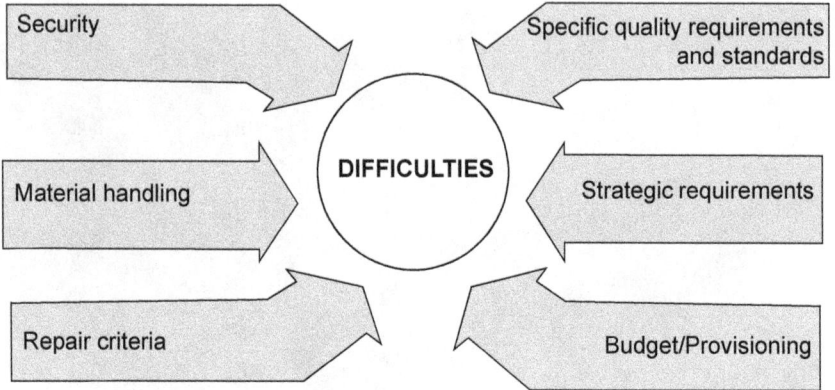

A study done recently on the Western European Military Fleet has revealed very interesting facts on outsourcing. It is worth noting that these countries have very aggressively outsourced many of their aircraft sustainment activities. Let us look at the following facts:

Fig 10: Over 40 Percent of the Fleet is Rotary Wing

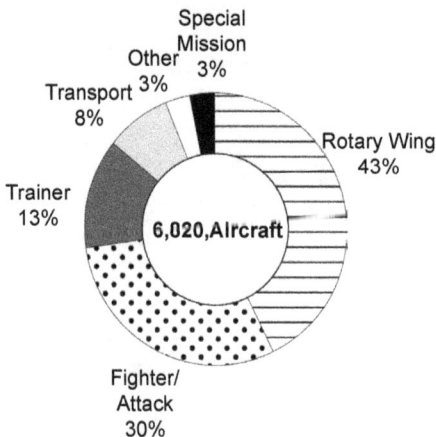

Fig 11: The Top Five Countries Account for Over 80 Percent of Sustainment Spend

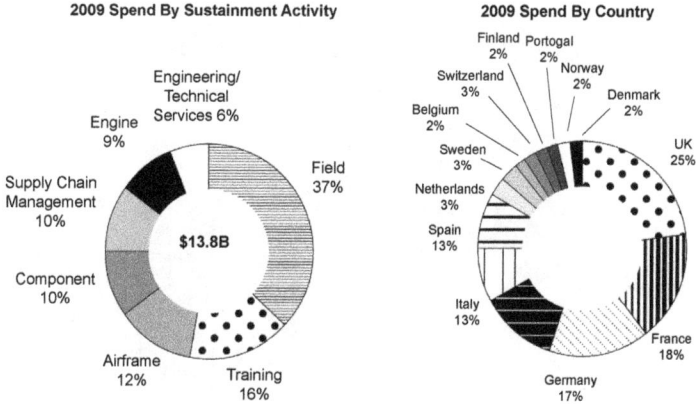

2009 Spend By Sustainment Activity

Engineering/
Technical
Services 6%

Engine
9%

Supply Chain
Management
10%

Component
10%

Airframe
12%

$13.8B

Field
37%

Training
16%

2009 Spend By Country

Finland 2% Portogal 2%

Switzerland 3% Norway 2%

Belgium 2% Denmark 2%

Sweden 3%

Netherlands 3%

Spain 13%

Italy 13%

UK 25%

France 18%

Germany 17%

Fig 12: This Spend is Projected to be Relatively Flat
2009-2013 Western European Sustainment Forecast

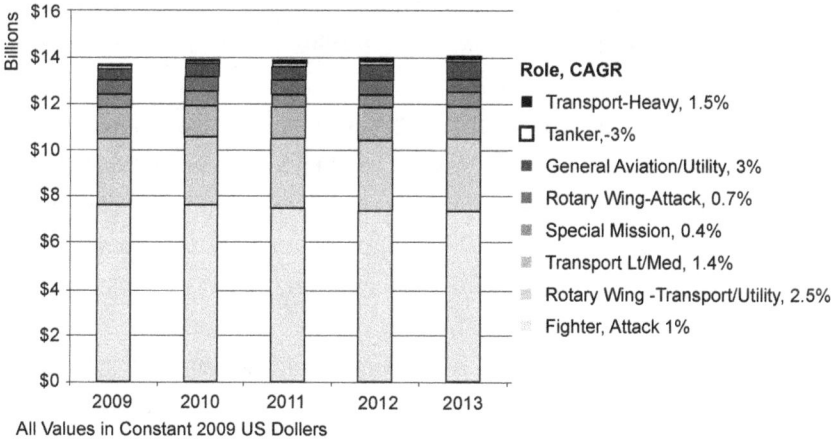

Billions

$16
$14
$12
$10
$8
$6
$4
$2
$0

2009   2010   2011   2012   2013

All Values in Constant 2009 US Dollers

Role, CAGR

■ Transport-Heavy, 1.5%

☐ Tanker,-3%

■ General Aviation/Utility, 3%

■ Rotary Wing-Attack, 0.7%

▨ Special Mission, 0.4%

▨ Transport Lt/Med, 1.4%

▨ Rotary Wing -Transport/Utility, 2.5%

▨ Fighter, Attack 1%

Fig 13: United Kingdom has Aggressively Outsourced Many Aircraft Sustainment Activities

2009 Western European Sustainment Market

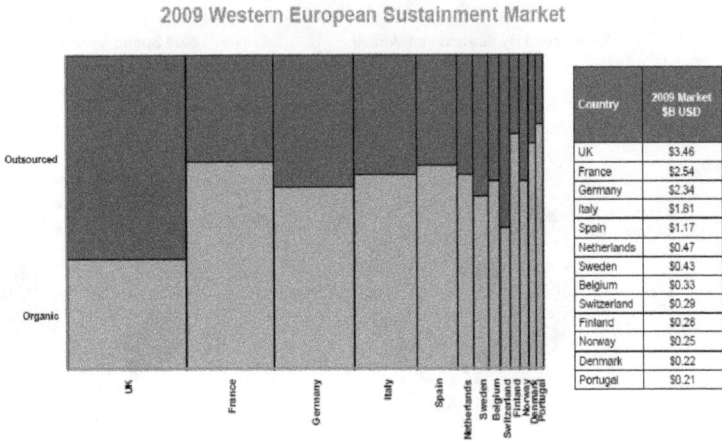

Country	2009 Market $B USD
UK	$3.46
France	$2.54
Germany	$2.34
Italy	$1.81
Spain	$1.17
Netherlands	$0.47
Sweden	$0.43
Belgium	$0.33
Switzerland	$0.29
Finland	$0.28
Norway	$0.25
Denmark	$0.22
Portugal	$0.21

Private Financial Initiative on Military MRO

Some of the programmes where private finance initiatives are already involved in Europe on outsourcing are:

- **IBERIA Maintenance:** Proving serious to the Spanish Navy and Spanish Air Force:
  - Close to 30 years ago, IBERIA Maintenance started to cooperate with the the Spanish Navy to maintain some of its engines.
  - At that time, Spanish Air Force (SAF) incorporated commercial derivatives for military applications (B707 tanker/troop's transportation/electronic war units, A310 head of state aircraft, Falcon/Cessna VIP units).
  - Once the industrial set-up was established around the defence business, IBERIA acquired capabilities to rework pure military aircraft types such as the P3 Orion and C-130.
  - In the future, other commercial derivatives such as the Airbus Military A330 MRTT and very large airplanes such as the A400M will be in the IBERIA Maintenance mid-term strategy.
  - Finally, IBERIA is supporting the Ministry of Defence with component repairs for all aircraft.
- **RUAG Military Aviation:** Founded in 1996 as a spin-off of the

Swiss Air Force. RUAG was privatised in 1999 and is expanding support to the Swiss Air Force.

Fig 14: RUAG Military Aviation

- Depot level organisation or Fleet Readiness Centre of the Swiss Air Force
- Founded 1996 as a spin-off of the Swiss Air Force

- Privatised in 1999, still belonging to the Swiss MOD by 100%
- Expanding support for foreign military customers

Fig 15

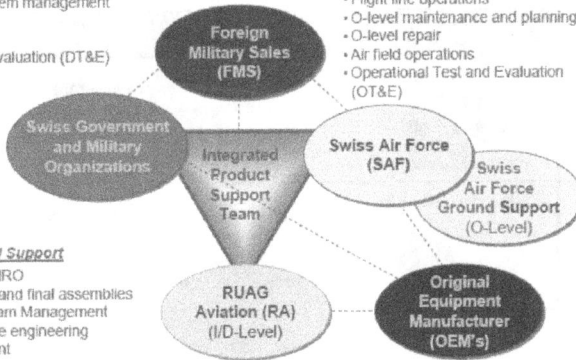

Evaluation and Systems Management
- Overall, lifecycle and system management
- Systems evaluation
- Air worthiness authority
- Development Test and Evaluation (DT&E)
- Budget authority

Operations
- Tactical operations
- Flight line operations
- O-level maintenance and planning
- O-level repair
- Air field operations
- Operational Test and Evaluation (OT&E)

Foreign Military Sales (FMS)

Swiss Government and Military Organizations

Integrated Product Support Team

Swiss Air Force (SAF)

Swiss Air Force Ground Support (O-Level)

System Maintenance and Support
- Aircraft and component MRO
- Retrofits of modifications and final assemblies
- Prime contracting / Program Management
- Systems and maintenance engineering
- Configuration management
- Logistics support
- Maintenance and technical publications
- Planning and Procurement of spare parts
- Functional Check Flight (FCF)

RUAG Aviation (RA) (I/D-Level)

Original Equipment Manufacturer (OEM's)

Fig 15: MTU Business Segment

MTU business segments

OEM business		MRO business
Commercial OEM	Military OEM	Commercial MRO
• Well-balanced portfolio • RRSP with all major OEMs • Complete thrust range covered; 30% of active fleet with MTU participation • Focus on LPT and HPC • Key programs: V2500, CF6, PW2000 • Latest programs: PW1000G, GEnx, GP7000	• Capability to develop and manufacture entire engines • Participation in key European military programs with systems design responsibility, and US military market • Partner to the German Armed Forces for practically all aero engines • Key programs: EJ200, RB199, TP400, F414, GE38	• World's largest independent engine MRO provider • Global network • Integrated repair solutions • Key programs: V2500, CFM56, CF34, CF6, PW2000, PW&C engines and Industrial Gas Turbines (IGTs)
1,054 m€ (40%)	532 m€ (20%)	1,058 m€ (40%)
MTU Group:	Sales 2,611 m€	¹ FY2009 figures

- Private Finance Initiatives (PFIs) are growing in Europe to reduce capital expenditures and manage life-cycle cost risk

Fig 16

Program	Comments
UK Tanker	• 27 year, $16B PFI to provide tanker availability • Supplier, AirTanker, will use14 Airbus A330-200 aircraft and provide tanking hours to the Royal Air Force on a fee-for service basis
Germany NH-90	• 18 year, 488m Euro PFI to provide at least 16,000 Training hours • Helicopter Flight Training Services (HFTS) is a JV between CAE, Eurocopter, Rheinmetall, and Thales
French Training	• 22 year, 422M Euro Helicopter training PFI • Supplier, Helidax, is a joint-venture between Defense Conseil International (DCI) and a local operator, Proteus Helicopteres.

There are two ends of the spectrum as far outsourcing of MRO is concerned. There are air forces like the IAF, which carry out the entire

MRO activity in-house (or through HAL). At the other end, are air forces like the Royal Omani Air Force, which outsource the entire MRO activity (including I Line servicing) to private enterprises. Fig 17 shows an increasing trend in outsourcing.

Fig 17: MRO Outsourcing—Trends

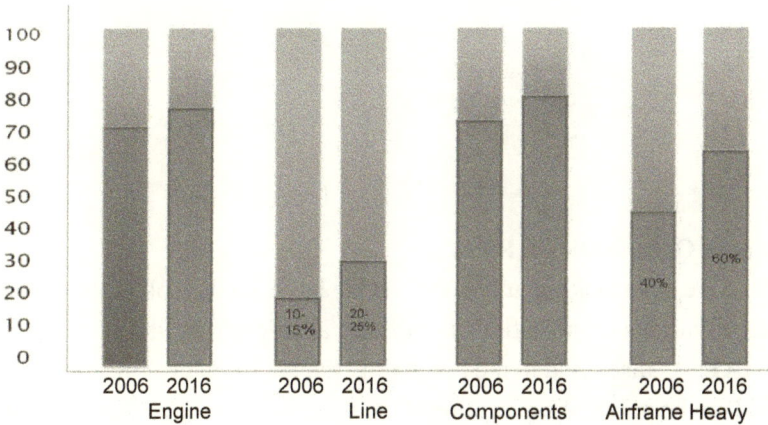

The OEMs of present generation military aircraft are, in fact, designing the MRO system as part of the D&D phase. A typical case is that of the Eurofighter—a programme involving four countries and over a dozen OEMs. They have devised an integrated logistics systems, MRO management (including on base support) based on cooperation between the operators and the service provider as shown below:

Fig 18: Time Scale Implementation Cooperative Model

Eurofighter/Typhoon introduction phase schedule

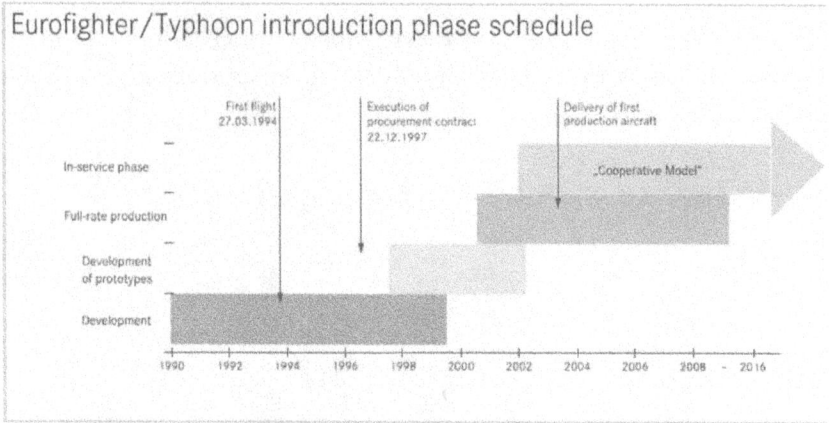

Defining Organisational Roles

Before we start looking at the options we have, let us look at the primary roles of various organisations in military aviation in India.

IAF: As discussed in the beginning, the IAF's role is force projection based on the political aspirations of the country. It needs to have a number of mission reliable weapon platforms available to it for this role.

HAL: The primary role of HAL is to design, develop and produce weapon platforms for the use of the Indian defence forces. This they can do by in-house D&D or even by absorbing technologies from abroad. A second role for HAL is to upgrade/modify the present weapon systems to enhance their operational adequacy.

The above clearly brings out that MRO is not the primary role of either of the two organisations. So what are the options available to us?

IAF Continues as own MRO provider.

Advantages

i.   Independent from industry.

ii. Process owner.

Disadvantages

i.   High costs of ownership.

ii. Diversion of resources.

Public-Private Partnership
Advantages
i.   Joint utilisation and streamlining of existing facilities and resources.
ii. Participation of Air Force manpower.
iii. Introduction of new products due to affordability.
Disadvantages
i.   High complexity of contractual and organisational set-up.

Outsourcing to Industry
Advantages
i.   No own cost risk and delegated responsibility.
ii. Efficiency and productivity improve due to industry leadership.
Disadvantages
i.   Lack of control over service (reliability and quality?).
ii. Downsizing costs (facility, staff).
iii. Loss of knowhow and expertise.
iv. Requires presence of industry manpower in crisis / war zone.

There are several key issues that will shape the way we need to develop MRO. The first issue is performance oriented contracts and a step-wise approach.

Fig 19: Performance Oriented Contracts

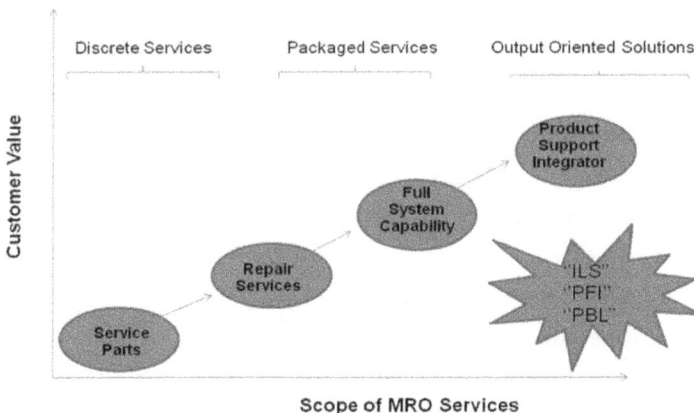

Scope of MRO Services

A prerequisite to the success of performance oriented contracts is the need to change the nature of the government-supplier relationship.

Old Model	New Model
Government is the customer	Government is the customer, partner and supplier
Government manages supplies	Government manages suppliers
Develop technical specifications	Develop operational specifications
Reactive	Proactive
Minimising acquisition cost	Minimising total cost of ownership
Manage maintenance costs	Maximise availability of aircraft at reasonable cost.

Lean transformation is a second key trend shaping the military MRO market. Governments the world over are struggling to do 'more with less'. Maintenance is, therefore, a key cost-cutting target. A number of countries are carrying out 'end to end logistic reviews' to cut costs by 15-20 percent.

There are numerous examples of European Performance Oriented Contracts (POCs), with the UK leading with POCs in place for the Jaguar, Canberra, Harrier, Tornado, Nimrod and other aircraft. France and Germany are also moving towards this trend.

Recommendations

I think now we have reached a stage where I would like to make some recommendations. The time has now come for us to move from total in-house MRO to public-private partnerships, due to the following reasons:

- Traditional approach is proving unaffordable.
- Realisation that 'we (IAF and industry) should be in this together'.
- Move from 'provide and forget' to 'whole-life support'.
- Availability contracting.
- Defence industry strategy.

What are the advantages of the partnership approach?

- Shared destiny.
- Fully integrated IAF/industry team.
- Joint ownership of challenges.
- Transparency and information sharing.

- Reduced risk.
- Improved availability.
- Long-term view.

Obviously, there are some risks involved when trying a new approach.

- New people-mindset change.
- Partnering behaviour can feel counter-intuitive.
- Over and above work funding constraints.
- Contracting for joint responsibility is a challenge.
- Completely now construct in the IAF/industry.
- Reversion to 'old ways' when the going gets tough.

The Way Ahead

It is time now that we started to take steps in the direction of public-private partnerships. May be we could start with inviting industry to participate in the MRO of some systems. We could start with some avionics or mechanical parts; even an engine overhaul line, where the IAF provides the infrastructure and the industrial partner brings manpower and spare parts. As we build confidence in the capabilities of private industry, the scope of partnership could increase. If we want this venture to succeed, we would need to support private industry, and build long-term relationships with them.

I think in the new millennium, the time has come for us to define now goals and find new ways to achieve them. Cooperation between the IAF and industry is the joint way into the future. I am sure we can succeed if we are willing to meet the basic needs:

- Mutual knowledge of, and respect for, capabilities and expertise.
- Readiness to share resources (human resources, infrastructure, equipment).
- Willingness to restrict capacities.
- Mutual trust.

I will end by projecting the key benefits for both sides in this model and leave the issue open for discussion.

Key Benefits for Both Sides

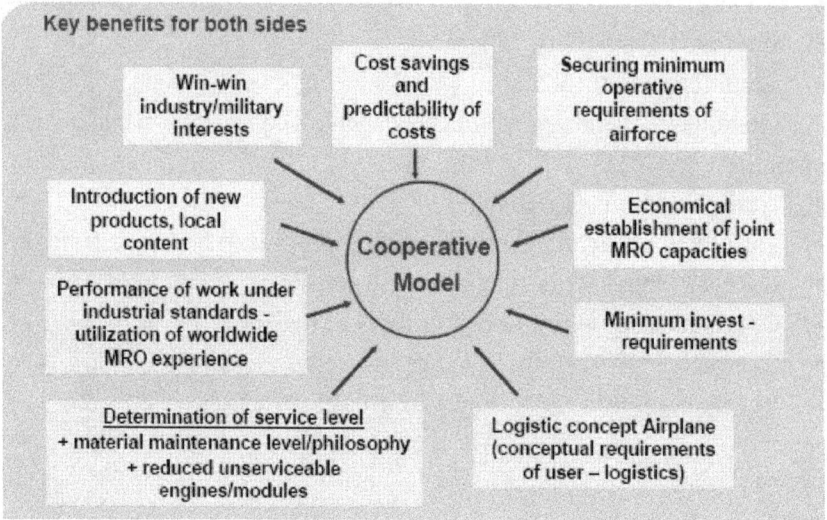

Key benefits for both sides

Win-win industry/military interests	Cost savings and predictability of costs	Securing minimum operative requirements of airforce
Introduction of new products, local content	**Cooperative Model**	Economical establishment of joint MRO capacities
Performance of work under industrial standards - utilization of worldwide MRO experience		Minimum invest - requirements
Determination of service level + material maintenance level/philosophy + reduced unserviceable engines/modules		Logistic concept Airplane (conceptual requirements of user – logistics)

Building Air Dominance

⚙ T.M. ASTHANA

Introduction

We have travelled the 'full circle'. There was a time when the emphasis of all air forces was on gaining 'air superiority' over the adversary, in order to permit the friendly air power to operate at will, while ensuring that the adversary's air power did not, or could not, interfere with the operations of the surface forces. When air superiority was not achievable because the adversary's air power was non-cooperative, air forces sought to achieve a 'Favourable Air Situation' (FAS), and in case FAS was not achievable, air forces sought to achieve FAS for specific periods. However, this emphasis of the air forces was contested by the surface forces, and they insisted on support from the air in their operations from Day 1 of the campaign, assuming non-interference of enemy air as granted. It has now dawned that this non-interference cannot be taken for granted, **it has to be earned.** The transformation of the mindset of the surface forces has taken a long time, and, finally, they have accepted that the state of air superiority is a virtue that air power has to earn. We have travelled from air superiority to FAS, to FAS for specific timeframes, and now, air forces consider air dominance as their prime objective. Hence, we have travelled the 'full circle' (Air Superiority = Command/Control of the Air = Air Dominance).

Winston Churchill once said, *"There is nothing wrong with change, if it is in the right direction. To improve is to change, so to be perfect is to change often."*

Transformation is a reality; however, transformation is not just change for change's sake, it is change in the right direction. Reality usually prompts ideas and innovation. Today's reality is that there are unique challenges facing our war-fighters—some obvious, some not so obvious. If we look at where our airmen fight, and their contributions, perhaps we can uncover some challenges that need to be addressed. Airmen are providing air dominance over Afghanistan and Iraq, allowing the North Atlantic Treaty Organisation (NATO) forces to operate in any capacity as an effective joint and coalition force with zero risk of enemy aggression from the skies. This air dominance is enabled by network-centric operations. We fly combat air patrols in a different way than we did 20 years ago. Fighters and bombers have become multi-role strike platforms with deadly precision. They carry versatile weapon loads in orbits over critical ground engagements and allow a level of precision never before achieved. Who would have imagined a few years ago that a B-1 crew would be flying a close air support mission? This is a great example of how air power has changed. The soldiers under fire gave their coordinates, bearing and range for the enemy fire. The B-1 crew found the target with synthetic aperture radar, received clearance to engage, and the crew released two Joint Direct Attack Munitions (JDAMs). The first JDAM destroyed the target. You can see how air power has been transformed.

Air dominance today is not only about air power but encompasses the entire gambit of aerospace power: large number of technological assets operating efficiently from the air and space to merge into a composite 'air picture', which provides the much required 'situational awareness'. This statement is only one half of the spectrum. Information seeking technological assets available on the surface also contribute towards 'situational awareness'. All these inputs need to be digested to ensure that "total situational awareness" is achieved. Total situational awareness is a prerequisite for air dominance. While air dominance enables the aerospace forces to operate at will, it also provides freedom and unhindered operations to surface forces, i.e. air dominance possesses the ability to dictate non-usage of enemy air to counter our Army and Navy.

Air Dominance: Offensive or Defensive?

In Desert Storm we had air dominance. That air dominance allowed our strike aircraft to devastate the enemy air forces and, at the same time, allowed our ground forces to operate without any enemy air interdiction. Desert Storm taught us something about air dominance. **We had it, we liked it and we're going to keep it.**

— Secretary of Defence William Perry

For this paper, it is presumed that every use of the term air dominance amounts to aerospace dominance. First of all, we must clarify the nature of air dominance. Is air dominance offensive in nature, or is it defensive? In the attempt to answer this question, let us consider all the categories or states of air effectiveness of own vs enemy air.

Air Denial

Friendly air forces may initially operate in a state of air denial at the start of operations when the enemy has air dominance. Air denial is the lowest air power state where friendly aircraft can conduct air operations sufficient to oppose the enemy air dominance while conducting those air power activities necessary to halt an initial enemy advance. The objective in this state is the denial of enemy air power *effectiveness* to the extent possible. The friendly abilities, through air defences or airborne threats, to provide protection to friendly ground and air forces are abilities which decrease the *effectiveness* of enemy air power. Enemy flak during the Korean War did not prevent air operations but it did make them more expensive. Despite air superiority at medium and high altitudes during the Vietnam War, the United States lost to North Vietnam, in part due to the condition of air denial in the low altitude environment with its Surface-to-Air Missiles (SAMs) and anti-aircraft artillery. The SA-2 SAM forced the US to devote considerable numbers of aircraft to defeat it. And, in many cases, the SA-2 forced aircraft to jettison ordnance in order to evade it, which, in effect, negated an aircraft's mission—thus, *effectiveness*. The bottom line consideration is that it does not matter why an aircraft cannot drop its bombs, what matters is that the target is not attacked – or that the mission was *not effective*.

Air Superiority
The next air power state is air superiority. Air superiority "rarely is an end in itself but is a means to the end of attaining military objectives". Air superiority is the degree "in the battle of one force over another which permits the conduct of operations by the former and its related land, sea and air forces at a given time and place without prohibitive interference by the opposing force." This state is not enough to ensure the *effectiveness* of air power.

Air Supremacy
The next state is air supremacy, which is "that degree of air superiority wherein the opposing air force is incapable of effective interference". Most theorists add that air supremacy is achieved when superiority is ensured just about everywhere, thus, allowing friendly aircraft the ability to fly anywhere within the theatre of operations. However, this air power state also does not adequately address the issue of air power's *effectiveness* at dropping bombs on enemy targets at will.

Air Dominance
The final air power state is the attainment of *effectiveness* in the conduct of offensive air operations. Air dominance is the highest air power state when the requisite *effectiveness* of air power is achieved: that 100 percent of the friendly bombs hit enemy targets while no enemy bombs hit friendly targets, that wars are won quickly (such as the Six-Day War of 1967 and Operation Desert Storm of 1991), that fewer friendly casualties are suffered. The lack of air dominance, on the other hand, may give the enemy time to use the "kill as many military personnel as they can" tactic. The low attrition of friendly military in Desert Storm seems to have established optimistic expectations about war, which may constrain some future commanders. The lack of air dominance will also make it significantly more costly for the military instrument of power to support 'The National Security Strategy'. The lack of air dominance will also make it more difficult and costly for the military instrument of power to conduct its growing role in deterrence and Military Operations Other

Than War (MOOTW). Air intervention plays a key role in the military's expanded role in MOOTW. Air dominance contributes to the safe accomplishment of these missions. The successful application of military power is dependent on uninhibited access to air and sea. Our forces will seek to gain superiority in, and dominance of, these mediums to allow our forces freedom to conduct operations and to protect both military and commercial assets. These demands require a capability to rapidly defeat initial enemy advances in order to seize the initiative and minimise the losses of territory and/or life. One is relatively well informed when it comes to defending assets and infrastructure through the use of air power, but protecting and ensuring that space capabilities continue to deliver in all, or, near all conditions, demands greater planning and money. Air dominance, therefore, delivers the following:

- Enables fullest range of operations.
- Secures the commanders' initiative and fulfills the "what-where—when".
- Provides operational freedom to "execute 'as you wish' not 'as you have to' operations".
- Provides opportunities for dominant manoeuvre and shields friendly mobility, while denying enemy mobility.
- Simultaneous "Offensive Sword" and "Defensive Shield".

Air Dominance: Platforms

Air dominance goes beyond air superiority and supremacy, in that it not only ensures that friendly aircraft can fly anywhere in enemy territory, but they can also be *effective* at performing their mission. Suppression of ground-to-air attacks, prevention of attacks on our air bases and forces, and overcoming domestic attacks on military and industrial infrastructure are all important in ensuring the effectiveness, or dominance of air power.

Combat Aircraft—Fighters and Bombers

Nearly four and a half decades ago, each aircraft of this category had a dedicated role allotted like air defence, ground attack, close air support and Electronic Counter Measure (ECM) (Wild Weasel). In addition, there were aircraft dedicated to the counter-insurgency role known as COIN aircraft. Gradually, but surely, aircraft were produced that were effectively used in more than one role, and the concept as well as the terminology "multi-role aircraft" began to take shape. Today, with the harnessing of a large number of technologies, lighter and more durable materials and miniaturisation, combat aircraft have the capacity to carry a variety of weapons, sophisticated avionics suites, concurrently demonstrating increasing agility and endurance. For the public, the wars and subsequent stabilisation efforts in Iraq and Afghanistan have accentuated the actions of ground forces, but air power has been a key behind-the-scenes factor all along. Air warfare will, if anything, grow even more critical to military operations in the years to come.

Modernisation of the Air Force is not only a strategic necessity, but also a fiscally sensible course of action. Significant new capabilities becoming available in the form of upgrades and munitions will help the Air Force bridge the gap from its existing fleet of ageing fighters and bombers to a force mostly of stealthy aircraft in the coming decade. The aircraft mentioned here are combat ready aircraft and not test or evaluation systems. Basically, the aircraft will be optimised for air superiority missions, but they will also be capable of strike missions with weapons like the JDAM. These aircraft should have the ability to pick up and go for 90 days to a deployed location and operate a dozen aircraft round the clock. The biggest conditional factor will be having sufficient spare parts for the war readiness kit that must accompany the unit to a deployment.

It is assessed in a US Air Force (USAF) study that the USAF needs 381 F/A-22s to be able to guarantee air dominance in any conflict from a terrorist hunt to all-out war. There is a strong lobby in the US that believes 381 F/A-22s in exchange for 880 fighters of earlier types, such as the F-15, F-117 and F-16 'is a good investment trade to make'. The F/A-22 fighter, despite just emerging from its development phase, is delivering a 78 percent mission capable rate and the aircraft has proved unbeatable even when outnumbered 2-to-1 by today's fighters. With the advanced radar, a new F-15 would have greater detection range but lack the survivability of the stealthy F/A-22 Raptor. Raptors are more cost-effective because more of them will survive combat, and each can destroy more enemies. It takes two to three aircraft to replace the killing capability of the F/A-22. An F/A-22 at $113 million a copy is a better deal than buying at least two $75 million F-15s to accomplish the same effects. The F/A-22 requires fewer personnel, fewer air-to-air refuelling tankers and can operate more frequently than earlier types, and so, will save considerable money in the long run. It is claimed that the USAF analysis and math supporting the 381 figure has been validated over more than a dozen independent reviews. There was a view that "if we can't afford it, we can't afford it, but, the threat does not get any smaller just because you can't afford to meet it". It must be noted here that the numbers quoted are the number of aircraft available for fighting, after deducting a certain number devoted to training, test, maintenance and attrition reserve.

The same study also quotes a similar figure for the F-35. While the F-35 is stealthy, it lacks the speed and altitude capability that allows the F/A-22 to so dominate air combat. It has been indicated that the larger percentage of F-35s acquired should be of the short take-off and landing variety to cater for some objectives. The air force does not have a vertical landing requirement. The main conclusion of the study was that **"air dominance continues to be a key enabler"** for the entire military, regardless of the kind of campaign under way. Another conclusion was that the in-service aircraft such as the F-15, F-16, and F/A-18 are at parity with threat aircraft or at a disadvantage because the overseas designs are increasingly stealthy and fitted with advanced avionics.

While we accept that the USAF is the leading air force of the world in terms of capability and its overpowering ability to acquire the state of air dominance, I personally, cannot reconcile to the logic of reducing the numbers of combat aircraft just because a more capable aircraft has appeared on the horizon. Any air force will always require the numbers of combat aircraft that it has been accustomed to. There should be no compromise on this issue.

The Indian Air Force (IAF) can today boast of a comparable or better fleet of fighters in the neighbourhood. Nearly all the fighters have proved their capabilities in national and international exercises. The IAF can also claim strategic reach now with aerial refuelling becoming a reality. However, we need to remind ourselves that modernisation of the fleet is an ongoing process and one has to continuously plan to remain ahead Along with the modernisation process, it is mandatory to upgrade and modify the existing platforms and integrate better and more accurate munitions with extended ranges. The absence of a dedicated bomber aircraft has often been adversely commented upon. In all fairness, it must be stated that no serious shortfall in the force's capability has been felt in the recent past, or indeed, will be felt in the near future. Not for a moment am I suggesting that the IAF need not acquire a fleet of dedicated bomber aircraft, because, as we have seen, today's bomber aircraft have also been pressed into service for close air support missions, provided the state of air dominance exists. In other words, the bombers of today and tomorrow will also be multi-role aircraft.

Sensors

Air dominance allows more deliberate, persistent and penetrating Intelligence, Surveillance and Reconnaissance (ISR). We need to develop the capacity to place ISR assets where and when the joint force needs them. Airmen provide persistent, dynamic and non-traditional ISR that benefits the entire military. ISR is everyone's job. This means that even fighters, strike aircraft and ground units are involved in building the battle space picture using on-board sensors connected to command and control nodes through networks. Today's ISR is unbelievably effective and timely. Developments in this field are providing and upgrading better data processing and storage technologies by the day. The progress is indeed rapid. The process of miniaturisation is well under way and in the near future, sensors will be available off-the-shelf as COTS. Until now, there was either a space or weight crunch when it came to how many sensors one could put on an aircraft/Unmanned Aerial Vehicle (UAV) or any other aerial platform With miniaturisation, nearly all the desired technologies would be easily accommodated on the platforms. In respect of ISR, one can be sure to include electro-optical, infrared and Synthetic Aperture Radar (SAR) imagery on a single platform, all thanks to miniaturisation. This will ensure that the limitations of one sensor will, to a large extent, be adequately covered by the other sensors onboard. In all likelihood, the same platform could also collect data for the required Signals Intelligence (SIGINT) and Electronic Intelligence (ELINT). However, it must be mentioned here that all these sensors only provide information. This information needs to be collated, analysed, and compared with available intelligence to convert this information into actionable intelligence.

Combat Support Operations

The mobility and flexibility of air power permits it to ensure that all operations desired to support the combat of the surface forces as well the Air Force are conducted swiftly and in the desired timeframes. Time is at a premium and when operations are assisted and/or precipitated at unbelievable timeframes, it may even take the enemy totally by surprise. The platforms for this part of operations are the transport aircraft and helicopters of air power. Significant and unprecedented movements of the surface forces to regroup, reinforce or augment the friendly forces at planned and random intervals provide the much-desired fillip to the operations of the surface forces. These operations too can only be executed with impunity when the state of air dominance is achieved.

Unmanned Aerial Vehicles (UAVs)

UAVs are here to stay. A mere glance at the interest generated by a number of countries to acquire UAVs reflects the international opinion in favour of the UAV. The suitability of the UAVs for the 'dull', 'dirty', and 'dangerous' missions cannot be disputed. However, for a long time from now, the manned aircraft and unmanned aerial vehicles will coexist and operate in a complementary manner to each other. We are aware of the tremendous contributions of UAVs in recent wars and names like Global Hawk and Predator are much too familiar to demand a repetition. I intend to cover some of the trends in the platforms of UAVs. These are:

- **Next Generation Sky Warrior's Maiden Flight a Success:** On June 18, 2007, resurrecting a great name from the 1950s, General Atomics completed the maiden flight of their Sky Warrior UAV. The new Sky Warrior will operate as an unmanned long-range surveillance, communications and weapon delivery drone. This will be able to run on diesel or jet fuel due to its heavy fuel engine and the Sky Warrior will form part of the US Army's extended range/multi-purpose UAV.

- **UAVs:** On June 28, 2007, Boeing successfully demonstrated the simultaneous command and control of multiple UAVs by a single operator. These UAVs will be able to operate through a central control point as well as having the ability to self-organise and make independent decisions.

- **Reaper UAV:** On August 31 2007, the USAF has announced the deployment of a new squadron of UAVs into the combat zones of Afghanistan and Iraq. Capable of carrying a payload of 3,759 pounds, the jet fighter sized Reaper can fly at 300mph, reach 50,000 feet and stay airborne for 14 hours at a time. This "hunter-killer" UAV also incorporates infrared, laser and radar targeting, and is capable of deploying precision guided weapons.

- **Fast Jet Pilots Direct Multiple UAVs:** On April 4, 2007, a new system was demonstrated which provides a single pilot with the ability to fly his own military fast jet while simultaneously directing up to four UAVs. The system gives the UAV an advanced level of autonomously independent decision-making, including self-organisation, communication, sensing the environment, identifying possible enemies, and targeting of weapons, with the final decision to shoot retained by the pilot. The project trials initially will take place exploring the use of UAVs for non-military operations. The flight trials were flown using a Tornado as the command and control aircraft and a BAC 1-11 trials aircraft acting as the 'surrogate' UAV. The Tornado pilot also had the responsibility of commanding a further three simulated UAVs. Working in combination, the Tornado and four UAVs carried out a simulated ground attack on a moving target. The sophisticated computer on the UAVs allowed them to target their weapons after an analysis of the environment, including possible enemies. However, the final decision to fire any (simulated) weapons was retained by the Tornado pilot. The system has been designed to provide the UAVs with a significant degree of independent intelligence in order to substantially reduce the workload of the pilot and also ensure that the most important decisions are retained by the human operator, viz, the Tornado pilot (in this case). Consolidation trials and development of expertise will take place in search and rescue, disaster relief and environment monitoring operations before full-fledged induction in military operations.

Space

The harnessing of space capabilities for military operations in recent wars has amply demonstrated the advantages that accrue. Space capabilities benefits are evident in our daily lives also with satellite-based TV and commercial communications. This has led to ensuring that most of the required equipment is of the COTS category. Better data processing and storage techniques, on the one hand, and miniaturisation, on the other, will permit the use of smaller, lighter and more sensitive sensors for the full range of surveillance and reconnaissance needs for electro-optical, infrared, hyperspectral and SAR imagery catering for all weather conditions round the clock. With miniaturisation maturing, we will witness a far greater capability on each satellite since weight will no longer be a restriction. Such attractive contributions cannot be ignored, nor can we permit any agency to interfere or deny us these lucrative benefits. Therefore, space control will remain our major objective wherein it will be ensured that our space platforms continue to provide us with the desired inputs. Aerospace domination implies aerospace control and requires build up of considerable aerospace capability. By the way, miniaturisation will also give us the opportunity to launch smaller satellites, as well as provide the redundancies that are so desperately planned for in every military operation.

Near Space

The contributions of space are much too expansive indeed. However, there are a few limitations that mainly pertain to persistence of observation and surveillance. It has been realised that launching satellites is an expensive proposition, and that, very soon we will witness saturation of space itself. It is with this background that we are travelling the "full circle" again by thinking of, and trying to launch, lighter than air vehicles, namely balloons, at altitudes from 50,000 to 70,000 feet. These balloons will have adequate space available and they could be charged with various sensors which will deliver all the information required on a permanent schedule, and that too, continuously. One may argue that with High Altitude Long Range Endurance (HALE) (upto one week), UAVs, we do not need balloons. But the UAVs will not grant persistence of observation of an area as well as a balloon will do. Once again, it may be argued that the balloon will be very vulnerable, but that is where the ingenuity of application of air power and ground-based defences would come into play to ensure their safety and survivability. These balloons could also be powered by relatively small motors, which could slowly, but surely, move them to locations as desired. Hence, near space platforms will also be major contributors in future wars. In addition, they will be inexpensive platforms, and launching alternates may be a suitable plan for redundancies. While accepting the elapsed time gap for the alternate to become operational, one may satisfy oneself by optimum utilisation of the information available through the other platforms as a stopgap measure.

Force Multipliers

The very mention of terminology terms like Airborne Warning and Control System (AWACS), Airborne Early Warning and Control (AEW&C) and air-to-air refuelling tankers ring a bell. In my logic, the days have arrived when cyber warfare (both offensive and defensive) should also form a part of this category. The reliance on goods delivered by avionics suites, communications (both line and satellite based), data transferring capacity and a host of other facilities have made command and control a relatively easy proposition. Any interference with this achieved comfort level would be most disturbing and cause serious discomfort to both plans and execution. Offensive and defensive cyber warfare must, hence, also be a major consideration for all military operations.

Network-Centric Warfare (NCW)

Converting the host of information collected into actionable intelligence is only half the work done. The other half, and the more important half is to ensure that the required intelligence data is transmitted to the correct agency/unit that would put this intelligence to use by converting it into well planned execution, with the optimum weapons, at the most opportune moment. Time is at stake and real-time intelligence makes it relatively simpler to plan and execute with the perfection and lethality that we desire, with the elements of surprise and shock effects thrown in as confirmed destroyers of the will to fight. The demands on avoiding collateral damage have increasingly become a trend in warfare. This would only be possible when all the participating forces and agencies are linked in a network which is capable of transmitting the required data and creating total situational awareness. This is achieved by NCW. We must also not forget that both the task of collecting the information undisturbed, and nil interference during execution by enemy air can only be achieved when air dominance has been secured.

Air Dominance Infrastructure

Immaculate and intensive planning needs to be undertaken for erecting the air dominance infrastructure, be it in the form of airfields, command and control nodes and installations, NCW infrastructure and all the associated hardware required for building air dominance to optimum levels. The air dominance infrastructure must be robust, survivable and capable of ensuring enough redundancies to cater for a determined enemy.

Conclusion

If you want to overcome your enemy, you must match your effort against his power of resistance, which can be expressed as the product of two inseparable factors, viz, the total means at his disposal and the strength of his will.

— Carl von Clausewitz, *On War*

The contest for air dominance is the most important contest of all, for no other operation can be sustained if this battle is lost. To win it, we must have the best equipment, the best tactics, the freedom to use them, and the best pilots. A potential enemy will also observe the history of air dominance and reach similar conclusions, but air dominance/supremacy/superiority (in that order) will be an absolute necessity in future conflicts whether they are big or small. The debate on how, and what weapons will be required, to gain air dominance will likely never end. As a nation however, as so aptly pointed out by Clausewitz, we must never forget that the enemy has a vote. Technological superiority alone does not, and will not, guarantee victory. Stealth has opened a window of opportunity, a window of hope, which offers air superiority with minimal risk to the pilots asked to gain it. It seems likely, therefore, that despite the cost, stealth is here to stay. Stealth, however, has not fundamentally changed how an air campaign is fought. It is unlikely that any stealth platform will fly into a high threat environment without airborne Suppression of Energy Air Defence (SEAD). We must continue to pursue additional technologies to fill the gap between stealth capabilities and limits in current SEAD inventories. One cannot win by fighting head to head.

We are not looking for a fair fight. Each weapon of war must be capable of achieving greater things in a war than the weapon it replaces. Options such as the unmanned high altitude Global Hawk with high loiter times and the ability to attack enemy radars and sensors should be explored and fielded. In short, a wide range of technologies must be fielded out of the thinning defence budgets. *"War is, thus, an act of force to compel our enemy to do our will"*. The advantage we hold must be so complete and so overwhelming that **air dominance is the only answer.**

Index

9 789381 904497